Language at the Boundaries

Language at the Boundaries

Philosophy, Literature, and the Poetics of Culture

Peter Carravetta

BLOOMSBURY ACADEMIC
NEW YORK • LONDON • OXFORD • NEW DELHI • SYDNEY

BLOOMSBURY ACADEMIC
Bloomsbury Publishing Inc
1385 Broadway, New York, NY 10018, USA
50 Bedford Square, London, WC1B 3DP, UK
29 Earlsfort Terrace, Dublin 2, Ireland

First published in the United States of America 2021
This paperback edition published 2023

Cover design: Namkwan Cho
Cover image: A National Historic Site near the needles area of Canyonlands NP in SE Utah.
© Jim Unterschultz

A catalog record for this book is available from the Library of Congress.

ISBN: HB: 978-1-5013-6365-8
PB: 978-1-5013-7188-2
ePDF: 978-1-5013-6367-2
ePUB: 978-1-5013-6366-5

Typeset by Integra Software Services Pvt. Ltd.

To find out more about our authors and books visit www.bloomsbury.com and sign up for our newsletters.

Unscrew the locks from the doors!
Unscrew the doors themselves from their jambs!
Walt Whitman, *Leaves of Grass*, 24

For Angela Biancofiore, Antonio D'Alfonso, and Rolando Pérez,
living thinking writing/painting the unending reconfigurations of
the boundaries of language

Contents

Figures

The images intercalated between chapters are by Angela Biancofiore (University of Montpellier):

Acknowledgments

I would like to thank the editors at Bloomsbury for considering this work, and Ms. Amy Martin and Ms. Katherine Bosiacki in particular for their watchful eye and support in making the book a reality. As well I want to thank the anonymous readers for their comments and suggestions. A thank you goes to Justin Hill and especially to Baxter Jephcott for their careful editing of the final manuscript. All the chapters originated in either a conference paper or an invited article. Though they have all been substantially revised, I would like to list the dates and places of their first appearance, almost as a map of incursions over the years in foreign territories. I take these chapters as exercises in rhetorical-hermeneutical *inventio*, and background to more political and institutional discussions about the future of the arts and humanities, as I express here and elsewhere. I take the opportunity to thank again the hosts of the conferences and editors of books for inviting me, and for permission to republish my findings.

Original Articles

"Tuning in/to the Diaphora: Lyric, Metaphysics, and the Reasons of Allegory," was the Keynote Speech at the annual Romance Languages, Literatures, and Film conference held at Purdue University, October 12–14, 1994; and published in *RLA: Romance Languages Annual*, 6 (1994): v–vx. An expanded Italian version was included in my volume *La funzione Proteo: Ragioni della poesia e poetiche della fine* (Rome: Aracne, 2014). The present text is a development from those earlier versions.

An earlier version of "Poetics of Paradox" appeared in Italian as "Diacronicità," in Stefano Baratta and Flavio Ermini (eds.), *I nomi della sincronicità*, 37–40 (Bergamo: Moretti & Vitali, 2007).

"Toward a Poetica Cosmographica" came out in *MM: The Sentence Commuted*, edited by Richard Beck (Norman, OK: Sentence of the Gods Press, 2005), 20–7.

"The Canon(s) of World Literature," appeared in Theo D'haen, David Damrosch, and Djelal Kadir (eds.), *Routledge Companion to World Literature*, 264–72 (Abingdon: Routledge, 2012). Reprinted with permission.

Lectures and Conference Papers

"The Journey and the Creation: On the Manifold Aspects of Existence and History," seminar at Sapienza University of Rome, Percorso di Eccellenza, Faculty of Modern Philology, May 30, 2018.

"Translation and the Hermeneutics of Culture," at AILC 2013 (International Association for Comparative Literature), Paris, Sorbonne, July 23, 2013.

"*Poiesis, techné, logos*," at the University of Hartford, guest speaker at a humanities seminar, March 31, 2011.

"Poetics and Linguistics: Marinetti and Gertrude Stein as Philosophers of Language," conference *Futurismo: Impact and Legacy*, Florence University of the Arts, Florence, October 16, 2009.

"Migration: The Engine of History," at conference *Migrations and Transnational Identities: Crossing Borders, Bridging Disciplines*, SUNY/Stony Brook, November 12, 2009.

"Hyphenated Poetry: Towards a Poetics of the Manifold," at *The CUNY Conference on Contemporary Poetry*, Graduate Center, November 3–6, 2005.

"Migration, History and Existence," Human Rights Defence Centre, Athens, 4th annual conference, *Migrants and Refugees*, Nafplion, Greece, September 6, 2003 (now published in Carravetta, *After Identity: Migration, Critique, Italian American Culture* [New York: Bordighera, 2017], 8–37).

"Political Aspects of Multicultural Poetry in the United States," at Faculty of English Philology, University of Salamanca, May 14, 2003.

"The Problem of Reference: Literature Between Philosophy and Politics," conference *Qu'est-ce que la littérature*, University of Alabama, Tuscaloosa, October 10–12, 2002.

The Cover

"Newspaper Rock" [close-up], Indian Creek Canyon, Bears Ears National Monument, Utah. Courtesy Jim Unterschultz / Wikimedia Commons / CC-BY-2.0.

Figure 1 "Discovering natural signs, 1" by Angela Biancofiore.

Introduction

Limitrophy: Approaches to Poetics

There it was, word for word,
The poem that took the place of a mountain.
Wallace Stevens

This book consists of a collection of research papers and articles that probe, analyze, and try to understand from a variety of angles, the elusive art of poetry, arguably the most synthetic or economic way of saying something through human language, but here also doubling as a synecdoche for all of the creative arts. They explore how language works at the limit, beyond which there is either silence or death. Or, less gloomy and more likely, various levels of misunderstanding. As the title of this Introduction suggests, perhaps we can only come so close, approach limit-situations, test *the boundaries of the sayable*, but never fully contact, possess, or explain everything about the poetic act. As we will see, there emerges a vocation in language when employed creatively to issue meaning-producing relations between the traditional big concepts of Western thought, such as essence and existence, between immanence and history, between creating and interpreting, and ultimately, between the known and the unknown. It is well known that after sound, at the origin of language there is the visual sign, from whence all different alphabets and eventually grammars derive over time. It seems that the very possibility of thought resides in this blurry continuum. Yet there hasn't been a dearth of interpretive schemes to make sense of it, as the history of philosophy in the West is replete with them. As philosophy became more and more rational, scientific, logical, or mathematical the solutions proposed apply to common speech, to "natural language," to a somewhat ordered principle, based on regional logics, metalanguages. One need only glance through Peter Ludlow's gargantuan anthology *Readings in the Philosophy of Language* (1997) to appreciate the variety of approaches and the specific issues tackled, especially in the twentieth century. Though I will occasionally draw on a few of them to explain my itinerary, in general the emphasis here is different: it concerns *what language does outside the rational and logical domains*, what happens—what and how something gets articulated—before the incommensurable, the untranslatable, the unsayable, the utterly foreign, the shocking new, silence. Faced with these topics, more than the linguist or the philosopher, we must turn to the actors themselves, the poets or writers who execute, who actually do, what the philosophers and the linguists can only talk about. This area of inquiry we call *poetics*, a term with a large and supple history, as we will see, but one that needs to sit between aesthetic/literary criticism and cultural hermeneutics proper. We want to hear what the practitioners themselves have to say about this limiting condition, this in-betweenness. For when language works at the boundaries and discloses a dynamic space for interaction between two beings, it enables thought and reality to connect, *somehow*. Poets actuate the synapse of the transaction. But there is no consensus on how it occurs, when it occurs, and whether it is good or bad? There have been some intriguing perspectives, as we will see, going from prelinguistic neurological bases of communication to the idea that language predetermines *what* we call reality, and *how* we can grasp it. But from this arena of often strongly antithetical positions what keeps reemerging are questions surrounding the meaning of interpretation itself, the dynamics of institutionalized paradigms over time (such as schools; publishers; relations between groups; aesthetic, scientific, or political currents), and the need to put the problem of *poiesis* back on the front burner.

As I explored each theme, my theoretical concern with how creativity and communication are structured and function brought me to consider not just *who* is communicating with *whom* but also the discourse generated and what gets launched outward from the interaction, what messages, and therefore ideologies, surface in the community. That is, messages beyond the creator's intention that become a cultural meme in the community. A recurring *topos* deals with how we speak about something for which there is no (or not yet a) language, relaunching reflection on allegory; another on how to understand someone who is not a functioning member of a community or cannot partake in the communicative exchange of that community, who may in brief not know the semiotic codes of the other, resident host. It's the problem represented by national versus foreign literature, which leads directly into inquiries about canon formation, translation, and migration. In this, the papers also double as an historical-philosophical inquiry into core values of the humanities, how they evolved in modernity in specific contexts such as the scientific, political, and ethno-anthropological communities, the slow but inexorable march toward reducing the space of action and philosophical relevance of the poetic, and look at the reasons of politicized authors, groups, or institutions who are trying to redefine the idea and function of literature in a nearly dystopian society.

This collection of writings is situated between three other works of mine of a more systematic nature, and I must beg the reader's patience if I occasionally refer to them, but when I happen to make some larger claims, they likely have been explored and tested in other works. First is the direct precursor of this book, my *Prefaces to the Diaphora* (1991), in which I tackle the debate over what is postmodernism, with readings of Nietzsche, Lyotard, Vattimo, and Vico and Heidegger. It is in this earlier work that I first question the "ancient diaphora," the ancient contest between philosophy and poetry, and attempt to reframe a trend that has dominated the West for over two millennia, at the expenses of the humanities. Further, in *Prefaces* I first tentatively advance a rethinking of allegory. I also researched a great number of critical currents and schools of thought for my "big book" titled *Del Postmoderno* (2009, but finished in 2004), which covers the years 1945 to 2001. Thus much of my research in the social sciences, minority discourse, postcolonial studies, feminism, and neohistoricism is contained in that volume. It also advances a theory about our dystopic twenty-first century, called the Orwellian Warp or the Age of Perennial Distortion. Third, in the background I worked on resolving some of the aporias in Western thought and developed my own theory of interpretation, an actual treatise, which is based on discourse as the co-enabling factor in the theory–method relation, *The Elusive Hermes* (2012). With this in mind as general background concerns, the chapters may nonetheless be read as self-standing essays, as explorations of the topos in question.

Chapter 1, "Tuning in/to the Diaphora: Lyric, Metaphysics, and the Reasons of Allegory" addresses the questions: if as some philosophers have held Western metaphysics is at an end or in irrevocable decline and loss of authority, does that impact the fate of the lyric poem, widely touted as the quintessentially philosophical poetic form? And, because of that, is poetry doomed also? Up to the nineteenth century, poets could still claim to be, or the community of experts asserted that in some guise they were, the *vox populi*. Even in their differences, poets still gave voice to the grand values: life, death, love, pride, the good, different values, or imagined worlds. This was no longer possible in the twentieth century. For the short answer has been: since Romanticism, poets only explore or know at best themselves, have little to teach the world, and do not introduce any new "knowledge." Then a half-century of positivism was followed by, and strangely encroaching on, another half a century of idealistic aesthetic (whether German, British, Italian, or French). Straddling the two World Wars, *Stilkritick*, formalism, New Criticism, and structuralism added to and embedded this cultural prejudice, so the "hostiles" of poetry (those who did not see anything resembling an "aura" in a poem nor its "usefulness") were to be found not only outside but also inside the precincts of the humanities. The question of poetry and science will be explored in a later chapter, whereas here I deal with how we arrived at the idea that a lyric poem is prone to pose and explore "big questions," what I call the metaphysical dimension of life and meaning. The essay rereads the evolution of this "universalist" understanding of the lyric composition through Leopardi, Emerson, Whitman, Baudelaire, Eliot, and Walcott to highlight the weighty philosophical questions at the very limit of linguistic expression. In the end, the dual challenge forces a rethinking of how we read these lyrical poems, introducing allegory not just as mode of language but also as necessary critical figura to sanction our very possibility of interpreting.

The idea that poets are the founders of society is typically associated with Martin Heidegger, and his readings of Hölderlin and other German poets. But this will be found to be limiting, claiming as it does that lyric poetry is the quintessential metaphysical expression on the question of Being, which means human beings will remain under the tutelage of the One (theological or not), which in history has taken on the transcendental attributes of the one, good, true (unum, bonum, and verum). Thus if substance is off the table, and One (unity, the en/closed essence) is no longer credible, how can a poem "found" anything, if it doesn't have an essence of its own? Yet writing nearly a century before the Romantics, Giambattista Vico had understood that the philosophical import of poetry resided in its giving voice to *being/s*—that is, the invention of god(s) and their undecipherable language was meant to explain *somehow* the unexplainable, at least give it a face. It is therefore marked for an anthropological, indeed materialist, dimension that concerns not solely the speaking deity, nor in later epochs the speaking "I," but the language of the tribe itself, the person(s) and phenomena and other referents both human and natural *outside* the poem. This is made evident the moment Vico seeks to understand myths and religious poems, which are inextricably tied to local/regional dynamics, links *necessity* and *cogency*, and describes the *Urgrund* of the class struggle in all societies. In the language of the myths, through the epics, Vico reveals how human cultures came about, how they discover agriculture, the spiritual, enact taboos, raise altars, pass or impose laws, and develop a basic ethos, a common vocabulary, and a system of symbols. These *arché* are the bedrock of our cultural models, they provide a basic enframing to allow us to link with and grasp what was previously mysterious, unknown, noncommunicable. Though Vico applied this theory to ancient and some preliterate societies, we can use the model to look at contemporaneous but foreign, in the sense of nonnational and more broadly non-Western, cultural texts and other artifacts. But with or beneath that we perceive the *human need to communicate something*, typically meant to persuade the listener about something else deemed important and meaningful. Vico's understanding of the evolution of human discourse, of language *tout court* (that is, of the modalities it developed to discover, transmit, and confirm and reconfirm or alter specific knowledge and ideas), from mere recognizable grunts on to words and metaphor as the foundational enabling trope, and then through the other more "evolved" tropes as "coded" for specific environments, to the highest possible expression, that of irony (which for Vico automatically means using language as the instrument of reason, that is, our idea of reason), has not been explored philosophically, or not enough, and is almost absent from professional discussion about poetics. (This would require a separate, very technical chapter, but I hope the thesis will be clear.) Thus to the critical trope that lyric poetry is concerned only with the self and has nothing to say about the world, we juxtapose a reading of poetry as "other-speaking" (the original sense of *allo-agourai* as we will see) that displays concrete, symbolical, and existential concerns about being-in-*this*-world-*with*-others. The claim that the earliest human, and poetic, language is *ab initio* allegorical will be picked up in other chapters.

The second research, "Poetics and Linguistics," explores the theories of language of two representative, and in fact very influential, authors who wrote in the early part of the twentieth century. The title reverses the key terms employed by Roman Jakobson in his milestone 1953 essay "Linguistics & Poetics" insofar as it privileges the creative side of language-use and not the rational (discipline-bound) aspect. In Jakobson's formulation, poetry (and literature in general) is essentially a *swerve* from a documentable convention in linguistic usage within a given community (or country if we think in terms of "national languages"). It turns out the two very dissimilar poets I analyze, Filippo T. Marinetti and

Gertrude Stein, undertook an exploration of the very boundaries of the capacity for language to say something new or somehow different, possibly disclose an "other" world, by pushing through and breaking the rules of what is public convention or, more pointedly, a number of accepted variations within a community (in this case, the avant-gardes). It is here where the poet's *inventio* is truly remarkable, and stimulated further formal study of language, including by Jakobson's himself in the 1920s, before he made it all cohere, in Aristotelean fashion, in what retrospectively is a too simple and limited view of literary art but still widely held by non-humanists. For one thing, the defense of the avant-gardists rests on the claim, shared by both Arthur Rimbaud and Friedrich Nietzsche, that one cannot invent, or say, anything new if one stays within the allowable range of existing grammars, not challenging the boundaries of the standardization of speech and specifically of rules governing style, acceptability, production of images, and fictions about oneself (or one's society). What emerges from these two paradigmatic avant-gardists is that untried pathways of expression bring with them undisclosed possibilities for understanding language *and* reality as well as history, given the memory couched in language, as both writers have precise ideas on some negative aspects of the tradition and of their respective national canons. That this "knowledge" is of practically no use to professionals in politics, governments, and public education is one general tragedy of our world culture at the dawn of the twenty-first century.

The third boundary I explore begins in a paper I was invited by a journal to contribute on the nature of paradox. Having recently finished a study of the role of aphorism in Nietzsche (Cf. Carravetta 1991: 17–87), I asked myself why is it that at a certain point the philologist-philosopher and master of the compressed prose form felt compelled to write an allegorical poem, *Thus Spoke Zarathustra*, in the Spring and Summer of 1881? The short answer here is that, as the aphorism by nature is not directed to anyone, or is meant to speak to everyone, it excluded *a priori* a possible response: it was a *sententia*, outside of practical or specific human time and place, and universalizing. When wishing to show how the modern subject can overcome the self and steer it toward a dynamic becoming, Nietzsche had no choice but to turn to allegory, where the self, the subject, is no longer spitting universal tokens of ultimate knowledge or sententiae about humanity but is rather intrinsically pluriform, mobile, subject to changes, to revelations, to blind alleys, wearing different masks, deconstructing the ego, admitting limits and excesses. To the claim, by Nietzsche himself, that the Zarathustra book is written for no one and for everyone, our answer has to be that the author himself had not paid enough attention to the question of temporality that is enacted when reading aphorisms and when reading allegories. The *Zarathustra* book demonstrates the *necessity* to (re)turn to Myth if the aim is to reach the greatest number of people, and be able to found the new language of the tribe, which involved circulating the message of the self-overcoming of the subject, the arrival of the *Übermensch* (the man who is "over" the existing nineteenth-century specimen), no matter in what culture. It's an ethical message to get over ourselves and try something else. But *it is* directed to *everyone*, Nietzsche's mock-irony notwithstanding: we can grasp what was so originary about writing an allegorical epic, and in typical grandiloquent fashion, Zarathustra echoes Homer and Dante and other great allegorists. Unfortunately this kind of writing/thinking has become a burden and a hurdle in Nietzsche studies, despite claims to the contrary by professional philosophers and experts in literature: philosophical poetry is complex, understanding it requires breaking boundaries. Let me elaborate further by way of a digression.

In a paper I delivered at an American Anthropological Association annual convention—but that is not included in this book—titled "Allegorical Poetics and Ethnography," I analyzed and became aware of the challenge anthropologists and ethnographers face when dealing with the highly symbolic speech and especially "literary" creations of non-Western cultures, and the problems that were thus raised for literary critics and hermeneuticists alike. Let us consider some basic traits or concerns ethnography and literary critique share, starting with:

1. the status and role of the interpreter;
2. the interpretation of codes and symbolic universes alien to ours; and
3. the necessity to rethink the subject (in philosophy as in psychology) in terms that become more explicitly *relational*, preventing blocking one side or the other for whatever methodological reasons.

This last requirement means we need to search and account for the activator or *ur*-generator of images and artifacts that necessarily inhabit two or more domains, two or more forms of thinking by a collectivity, transgressing the boundaries set up (often unwittingly) by interpreters who deploy logical grids and erect epistemological or even aesthetic castles. We will find that the *relation* remains, whether obscured by superimposed, typically Eurologocentric models or paradigms (or prejudices), or brought to light explicitly in some of the poetics we will look at, such as translation as migration, or bilingual writing, or immigrant poetics. Ethnography furnishes crucial proof of the *essentially relational nature of discourse*, even when—in the lyric as well as, and for different reasons, the avant-gardes—poets essay to speak without addressing anyone in particular.

As we will see, this condition requires that we understand language itself as fundamentally allegorical, not (as we find in most manuals, and even in Angus Fletcher and Northrop Frye) the "saying this to mean that [particular meaning in the master code of the reader]" but, rather, and by our reading, the "saying this and *then* something else not immediately evident," and *for whose intellection the reader/critic must participate, take a chance, risk assigning a value to the initially incomprehensible icons, symbols, figuras*. To proceed we must therefore first:

1. Restore a meta-critical consciousness to the critic, as they will approach the foreign text from within a set of parameters, such as the academy or the public press, and typically from within one master code (i.e., a particular national language). The interpreter must be ever aware from where they are speaking.
2. Attempt to come up with a preliminary conceptual/topical map of the universe disclosed by this/a particular foreign work. Basically, a first reading listing recurring themes or other traits (as Descartes tells us in rule number two of the *Discours sur la Méthode*).
3. Much like the anthropologist, the ethnographer, or the mythographer, we hermeneuticians and cultural critics must essay to establish a contact and enter the world of the foreign culture/text, by becoming a *participant observer*, a mediator between being (and learning from) an insider, and being (and bringing learning models from) an outsider. This is a very complex relation, and though we soon discover much is not "getting through," and there are subtle but known issues with the notion of participant observer, it is nevertheless the *initial enabling condition* for any sort of communication and therefore for the creation of meaning. It means being aware of one's unconscious cultural grids, one's biases.

The point revolves around the necessarily public or audience-enabled, temporal, nature of allegorical discourse, as well as around the recurring situation, in philosophy or science and any strict methodological pursuit, to have to explain certain concepts (even epistemes) by the use of images, metaphors, examples, analogies, parables. Think back for a moment to Bk X of the *Republic*, where after the reasons for the disbanding of poets Socrates goes on: (1) to make exceptions of certain forms of poetizing, and (2) construct a whole allegorical fable himself, with the Myth of Er. In any case, these openings that see the divide as actually a conjoining enabling location for science and humanities, philosophy and poetry, should allow us to recover the symbolic-cognitive mapping present in all exchanges, especially in those that extend *beyond* the I-Thou field. The chapter on the poetics of science in part explores these issues.

The "other-speaking" implicit in *allo-agourai* is the figurative locus or terrain where even totally alien cultures and subjectivities can meet and expect an even handed exchange (both are foreign to one another, so to speak), within and reassured by the right-then-and-there inscribed semantic and existential realm of what can be called *the included third*, the basis for a societal reality. Except that, like Hermes, the third person is forever in transit, switching passports, speaking many foreign tongues, and evoking uncommon memories.

I came away from that research thinking that maybe what is meant by allegory should be rethought through and through. In the older, more thorough manuals (of the Erich Auerbach, Ernst Robert Curtius, Heinrich Lausberg generation) allegory was glossed not only as a *figure of speech*, a subgenre, suitable (that too by convention) to convey certain pre-established ideas but, remarkably, also posited as a *figure of thought*, a way of structuring and organizing an entire world, or one of its manifestations, as idea, as a cognitive vision. It entails thinking something, a society, humankind itself, from the barest materials, asking the simplest questions! My take on this is to rethink the meaning of allegory, not as a semiotic (for Umberto Eco as well, in allegory "this means that") but as the founding language of cultures, in a Viconian sense, as "diversiloquium" … comprising "diverse species or the diverse individuals comprised under […] genera […] [or] imaginative class concepts." This way the myths and "foreign" figures of different or primitive cultures can be engaged linguistically in that a *cognitive schema* is inscribed in the work and can be engaged and developed to disclose newer and fruitful pathways (even if we have limited knowledge of the original language; see Chapter 7, below, on poetics of translation).

Chapter 4, "Poetics of the Manifold and the Hybrid: Poets between Cultures," is subdivided into two parts. The first part deals with the notion of the manifold, again a big concept in Heidegger, but with the intent of showing how metaphysical it is and therefore in need of being anchored to specific cultures, to given poetological experiences, to an *Urgrund* rather than an *Abgrund*. The case of the poet between two or more languages/cultures offers a special viewpoint in the relationship between creativity and the social, political, and institutional frameworks that legitimate the artifact. In investigating these concerns, an effort is made to rediscover or rethink the rhetorical as not simply aesthetic decorum but as actual *lived experience through language*, as a setting-into-speech and as such requiring and validating *inventio* and ex-pression through *loci*, or more broadly, a cultural topica. Now, these linguistic or poetic embodiments are space and time specific, that is, culturally determined and historically contingent: poems are written/created for someone else (even when they seek the gods or the unconscious: the other is a necessary and co-enabling presupposition of any speech act). Once again, after references to J. L. Austin and Émile Benveniste, we will see how Vico's understanding of poetry and allegory counters Heidegger's.

Chapter 5, "Poetica Cosmographica: An American Poet in Taiwan" takes as its task the possibilities of poetry after the destruction of tradition and the lyric by the avant-gardes. In particular, the self-exiled writer Madison Morrison, who in the tradition of William C. Williams and others writes poem with the linguistic detritus of our society. Teaching English literature in Taiwan for nearly thirty years, he launched a major project, in twenty-six books (I wrote the present chapter when he had written the first half of these), which includes so many elements from Asian philosophy and culture, as well as reinterpretations, in a non-Eurologocentric way, of his own avant-garde tradition. Madison's writings show the interpenetration not only of East and West but also, in their layering, of high and low culture, and the background drama of the individual utterance in a sea of overlapping institutional discourses, themselves basically transnational (as are Buddhism, the Vedas, Christianity).

Chapter 6, "Poetics and Science: *Poiēsis, technē, logos*," is derived from an invited humanities lecture on autopoiesis given at the University of Hartford in 2009. It tackles the complex relationship between scientific knowledge and poetic knowledge. The claim is made, against over two centuries (but with roots in the seventeenth century) of theorizing that poetry is rhetorical and science is methodic, that actually *poiesis* is the greater of the two categories, and that it informs the construction of method. (I explored this at length in my *The Elusive Hermes*.) Moreover, by relying principally on the image, poetry sets the stage for the specific uses of images in culture, and this includes the metaphors used in science to explain phenomena. This allows us to consider the possibility that the difference between the two is more a question of institutions, of the discourse and politics of the disciplines (in a Foucauldian sense) and less a matter of some intrinsic ontological difference between language and knowledge. Materials are drawn from the emergence of this differentiation, which wasn't so clear-cut up to Goethe, when it was still commonplace for a poet to know about science and a scientist to be able to versify. But generally from the end of the eighteenth and through the nineteenth century rise of scientific "disciplines" (geology, evolutionary biology, chemistry, and more broadly positivism as the philosophy of science) onward all the way to C. P. Snow's "two cultures," knowledge has been removed from the poetic realm. This huge historical trend is here critiqued and in part demolished: poetic knowledge is broader and more fundamental than scientific knowledge. Without an array of expressive means available to and fine-tuned by the poet, the scientist would never be able to speak/write to anyone about her/his discoveries or knowledge in general.

Chapter 7, "Poetics of Translation as Migration," delves into the problem of translation and the parallels between the critic's task of extracting, synthesizing, and bringing to a new audience the meanings of texts, and the socially concrete experience of crossing boundaries by poets and their own books. The study finds a correlation, symbolic at least, between migration and translation. Theoretical premises point toward the literature produced by expatriates, exiles, emigrants, and refugees. The question of which "national" or "regional" language to employ impacts profoundly on what can be imagined and embodied in (poetic) language. Here the thought of Benjamin L. Whorf is key: knowledge is dependent on its possibility to be articulated in a given idiom. But when this knowledge is brought into a social/cultural world in which it must be rendered in a profoundly different language, as happens factually to migrants with their own life experiences (which is thought to be the unassailable source of knowledge), what are the implications for poetics, for philosophy, for politics? I will make a case that George Steiner had it right when he argued that translations, because of their materiality, are a better index of how a culture constructs its own national mythology. But he also made the case that translations *are* possible, despite what most argue is a "loss" of sort in the transition. The ideas, the concepts, and the references can and do go across in a translation (it's often a question of finding the competent translator). What is debunked is Walter Benjamin's theory of translation with its theocentric assumptions.

Chapter 8, "The Canon(s) of World Literature: Premises to a Postcolonial, Transnational Poetics," deals with two interconnected topics: first, the very reason for being of a national literature canon, and consequences of that; and, second, the challenge to hermeneutics and critique in general as it goes through the nonexistent yet historically reiterated need for a criterion, or a "measure," to determine and compare works published in very different ages and even more different cultural milieus. The hypothesis is advanced that though literature must always be linked to a concrete sociohistorical reality in the twenty-first century it can benefit by moving away from both the "national literature" paradigm as well as, on the opposite end of the spectrum, from the "World Literature" or transhistorical aesthetic in- and for-itself paradigm. This critique of a metaphysically grounded World Literature is different from E. Apter's criterion of "untranslatability," which is heavily invested in deconstruction, and is more about delinking than connecting. In its place, and to regain a sense of the existential and regional circumstances of the creation of the text, we might consider looking at the figura of migration as a fluid, polysemic, and yet realistic approach to interpreting cultural artifacts in their ebbs and flows, concretizing and dissolving. After looking at the contribution made to this aspect of poetics in its broadest possible horizon, indeed being literally planetary, and integrating insights from postcolonial studies, a plethora of representative materials can be drawn from lesser-known European, South American, African, and Asian texts.

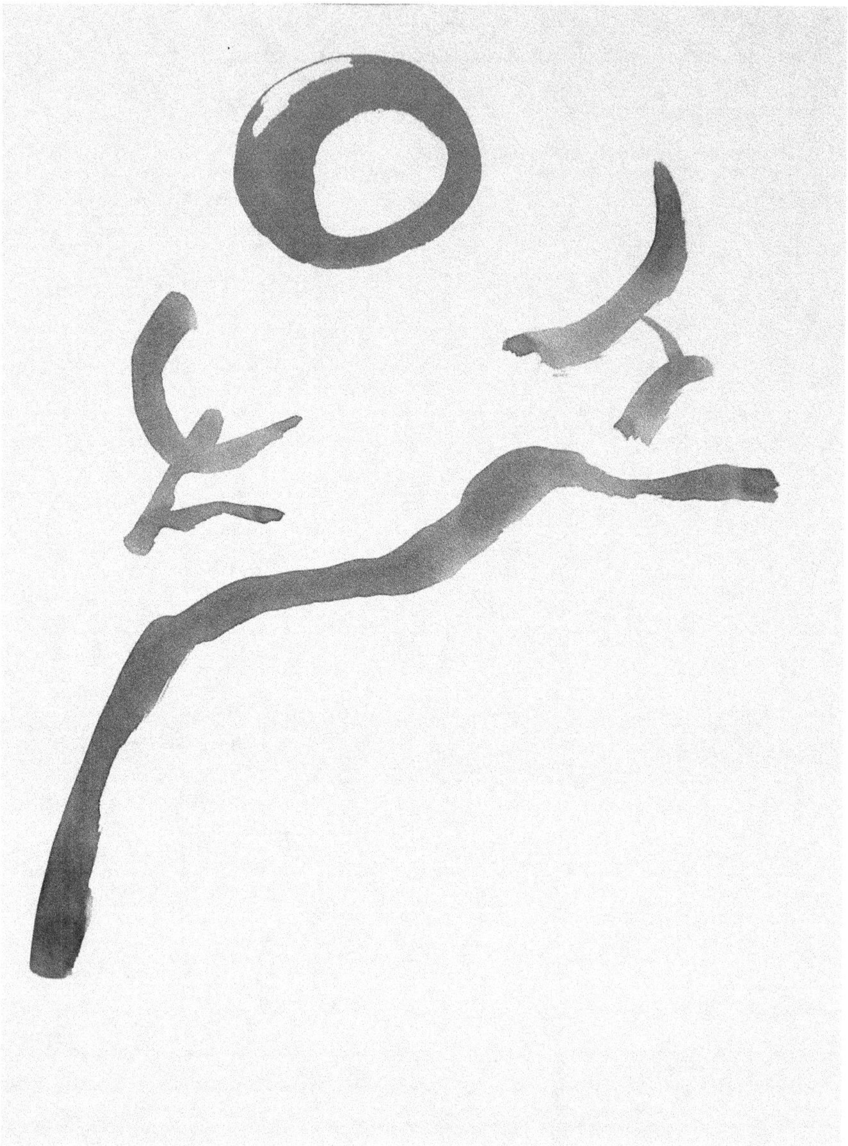

Figure 2 "Discovering natural signs, 2" by Angela Biancofiore.

1

Tuning in/to the Diaphora

Lyric, Metaphysics, and the Reasons of Allegory

Mirate la dottrina che s'asconde
Sotto il velame de li versi strani.
Dante, *Inferno* IX, 62–3

Questions

My initial working hypotheses are simple if sweeping. First, lyrical poetry is quintessentially metaphysical.[1] As a form of literature that speaks to the emotions, is traditionally complemented by music (specifically the lyre, in earlier centuries), and puts in language ideas, images, feelings, that yearn for a universal sense or meaningful expression for all and for all times, the lyric is quintessentially metaphysical, with variations that stretch from the momentary to the transhistorical. To flesh out the hypothesis, a number of contextual questions need to be asked: if this is the case, what happens to the lyric in the age of the decline and/or rejection of metaphysics, in the epoch of the forgetting of Being, the "end" of philosophy, and the confrontation with the *Ab-grund*, the foundationlessness, of the technological worldview?[2] Further, if we are not

[1] I am taking the word-concept "metaphysics," initially, in its broadest acceptation, starting from Aristotle: "a science which investigates being as being and the attributes which belong to this in virtue of its own nature" (*Metaphysics*, IV, 1003a), since "all men suppose what is called wisdom to deal with first causes and principles of things" (981b), so that "Philosophy should be called knowledge of the truth. For the end of theoretical knowledge is truth, while that of practical knowledge is action" (993b); and on to Heidegger: "Metaphysics is inquiry beyond or over beings which aims to recover them as such and as a whole for our grasp" (Martin Heidegger, "What Is Metaphysics?," in David F. Krell (ed.), *Basic Writings*, 91–112 [New York: Harper & Row, 1977], 109).

[2] This is a Heideggerian perspective on the twentieth century, reformulated from the 1970s through the 1990s by the likes of Jacques Derrida, Gianni Vattimo, and Richard Rorty. But I will continue to refer to Heidegger's views of our *Zeitgeist* as they provide the necessary background to our engaging his readings of poetry, further down.

experiencing an "end" of modern man, is it still plausible to speak of a decline of the presence and meaningfulness of poetry and the literary arts in general? Is there a connection between the decline of poetry and the decline of metaphysics? What were the stakes when amidst so many "crises" and "ends" of this or that, a notion of the postmodern started circulating basically from the 1950s on, but strongly from the 1980s?[3] In this scenario, can we rethink the possibilities of the poetic, of poetry as once again a way of distilling in language the very meaning of being, can it become (again) a form of thinking, a *Denkungsart*?

From this stems the second critical hypothesis and research objective, namely, if the above is true, perhaps we need to rethink the limits of the lyric in terms of an alternative vision of the language of poetry and explore yet again meaning and possibilities of the allegorical. Briefly, approach the texts through a keen rhetorical awareness aimed at rehabilitating *inventio*, role of *topoi*, and expansion of the idea of *dialogue*, downplaying the long-dominant notion that rhetorical language focuses solely on *ornamentum*.[4] To carry this out, we have to juxtapose what the actual texts say to what the authors state in their programmatic writings, in their "theorizing" about their art and activity. These writings are properly called poetics, to contrast them to, and distinguish them metacritically from, critique or critical theory, which has a specific requirement of a *formal* rhetorical structure as determined by convention and tradition, and a clarity about its metalanguage.

A poetic belongs to its author and the sphere of other authors it inspires, as when it becomes a current, or mode of dealing with the creative arts, or an activity within the intellectual world. Occasionally, depending on the school of criticism one subscribes to, a style or a dominant trope. The activity-participation aspect is built right into the words *poiesis*, *technē*, as opposed to critical *theory*, where the word "theory" suggests, etymologically, distance, regard as if a spectator, and ultimately illumination as if the deity, *theos*.

The questions being complex, they must be framed, situated (even if ad hoc) so that we may talk about the problems raised at all. To satisfy this hermeneutic prerequisite, I shall proceed by sketching four poetological scenarios.

3 See on this my previous works *Prefaces to the Diaphora* (1991) and *Del Postmoderno* (2009), where much of the literature on this very broad topic is discussed. For recent attempts to go "beyond" the amorphous designation of postmodern, see the intriguing proposals gathered by David Rudrum and Nicholas Stavris, eds., *Supplanting the Postmodern* (New York: Bloomsbury, 2015).

4 See Craig Owens, "The Allegorical Imperative: Toward a Theory of Postmodernism," *Oktober*, 12 (Spring): 67–86, and some of the studies referenced later inspired by Walter Benjamin and Paul de Man's work on allegory.

Historiography: Identity and Narration

"I look in vain for the poet whom I describe," concludes Emerson's 1844 essay "The Poet,"[5] articulating a desideratum in terms that reflect the at the time pressing question of the yet elusive identity of a national literature, a voice that could speak to and for the new great land without feeling inferior and/or submit to forms and contents from the European traditions, which were rich, complex, and proud of their inimitable geniuses. He goes on to say:

> Time and nature yield us many gifts, but not yet the timely man, the new religion, the reconciler, whom all things await. Dante's praise is that he dared to write his autobiography in colossal cipher, or into universality. We have yet had no genius in America, with tyrannous eye, which knew the value of our incomparable materials, and saw, in the barbarism and materialism of the times, another carnival of the same gods whose picture he so much admires in Homer; then in the Middle Age; then in Calvinism … Yet America is a poem in our eyes; its ample geography dazzles the imagination, and it will not wait long for meters.[6]

We know that this wish, exhortation, or wager to meet the "colossal" challenge, was to be answered eleven years later by Walt Whitman with his *Leaves of Grass*. The literary history of the United States is deeply marked by this preoccupation with inventing or developing a distinctly American poetics, which begins actually during colonial times, with Michael Wigglesworth's "Day of Doom" (1662), and Timothy Dwight's "The Conquest of Canaan" (1785). After the founding of the republic, John Barlow produced "Vision of Columbus" (1797), rewritten in 1807 with the title "The Columbiad." The tradition of course is by now ample

[5] Cf. Ralph W. Emerson, *Selections from Ralph Waldo Emerson*, edited by Stephen E. Whicher (Boston: Houghton Mifflin, 1960), 238. On Emerson and language, see now Thompson 2017.

[6] Ibid. In a journal entry from Autumn 1845, "Native Americans," Emerson writes: "I hate the narrowness of the Native American party … Man is the most composite of all creatures … in this continent – asylum of all nations – the energy of Irish, Swedes, Poles, and Cossacks, and all the European tribes, – of the Africans and the Polynesians – will construct a new race, a new religion, a new state, a new literature, which will be as vigorous as the new Europe which came out of the smelting pot of the Dark Ages, or that which earlier emerged from the Pelasgic and Etruscan barbarism. La nature aime les croisements" (Emerson, *Selections*, 280). Impossible not to fast-forward to Israel Zangwill's 1908 play, where "America is God's crucible, the great Melting-Pot where all races of Europe are melting and reforming. Here you stand, good folk, think I, when I see them at Ellis Island, here you stand" (Israel Zangwill, *The Melting-Pot* [Charleston, SC: BiblioBazaar, (1909) 2008], 35). But in the background, let's bear in mind the proposals or manifestoes, some literary and some critical or historical, on the birth and influence of other paradigms, such as the "imperial self," the "Adamitic strain," and the "frontier mythology" as well as the trajectory from the (presumably) absolutely free self in Whitman to its imprisoned or splintered counterpart in most post-Second World War poetry and fiction, to which we will have occasion to refer.

and diversified, and includes other exemplary texts of what we might call the modernist epic or the modern long poem. Some works became synonymous with a movement, with a turn or interstice in the evolution of different but influential poetics, and inroad into cultural politics.[7]

Let's continue by reflecting on what is embedded in the cited passage: poetic "autobiography" written in colossal cipher and elevated into "universality."[8] Retrospectively, the latter two requirements are no longer desired, or even possible.[9] Ezra Pound, William Carlos Williams, and Allen Ginsberg do try different solutions but they are consistent in programmatically ripping apart and reconfiguring a shattered self, a vanished or vanishing origin, a too-long-honored belief in unity, revelation, or emancipation. The pulse of the subject is irregular and borders on, the images an endless interplay of mirrors, certainties of any type (scientific, metaphysical, political) no longer trustworthy, alienation a quotidian reality, nihilism an uncanny possibility. Strangely enough, this has actually been beneficial to the genre of autobiography, which has witnessed a resurgence especially in communities that found a voice during the 1960s and the 1970s, and received wide critical attention. Autobiographies, and the memoir in particular, share this with the lyric: they concern the self, the "I," no matter how defined, above and beyond the formal differences between the two kinds of writing. In both there is no preliminary necessity to refer *factually* to anyone or anything outside the speaker or narrating persona. It's the question of the referent. But to continue.

Whether in continental philosophy or in cultural studies broadly understood, subjectivity, grand values, and national allegories have been in profound crisis for

[7] In this horizon we can then situate a number of philosophic-mythical topics, such as that of discovery, the quest, the struggle against nature first and culture later, and the vision of a final harmony. These dominant topics can be critically culled from the earlier Daniel Bryan's *Adventures of Daniel Boone* (1813), to Thomas Ward's *Passaic*, to Longfellow's *Song of Hiawatha* (1855), and so on through the great revolutionaries of the twentieth century, such as Pound's *Cantos*, Crane's *The Bridge* (1930), Williams's *Paterson* (1946–63), till we reach Allen Ginsberg's 1972 long poem *The Fall of America*. The recent *Ellis Island* (2013) by Robert Viscusi should be added to this list.

[8] Not to speak of terms that today we cannot but either dismiss, deconstruct, or reframe in relation to other concerns going on at the time. I mean, "tyrannous eye," "incomparable materials," "barbarism," and the implicit faith in a historical *telos* nourished by notions such as progress, power, identity, supremacy. It may be sheer coincidence, but John O'Sullivan's "Manifest Destiny" idea comes out the very same years, in 1845 (prompted primarily to favor the annexation of Texas).

[9] Refer to the now widely circulated critical and philosophical literature on the subject (most of them listed in the Bibliography, below, and analyzed in my other works, specifically in *Prefaces to the Diaphora* [1991], *Del postmoderno* [2009], and *The Elusive Hermes* [2012]). I have in the background of these remarks key writings by philosophers such as Jean-François Lyotard, Michel Foucault, Julia Kristeva, Michel Serres, David Harvey, Gianni Vattimo, Richard Rorty, and Robert Margolis.

the past half a century, following another several, pre-Second World War, decades where this crisis, though brewing, was only barely heard and felt (except perhaps to existentialists). But it has become a truism across different critical traditions that subjectivity, and master objectifying narratives of one's country or ethnic group, have been considered suspect, deviously pretentious and ontologically foundationless, in dire need of revision or debunking, and have consequently spawned frenetic theoretical and political revolutions in the various disciplines and throughout society at large.[10] In this world picture, some historical narratives on the life and health of poetry have been pieced together from shreds and shards of the more canonical long narratives mentioned above, and which show that poetry is, nevertheless, still alive, at the molecular level, albeit weakened (but not on the internet), and by and large marginalized, confined to the cognoscenti, a filler in more mundane humanities publications. What's more, their "contents" (if I may be allowed to use this term, for clarity's sake) point to pursuits that are confusing, excessively personal, and often chimerical. Not that the lyrical poets variously anthologized and studied are totally alienated from the *humus* of their cultural unconscious. As we will see in this and subsequent chapters, twentieth-century poetics wrestled with concrete realities in dramatic, inspiring ways. And each and every time, the boundaries of languages itself became a problem and challenge.

To open up the field within which to continue our search, let's look at James E. Miller's thorough reconstruction of the specifically American ("Whitmanesque") "Personal Epic." We learn that there are many branches within the canon, from (1) the motivations and literary techniques adopted when confronting the expression, embodiment, and characterization of the consciousness of the times (Hart Crane); (2) to the rewriting of history in a dilated present (Pound); (3) the relationship between personal mood and its fragmented global picture (T. S. Eliot); (4) the inability in the twentieth century to (re)locate the dream (as in John Berryman's *Dream Songs* or Ginsberg's *Fall of America*); (5) the impossibility of finding "My Being" even when conflating America with its

[10] I am making this necessary generalization in order to sketch a broad scape for analysis, on the basis of a number of articles that have appeared, during the 1980s and 1990s, in Anglo journals such as *Cultural Critique*, *Critical Inquiry*, *Representations*, *Boundary 2*, *Social Text*, *Rethinking Marxism*, *New Literary History*, *Representations*, *Popular Culture*, and other collections, and in other languages as well as in publications in the areas of anthropology, ethnic studies, and philosophy. See Bibliography for some representative titles.

pre- or non-European heritage (as in Charles Olson's *Maximus Poems*); or (6) acknowledging the failure of language when it meets up with chaos (Williams's *Paterson*).

One can argue that the catalog of iconic texts/authors thus far referenced would best serve as a way to enter into an interminable discussion on the double, bifurcate soul of America, polarized between the Enlightenment dicta of universal democratic egalitarianism and free individual choice. That is, between "we are all created equal" and the unimpaired individual will in the frontier mythology of self-reliance, sacrifice and competitiveness, survival of the fittest, and folding back to community values, living and dying the just battle. Yet if the nineteenth century struggled to find its national identity with the corresponding "representative man," the twentieth century struggled to isolate, describe, and place (or situate in a broader context, society, or world) the innermost soul of the individual, that "something" typically called "self" that the developing disciplines, the new epistemologies on the horizon—such as devised and developed in psychology, phenomenology, physics, and biology—in their various ways probed, scanned, experimented with, and finally parceled out into the different fields of inquiry. The picture is obviously more complex, owing to the asymmetrical appearance, in Western societies at least, of any number of innovative and yet conflicted poetries, all trying to define themselves, or achieve an identity and visibility for newer subjectivities, under the pressure of extra-poetic yet dominant or hegemonic ideologies.[11]

Nevertheless, even at this level of abstraction, these "personal epics" speak to and refract the three words of my title: lyric, metaphysics, and the reasons of allegory. What is it about the lyric that may prompt us to declare it finally moribund—like metaphysics—and look to the allegorical as the task of investigation in poetics, cultural critique, and ultimately hermeneutics?

Theory of the Lyric: Leopardi as Paradigm

Let me illustrate with an emblematic example. In a note written in 1819, the Italian poet-philosopher Giacomo Leopardi (1798–1839) observes that

[11] See, for example, the works of Homi K. Bhabha, Edward W. Said, the anthology by Abdul R. JanMohamed and David Lloyd, and the special issues of journals dedicated to "Post/Colonial Conditions."

"Everything has been perfected from Homer onwards, except poetry."[12] The statement is sweeping, categorical, and yes, metaphysical, in the sense that it claims an essence to poetry that is impervious to human-historical time, to change and development. But in order to not pluck it out of the four thousand pages of the *Zibaldone* and use it arbitrarily to support any claim I might be tempted to make concerning the nature and history of lyric poetry, let us read it first in the context of the period, in the wake of Friedrich Schiller's essay on *Naive and Sentimental Poetry*, against the background of the polemic between the promoters of a Romantic poetics (which Leopardi critiques and rejects) and those of a classicist or "Hellenistic" poetics (which Leopardi values and supports). Moreover, we cannot ignore some of the other tenets of Leopardi's own complex personal poetics either. The following year (September 18, 1820), Leopardi in fact writes: "The lyric can be said to be the peak, the pinnacle, the summit of poetry, which makes it the highest point of human discourse." In yet another *Zibaldone* entry written six years later, we find similar observations:

> As far as genres are concerned, poetry is essentially made up of three true and great subdivisions: lyric, epic, and dramatic. Proper of any nation, even savage ones, *the lyrical mode* [il lirico] *is the most noble and is more poetic than the rest*. It is proper of any man, even the unlettered, who wishes to recreate or console himself through song, and with words measured in whatever way, and with harmony; a frank [*schietta*] and free expression of any true and deeply felt human feeling. *The epic is born after and from this*; it is in a way nothing more than an amplification of the lyrical.[13] (my emphases)

But is it really true that the lyric is more "original" than or precursor of the epic, a genre eminently allegorical? In this same passage he also offers a definition of the epic, which I cite at length because I will utilize some of his statements later when I reframe the allegorical basis of poetry:

[12] Giacomo Leopardi, *Zibaldone*, in *Tutte le opere*, 2 vols. (Florence: Sansoni, 1965). "Zibaldone" means hodge-podge, an "immethodical miscellany" Coleridge would say, basically a collection of scholarly notes, drafts, projects, philosophical and historical reflections, a sort of *Nachlass* posthumously published (Samuel T. Coleridge, *Biographia Literaria*, edited by James Engell and W. Jackson Bate, vol. 1 [Princeton: Princeton University Press, 1983], 88). See now the English version, Giacomo Leopardi, *Zibaldone*, edited by Michael Caesar and Franco D'Intimo, revised edition (New York: Farrar, Straus and Giroux, 2015), δ 4234–5.

[13] After the Hellenistic and Latin period, in the late Middle Ages Dante also defends the superiority and primacy of lyric poetry, understood as "canzone"; cf. Dante, *Literature in the Vernacular*, translated by Sally Purcell (Manchester: Carcanet New Press, 1981), II, iii, *et infra*. On the other hand, his greatest work is the grandest allegory of them all, *The Divine Comedy*: quite an "amplification" of the lyric! Except where noted, all translations from the Italian are my own.

> The epic poem also was sung accompanied by lyre or with music, in the streets, for the people, like the earliest lyric poems. It is nothing more than a hymn to honor the heroes and the nations or its armies; an extended hymn. See for instance the songs of savages, and those of bards of earlier eras, which partake of both the epic or the lyrical, wherein often we cannot tell to which of the two genres to assign them … The dramatic is the last of the three genres both in terms of time and nobility. It is not an inspiration, but an *invention*, it is the daughter of civilization, not of nature, the poetry is framed within convention and the will of its author/s, not on the basis of its essence … Drama is not proper to uncultured nations. It is spectacle, the offspring of civilization and *otium*, the creation of man's ingeniousness, not the inspiration of nature … All others can be reduced to these three heads, or are genres distinguished not by poetry but by meter or some other external device. The elegiac is the name of a meter … the didactic, insofar as is embodies true poetry, is either epic or lyric.[14]

In this hierarchized poetology, drama does not fare well, as it is historically and genealogically considered a derivative art, the product of contrived intelligence, a pastime. Drama is not "natural" and moreover it deals with minute details and with situations that are ultimately simple. So while it speaks to something considered to be "the truth," this truth is irregular and disharmonic, says Leopardi, and rests on imitation. Implicitly, imitation in time and place, according to dominant taste and protocols, as drama is performed by actors on a specific stage. But poetry is not this kind of imitation, says Leopardi. *Poetry imitates something of or from nature that produces an expression of the most profound feeling (*sentimento*)*. There is not much of a concern with the truth, understood philosophically (or theologically), but the "true" of the sentiment being embodied in poetic language, in other words, that it is, it exists *as such*.

Now, for a comparative critical context,[15] let us recall for a moment the apparently antithetical position of his fellow poet on the northern shore of

[14] Ibid.

[15] On the complex evolution of the lyric and its turning, through Western history, into a self-effacing literariness, see the insightful study by Walter R. Johnson, *The Idea of the Lyric: Lyric Modes in Ancient and Modern Poetry* (Berkeley: University of California Press, 1982), especially the Introduction, where it touches on the problematic "you" of the speaking lyrical persona, which is presented through an essentially monodic voice, and the foibles of the eternally exiled self in twentieth-century poetry in "search for this invisible ideal" (2). Interestingly, Johnson opens with a reference to the T. S. Eliot of "The Three Voices of Poetry" who, manifesting a certain continuity with Leopardi and Baudelaire, argues that "the first-voice poet is expressing 'his own thoughts and sentiments to himself or to no one.' This voice, this poetic genre, he elects to designate as 'meditative verse' and it is meditative verse that for him replaces outmoded lyric, which was perhaps never quite genuine in any case."

the English Channel. In the "Preface to *Lyrical Ballads*" William Wordsworth (1770–1850) conceives of the language of poetry as imitating "the very language of men," downplaying genre differences and laureate diction. From this stems his other corollaries concerning the need, in poetry, for description, the focus on a subject, the acceptance of an intermediary structure like the image—"poetry is the image of man and nature"—and finally the much cited passage:

> Poetry is the spontaneous overflow of powerful feelings: it takes its origin from emotion recollected in tranquility: the emotion is contemplated till, by a species of reaction, the tranquility gradually disappears, and an emotion, kindred to that which was before the subject of contemplation, is gradually produced, and does itself actually exist in the mind.[16]

In view of what will be argued later is the necessity, in our time, to restore that referentiality to poetry that is typical of prose and allegories, we could read Wordsworth as a subterranean precursor for those poetics which cannot exist independently of their sociohistorical context, their surroundings, in his case prominently the Lake District. But its object is still

> the truth, not individual and local but *general and operative*; not standing upon external testimony, but carried alive into the heart by passion; *truth which is its own testimony*, which gives competence and confidence to the tribunal to which it appeals, and receives from the same tribunal.[17]

Quite complex a thought, for if truth in poetry is being its own self-same expression ("testimony"), that is, a self-generating and self-referential expression, it means the poet speaks as if they were God or a medium, or the oracle at Delphi: no interlocutor needed. It may seem the circuit is closed: "beauty is truth, truth beauty," ends Keats's "Ode on a Grecian Urn."

In any case, we have a dilemma: on the one hand poetry is "philosophical"[18] and bears upon what is "general"; and on the other it rests on the individual's passion, though it may have to be toned down and *re*created. Wordsworth explicitly addresses the need to seek for the right word or expression *within the language of the tribe*, and work in a median register (which later critics claim is what makes his diction "revolutionary" vis-à-vis his eighteenth-century precursors). But a space or abyss between the self and the world is still present,

[16] Cited in Charles Norman, ed., *Poets on Poetry* (New York: Free Press, 1962), 154.
[17] Ibid.
[18] Ibid.

as if there were a mysterious connection or *relation* between a general truth and a particular true, or what Giambattista Vico would juxtapose as the "true" and the "certain."[19] What I think is relevant here is that in his poetics as in his poetry, Wordsworth claims nonetheless to refer to something outside the poem, outside of language, which is revealed by that concern for "the language of men," that is, the speech (tones, variations, etc.) of his community.[20]

By contrast, in a *Zibaldone* note from August 1828, Leopardi writes that imitation bears with it something "servile." *It is false to consider and define poetry as an imitative art* and to compare it with painting, for example. *The poet imagines: imagination sees the world as it is not, it constructs a world that does not exist, it makes believe, it invents, but it does not imitate,* I mean it does not *purposely* imitate: this is the essential character poets express in poetry.

To make the horizon of understanding clearer, I hope, we can now turn to a third position, from nearly the same years. In his "A Defence of Poetry," Percy B. Shelley writes:

> A Poem is the very image of life expressed in its eternal truth. There is this difference between a story and a poem, that a story is a catalogue of detached facts, which have no other bond of connection than time, place, circumstance, cause and effect, the other, *the poem, is the creation of actions according to the unchangeable forms of human nature*, as existing in the mind of the creator, which is itself the image of all other minds. The one [the story] is partial, and applies only to a definite period of time, and a certain combination of events which can never again recur. The other [that is, poetry]—*is universal, and contains within itself the germ of a relation to whatever motives or actions have place in the possible varieties of human nature.*[21] (my emphases)

19 See Giambattista Vico, *The New Science*, translated by David Marsh (New York: Penguin, [1744] 1999), δ 138: "Philosophy contemplates reason, from which we derive our abstract knowledge of what is *true*. Philology observes the creative authorship and authority of human volition, from which we derive our common knowledge of what is *certain*" (emphases added).

20 That this "language of men" is ultimately a fiction, not duly analyzed by Wordsworth, was already pointed out by Coleridge in the *Biographia Literaria*, vol. 2, chs. 14, 22 *et infra*. About the origin and "construction" of a language for a community within certain geohistorical spaces, Coleridge references Dante's *De Vulgari Eloquentia*, bk I, ch. 9, who had first described the process whereby from many regional variations *and* differences among specific languages of trades and activities, a koine is eventually built. But they change over time. This gives language at once the character of convention *and* that of history (understood minimally as modifications in usage over a span of time).

21 Percy B. Shelley, *Shelley's Poetry and Prose*, edited by Donald H. Reiman and Sharon B. Powers (New York: Norton, 1977), 485. Also in Norman, *Poets on Poetry*, 180.

The poet, concerned with "the unchangeable forms of human nature," yet fully in touch with his self, as "creator" of something beyond himself, is the man transformed into Man, the paradigm, which explains why the poet can be lyrical and epigraphic at the same time, as in his *Adonais*. But this concern with the "universal" is eminently a metaphysical issue, it's an ontology that underlies all the ontic manifestations: "a relation to whatever motives or actions." Later, in the *Defence*, we read "Poetry [is] … the expression of the imagination: and *poetry is connate with the origin of man.*"[22] (We will return to this last observation made by Shelley.)

The "Ancient Diaphora" in Modernity

If we look at what Leopardi thinks of metaphysics, which is often equated with philosophy *tout court*, it shouldn't surprise us to read that "it is the exact contrary of poetry" and, moreover, (1) that "its foundation is that everything is relative,"[23] (2) that "without ideology it becomes an uncertain, frivolous science, full of dreams and unsustainable conjectures," and (3) that its endless questions concerning time and space "are nothing more than a logomachy born out of little clarity in ideas and even less capacity to analyze our intellect."[24]

Let us reflect on what we have here thus far. We are in the throes of a nature/culture debate, of an inspiration versus imitation dialectic, and of a poetry versus philosophy quarrel. Considered from a different angle, there existed in Leopardi's cultural milieu a near cult for a supposed authenticity and primacy of the ancients, incidentally shared by Friedrich Hölderlin and that, at the time, was marshalled against the coming "barbarism" of the affected, journalistic, urbanizing reality of the early nineteenth century. We are not interested in evaluating Leopardi's overall poetic, or whether there are or aren't "contradictions" in his position. Poetry, and the lyric in particular, is not history. We do know that elsewhere Leopardi displays a hermeneutic sensibility concerning changing mores and values. When he prefaces collections of poems

[22] Ibid.

[23] We will pick up and develop the concept of relation further down.

[24] This less than laudatory assessment of what philosophy is echoes unwittingly an earlier position by William Blake, who also struggled against and critiqued Enlightenment Reason, as in the early "There is NO natural Religion," last lines: "If it were not for the Poetic or Prophetic character the Philosophical and Experimental would soon be at the ratio of all things, & stand still unable to do other than repeat the same dull round over again" (William Blake, *The Poetry and Prose of William Blake*, edited by David V. Erdman [Garden City, NY: Doubleday, 1970], 1).

or translations, he reveals that he is ever wary that the edition is meant for a specific contemporary audience.[25] But the conclusion is therefore inescapable: *poetry is not philosophy*, as it does not deal (ideally, in its most perfect exemplars) with concepts, relations, explanations, and justifications. Compare once again with Wordsworth: "Aristotle, I have been told, has said, that poetry is the most philosophic of all writing: it is so: its object is truth, not individual and local, but general and operative."[26] Note that this would be consistent with a poetry that, in Wordsworth's later poetry, intends to teach moral precepts, an augmented sensitivity, or a way of looking at nature. Further, this is diametrically opposed to Coleridge's observation in the *Biographia Literaria* whereby "a poem is that species of composition, which is opposed to works of science, by proposing for its immediate object *pleasure, not truth*."[27] At the same time, though, if we continue with the above Wordsworth passage, we cannot miss the simultaneous claim to an independent poetic world, one which is informed by an absolute autonomy, a self-sustaining whole: "[truth …] not standing upon external testimony, but carried alive into the heart by passion; truth which is its own testimony, which gives competence and confidence to the tribunal to which it appeals, and receives them from the same tribunal. Poetry is the image of man and nature."[28] Clearly either Wordsworth is confused, or philosophy must try a different critical approach, as the claim is made that *poetry is philosophical*, concerned with *universals*, but at the same time *it is not philosophical*, as it expresses one subjectivity in relation to ambiance, nature, people, things *as* things, which elicit images and thoughts that are marked for place, with context for each occurrence.

The lyric, of which the idyll is a finely honed, crystal-pure form, expresses "situations of the soul, personal feelings, adventures of my soul" and is ultimately not concerned with the reader, with anyone other than oneself (or One's Self). Leopardi implies as much when, in an early entry in the *Zibaldone* (August 25, 1820), he writes:

> The only thing the poet must show is that he doesn't understand the effect which his images, descriptions, feelings, etc., will produce in his readers. This

[25] Cf. "Dell'errore attribuito a Innocenzo per aver dipinto Apollo piuttosto col violino che con la lira" (Leopardi, *Tutte le opere*, 1:964–5), and several of the "Prefazioni," "Manifesti," and "Appunti," written between 1825 and 1836.

[26] "Preface," in Norman, *Poets on Poetry*, 146–7.

[27] Norman, *Poets on Poetry*, 163; from Coleridge, *Biographia Literaria*, 2:14, my emphasis.

[28] Ibid., 147.

is true of the orator, and any writing of beautiful literature, and it could be extended to any writer in general.[29]

If any affectation is permitted the writer, this consists in *not* being … there, aware, ears pitched; or in his/her not foreseeing the beautiful effects which the words will have on those who read or listen, and of having no will or specific aim beyond that of narrating, celebrating, etc.[30]

And yet despite their own poetic, the verse they wrote ponder the most profound philosophical questions, reconducible to the ultimate question: What is being? What is man? In the contemporary acceptation: What is a human being? What is the meaning of existence? Consider briefly analogous metaphysical questions emerging from the heart of poems of the same era, starting with Leopardi himself:

What are you doing up there, in the sky, o moon,
Tell me, silent moon?

(Leopardi, "Night Song")

But who wast thou, O happy, happy dove?
His Psyche true!

(Keats, "Ode to Psyche")

What immortal hand or eye,
Could frame thy fearful symmetry?

(Blake, "The Tyger")

You spur my thoughts to tread the tracks
That lead to eternal nothingness

(Foscolo, "To Evening")

Where are you, young one, who would always
Wake me in the morning, where are you light?

(Hölderlin, "The Blind Singer")

[29] Leopardi, *Zibaldone*, 161.

[30] Leopardi expressed his distaste for the employ of all those diacritical devices he found in the work of Byron, which he holds to be self-indulging and self-aggrandizing, disrespectful of the reader, in a way excessively meta-textual. He feels this detracts from the proper evaluation of a poet he otherwise considers a fine mind and with deep poetic sensibility. The fundamental distinction here is that poets are "inspired" and attend to saying, whereas orators and everyone else writing/speaking prose typically Explain, and must be concerned with the effects the words have on the reader/listener. On the difference between saying and explaining, as derived from Heidegger's thought, see Richard E. Palmer, *Hermeneutics: Interpretation Theory in Schleiermacher, Dilthey, Heidegger and Gadamer* (Evanston, IL: Northwestern University Press, 1980), 13–32.

Leopardi's reflections on the lyric as the quintessence of poetry and of philosophy as what deals with concepts, relations, descriptions, and justifications is a Romantic (per)version of Plato's "ancient quarrel" between poetry and philosophy from *Republic*, book X.[31] There, however, it is philosophy that seeks the universal form, true knowledge, and poetry is understood as a derivative social art, an imitation of an imitation, a form of discourse that may, however, excite the lower ("Dionysian," Nietzsche would say) pulsions in humans, unleash an *eros* that may not be controllable, and would likely disrupt the ironclad *polis* Socrates was designing.

But as we saw in a few representative major poets from the Romantic period, poetry does bear in its bosom a philosophical afflatus, a yearning, the need to touch either universal ideas or concepts, or pretend at the same time that it is anchored to the specific givenness of whatever is embodied in the language, where it still triggers metaphysical reflection. One need only think of Martin Heidegger's readings of the major German poets, in his mature years.

Historiography and Hermeneutics: The Turn

Staying close to recent critical theory, philosophy of language, and hermeneutics, we ought seriously to consider whether perhaps lyric poetry never meant to communicate anything at all! Hugo Friedrich, in his classic study *Die Struktur der modernen Lyrik*,[32] identifies and describes many traits of twentieth-century lyric, such as

1. depersonalization,
2. emptiness of ideals,
3. the highlighting of the ugly, and
4. the incongruent, the ironic, the absurd, and so on.

But it doesn't escape his notice that *perhaps the obscurity, the incomprehensibility, the disinterest in the reader or the others* (as opposed to a metaphysical Other)

[31] Plato, *The Collected Dialogues*, edited by Edith Hamilton and Huntington Cairns (Princeton, NJ: Princeton University Press, 1975), 832, para. 607b5. See in this context Stanley Rosen, *The Quarrel Between Philosophy and Poetry* (New York: Routledge, 1988), 1–26. For a background analysis of the "quarrel" see my chapter "About the Ancient Diaphora" in *Prefaces*, 169–88.

[32] In the English version, the slight change in rendering "lyric" with "poetry" tout court is emblematic of how in modernity poetry means essentially lyrical poetry: Hugo Friedrich, *The Structure of Modern Poetry*, translated by Joachim Neugroschel (Evanston, IL: Northwestern University Press, 1974).

may be something tied to a deeper problem of language. Charles Baudelaire wrote: "there's a certain glory in not being understood," echoed decades later by Eugenio Montale: "No one would write verse if the problem of poetry were that of being understood."[33] As I have explored elsewhere,[34] the response of criticism to this disdainful intransigence has been misguided. Some have attempted to reconfigure criticism into a *poetology* to take into account this fundamental realization,[35] while others have redrawn the map to demonstrate that poetry as a genre is itself headed toward a merger with prose.

The paradigm, however, points to the conclusion: a poem that speaks of the person's ego/Ego, his/her emotions, or self, or seeks Being, is by definition a lyric poem. Yet a metaphysics is always presupposed, less often clearly stated, and occasionally is even declared antithetical to poetry, as both critics and poets have presupposed that the two cannot coexist. In any case, the poem still discloses a world of (non-)Being, posing ultimate but not always answerable questions: Why do I live? What do we do before death? Why does time elude us? Why is love so difficult? What does it all mean? It is true that poetry and philosophy have a common origin in wonder, then they may be thought of as two different ways of seeking the same thing. Namely, an essence (whether transcendent or transcendental is a different question, not taken up here). To give one brief but canonical example, let's pick up Keats's "Odes" again, replete with wonder or exclamations at the unsolvable yet immanent paradoxes of existence. In "Ode on a Grecian Urn" (1819), we read

> What men or gods are these? What maidens loath?
> What mad pursuit? What struggle to escape?
> What pipes and timbrels? What wild ecstasy?

This is followed by a realization that the image on the urn is actually freezing a moment in time with all its potential energy available and spread over a different kind of temporality, eliciting if not rescuing a sense of the desire of wanting to live *forever*, but now embodied in the *figuras* to which we can relate.

[33] Cited in Friedrich, *Structure of Modern Poetry*, 14 *et infra*. Still relevant for a phenomenological explication of the dynamics between poetry and aesthetics, and how it evolved from the Renaissance through the major avant-gardes, is Luciano Anceschi's *Autonomia ed eteronomia dell'arte* (Milan: Garzanti, [1936] 1976). On Anceschi's crucial role in launching the last Italian neo-avant-garde, the *Novissimi*, see Peter Carravetta "Luciano Anceschi," in Frank N. Magill (ed.), *Critical Survey of Literary Theory*, vol. 1, 29–35 (Pasadena, CA: Salem Press, 1988).

[34] See Carravetta, *Prefaces*, esp. chs. 1 and 2.

[35] See the intriguing suggestions made by the Portuguese poet and critic Alberto Pimenta, *O silêncio dos poetas* [The Silence of the Poets] (Lisbon: A Regra do Jogo, 1978), which would deserve closer analysis.

Image and concept coincide:We might say that the being of existence rests in its having been a yearning since forever:

Ah, happy, happy boughs! That cannot shed
Your leaves, nor ever bid the Spring adieu;
[...]
                    happy, happy love!
Forever warm and still to be enjoyed,
Forever panting, and forever young;

Until the poem closes by folding back upon itself, with a final resolution: an acceptance that anchors some sort of universal truth:

"Beauty is truth, truth beauty,"—that is all
Ye know on earth, and all ye need to know.

Similar lines can be found in other poems, for instance "O latest born and loveliest visions far / of All Olympus' faded hierarchy!" ("Ode to Psyche"), and of course in other poets, such as Hölderlin. The lyric seems to be the preferred choice of genre or form for most literary critics and basically all philosophers who intend to forage in aesthetic and poetological territory.

But now let us ask: what about ... the *other* implied in any linguistic exchange? The one to whom you tell the tale? Or the one from whom you hear it told?

The reasons of allegory have in part been already introduced, albeit in an allusive manner, but inferences can now be made. As opposed to the lyric, the epic is almost by definition allegorical in that its capacious temporal frame requires and then employs certain poetological conventions, such as personification, prosopopeia, plot development, and alternating first and third persons. In short, *allegorical poetry (typically epic) exists and makes sense primarily owing to its constant referencing to a broader, non-textual set of concerns, values, symbols.* The reasons for *the presence of allegorical language* are also embedded in these external, contextual frames of reference, and therefore, I will argue, *represent the cofounding, co-enabling force for movement, change, metamorphosis, the very possibility of otherness.* In terms of semiotics and the philosophy of language, a rethinking of what allegorical language might actually be (as opposed to the textbook version of it, as we will see below) requires that the very notion of the sign, which underlies our contemporary ideas about language and how we interpret its workings, be altered, shifting from a dualistic signifier/signified (or token/referent) model to an unstable triangle in which the referent, the third apex of the older models (and of which C. S. Peirce's remains the most elaborate)[36] regains its role, and permits relinking with whatever situation, indeed conception, of reality or society or history the interpreter embodies when she chooses to analyze specific texts.[37] I will return to the rehabilitation of the interpreter-in-society further down. It is true that allegorical writing has witnessed a decline during the modern period. Progressively in the second half of the nineteenth and more intensively in the twentieth century both poets and critics have repeatedly shunned it. Part of the rejection was probably due to the automatic association of allegory with the millenary traditions of the epic and then, in early modernity through the Enlightenment, didactic or moralizing poetry. Perhaps the explosion of patriotic or nationalistic poetry that swept through Europe and South America rendered allegory pretty much "instrumental," too easy to decode because it had to appeal to a variety of listeners bent on creating a literary tradition, a foundational "national epic" to go with the new nation-states.[38] Moreover, another truism of modernity considered the novel the true heir of the epic, and the novel is not particularly suited to allegories,[39] at least insofar as the dominant schools turned to realism, naturalism, introspection, and "lyrical" prose symbolism.[40] The story of this near disinterest is well known. To give two eminent examples, from influential yet opposing aesthetic and critical grounds, both Benedetto Croce and György

[36] For a more detailed articulation, see my *The Elusive Hermes*, 29–38, 257–73, and a shortened version in Peter Carravetta, "After Thought: From Method to Discourse (Rhetoric)," *RSAJ: Rivista di Studi Americani* 26 (2015): 121–40.

[37] Again, I am summarizing in perhaps too formulaic a manner researches and readings done at different times and for different occasions, mostly in my *Elusive Hermes* (2012) book. It is understood that my attempt at recapturing the referent, the "excluded middle" (see Michel Serres, *Hermes: Literature, Science, Philosophy* (Baltimore: Johns Hopkins University Press, 1982), 67, 69 *et infra*), is hardly Hegelian, coming in fact *after* the "age of suspicion" (Paul Ricoeur), and "the end of Philosophy" (Heidegger). From this derives the exploratory nature of my article.

[38] Consider that "national(istic)" poems that were practically written for every battle and war, praising generals and ideologues, and some of which have endured and become cultural reflexes through school adoptions. Though they indubitably contributed to the banalizing of the required allegories, most of them have disappeared from the canon (though in Europe their "fortune" among the general populace has often been a function or result of the political orientation of the ministries of education, for instance, under totalitarian regimes). For our purposes, however, particularly instructive would be to follow Baudelaire's struggle against the allegoricism of Victor Hugo (especially in the *Contemplations*), in an effort to cancel out "allegory" as style, tropology, or reservoir of traditional mythemes. But Baudelaire may also have prepared the path for a deeper understanding of the allegorical, as in his "Correspondences" and "Spleen," which implicates the gesture and materiality of the poet as well as the situatedness and interest of the interlocutor/interpreter, the famed "my brother, hypocritical reader."

[39] Not that one could not read a given novel as an allegory of some major topos, but that is a problem that concerns the method and theory adopted by the interpreter, not the studied poietic intent of the writer.

[40] A related topic that we cannot develop here is the curious evolution of the prose poem.

Lukács condemned allegory as "artificial," a structural, architectonic scaffolding, an extrinsic component, not really poetry. On the one hand, then, the epic and its allegorical sign system had metamorphosed into the novel, wherein the object of narrative was no longer overarching themes such as religious or ethical values, or the singing of praise or demise of larger than life characters, but rather microscopic, introspective, and localized events and accidents. Yet, we might interject, can anyone not call Herman Melville's *Moby Dick* America's grandest allegory? On the other hand, despite and in part against the major figures who still wrote poetic histories and paid homage silently to Clio and overtly to Calliope—think of Ugo Foscolo, Lord Byron, Victor Hugo, Dosso Dossi, Robert Browning, H. W. Longfellow—the crown of the writing arts was passed on to lyrical poetry, which allowed other muses to step in/to the poet's ken: Euterpe, Terpischore, Erato.

I took Leopardi as representative of an idea of the lyric that I believe is quintessentially Romantic and that will founder in the throes of Modernism or avant-gardism. Its assertions are categorical and totalizing. Its questions are about the transcendent meaning of it all: ultimate knowledge and bliss at once. Again, not that there weren't other Romantic poets whose notion of the lyric was somewhat different, argued on the basis of a less axiological or hierarchical subdivision of the three primary genres. We referred to Wordsworth above, author of a little-studied epic poem *The Excursion* (1814), but we could easily recall the poetics of Keats or Foscolo or Hugo. Further, we cannot exclude the impact made by the Jena School, including the Schlegel brothers' *Athenaeum* (1798–1801).[41] By the time we get to H. W. Longfellow (1807–1882), allegorism begins to wane. The last great (and perhaps greatest) allegorical writer on the European scene was Gabriele D'Annunzio (1863–1938), whose *Laudi* (1902–1912) aimed to be "the total poem."[42] But in a number of communities allegorical epics were read reductively, at best read ironically, at worst as props, pretexts.

[41] See, for example, Gerald L. Bruns, "The Invention of Poetry in Early German Romanticism," *Wordsworth Circle*, 47 (2–3) (2016) (Spring/Summer): 110–14 (available online: https://www.questia.com/library/journal/1G1-460573840/the-invention-of-poetry-in-early-german-romanticism [accessed October 7, 2020]): "I would like to propose that we think of the early German Romantics–specifically the *Athenaeum* group (1798–1801)–as the first avant-garde of literary Modernism, where poetry is an instance of art 'as such,' a form in itself and not (simply) an instrument of mediation in behalf of signification, representation, or expressions of subjectivity. Indeed, the celebrated post-Nietzschean critique of instrumental reason really has its origins in this period (1792–1803). As Friedrich Schlegel's brother, August Wilhelm, responding to Kant's *Critique of Judgment* (1790), argued in his 'Theory of Art' (1798), 'it is necessary not to treat language in poetry as a mere instrument of the understanding' (1997: 205)."

[42] On D'Annunzio, see the chapter "From Ulysses to Zarathustra to Hermes" in my *Prefaces*, 79–129.

The rhetoric of the lyrical is predicated through an expression, and upon an underlying metaphysical assumption, which attracts and subsumes the world to itself, as the meanings tweaked out of experience conflate in the unity of the I, and the obsessive need to embody in language a general, universal, sweeping gesture or ultimate (often tragic) truth.

In the decades following Leopardi, Shelley, and Wordsworth, there occur a series of complementary revolutions, which can be identified with signal works by Edgar Allan Poe, Charles Baudelaire, Arthur Rimbaud, or with "movements" such as symbolism and *l'art pour l'art*. In Europe, with the ultimate radicalization by Stéphane Mallarmé, and then Paul Valéry, *the autonomy of the work of art finds in the lyric the crystallized isolation of its own revelations, the overload of apocalyptic illuminations.* It's as if language folds upon itself, the signifier swallows up all possible signified, while the serpent eating its own tail implied in self-referentiality evokes by indirection the "eternal" self-consuming voice of a (non)Being. Its words stand for themselves, its naming is nondirectional, its sense often meanders in unintelligibility. Now let us ask: was this an undisclosed intention, a practical "de-fense?" Historians of literature typically point to the regimes that overtook Western societies in the interim between the two World Wars as one principal reason why poets became obscure, hermetic, minimalist, beyond their symbolist precursors. But it could be attributed as well to the rise of mass society, to the exponential growth of other media, such as newspapers, film, periodicals, radio. Decades later, Gadamer would muse:

> In the end, it is easy to appreciate why in the age of mass communication … lyric poetry necessarily has a hermetic character. How can the word still stand out amid the flood of information? How can it draw us to itself except by alienating us from those all too familiar turns of speech that we all expect?[43]

This doesn't mean, again, that a philosophy is not lurking somewhere, that a metaphysic isn't negotiated with that disinterested, unimportant reader. One need only to think of some poems by Eugenio Montale, Antonio Machado, T. S. Eliot, Jorge Guillén, and Wallace Stevens to retrieve the common origin of both poetizing and thinking, of the *poetic petitioning for a sound philosopheme.* But such coincidence inevitably highlights the *relation to* a unity or whole that, whether absent, bygone, or projected, speaks of a supernal *eidos*.

[43] Hans-Georg Gadamer, *The Relevance of the Beautiful and Other Essays*, ed. Robert Bernasconi (Cambridge: Cambridge University Press, 1986), 135, from the chapter "Philosophy and Poetry," 131–9.

No different is the fate of that alternative to pure poetry that claims to *speak to* or *address something* variously called reality, such as in political or "committed" poetry. But in this case the problems are of a different nature, since a "mimetic" or "representational" imperative lurks beneath the very construct and is accepted as an *a priori*. In fact, committed or political poetry suffers when it actually names specific ideologies and, as in ancient times or during the Enlightenment, wishes to philosophize in verse. Leaving this juggernaut aside for the moment[44] we can say that whether philosophical or political, referentiality in literature has been the great victim of modernity. As Gadamer aptly puts it:

> For all direction to a goal as we find it in military or revolutionary poetry is clearly distinguished from what is to be called "art," and for no other reason than that insofar as it is purely directed to a goal, it manifestly lacks the concentrated form of poetry.[45]

My question at this juncture is the following: what happens when we turn our critical glance from the diachronic to the synchronic axis? How do we read literature that comes from a world, from a social, personal, historical experience totally alien to ours. Consider the literature of minorities, marginals, foreigners, exiles, immigrants, border-crossers, polyglots, mestizos, bi-nationals, technocratic world travelers, electronic virtual arts … and the reticence or better resistance they encounter on the basis not only of falling short of our tried but worn Romantic and then modernist forms, but perhaps primarily owing to their inability, at the level of "content," to strike a note of recognition, promise a utopia, or redeem us somehow. But at this juncture, in the background we can hear the shrill "defenses" of the Great Canon of Western Literature. Even Harold Bloom, in the end, caved in. Rather than list the main advocates pro and con in the debate, I should like to point out in passing that the issue is not so much one of inclusion/exclusion of certain texts but rather of *how to read them* … there are ways of rereading our own deeply embedded master plots and symbols as to make them appear … foreign, or anti-canonic, or at any rate still potentially able to disclose views both ethic and aesthetic that go against the grain. But in this outlook, the onus falls on the critic much more than on the poet.

[44] See below, Chapter 6, "Poetics and Science."
[45] Ibid., 136.

Difference and Narration: Detour

If we look at Native American literature,[46] for example, we discover that, much like pre-Socratic poetry according to Hölderlin, words are imbued with "magical powers," they exist in their own right, conserve a sacrality and a connectedness with Spirit, their equivalent or analogue of Being. But unlike Western poetry it does not know the "evolution" toward a hierarchy of values or a subdivision in different genres with rules or, more broadly, as a distillation of something called the self or the ego. Nor does it seem to register a progressive alienation from the surrounding environment, be it nature or culture, as we witness instead in Europe and America after the modernist poetics dissolve into so many strands. Native American literature is by and large predicated upon an idea of language that reflects a fundamental *connection between beings and entities*, transcending the supremacy of a (politically or juridically defined) "people," revolving in cyclical time, seeking junctures and relations among all things created and imagined. Indeed, the very organization of ideas is radically different from our own.[47] There is hardly a "master plot" in our Renaissance or Enlightenment or modernist sense of the expression, though they are rich in creation myths, founding allegories, highly symbolic forms of transmission. Characters are defined more by the number of worlds they inhabit, the boundaries they cross, the obstacles to spiritual balance and interconnectedness, than by the obstacles to attain a goal, a quest for truth, a search for one's self. *One's self is fundamentally a self-in-relation-to-the-all*, the locating of a particle in simultaneous contact with all realms, beyond hierarchies, before the arrival (and imposition) of "civilized" norms and "laws."

Now this may lead someone to view Native American Indian literature as possessing a metaphysics of its own. Yes *and* no. Insofar as it expresses a worldview, yes, it's implied: if you can narrate, you have a theoretical assumption at work, you can cut and shape your world. But insofar as this poetry is eminently out-looking through time and memory, insofar as it needs an external component—nature,

[46] This reflection derives from a course I did at Queens College on reading across cultural and linguistic barriers. For historical panorama, still very useful is Frederick W. Turner, ed., *The Portable North American Indiana Reader* (New York: Random House, 1986).

[47] Besides various studies in Native American literature, I have been inspired by the ideas of Benjamin Lee Whorf, Edward Sapir, and Émile Benveniste. In particular, Whorf's *linguistic relativism* (the "weak" version), which we will return to further down, in Chapter 4, is here implicitly contrasted with the *Cartesian linguistics* of Noam Chomsky and Stephen Pinker, who beyond their differences support the universal innate grammar theory.

mineral, spirit, symbol, magic, and for (given) listeners—and insofar as it essays to transcend or circumvent the West's obsession with entities and manipulable effects, with further proof of abstracted emotional, social, and political values, then it is *not* metaphysical. American Indian literature foregrounds a *lived* temporality, binds myth back to the unconscious of a/the people from which it sprang, requires at the rhetorical level an audience, a memory, and finally will not be blinded by the light of its own revelations.

The critically legitimate doubt that may arise here is whether we as Euro-American modernists are unwittingly drawing closer to an idea of literature in touch with theological beginnings, which entails a movement toward a founding or the establishment of a sacred saying, an all-encompassing breath of life, a *pneuma*. This is not necessarily negative, provided we do not fall back into one of the many instrumental poetics of Modernism, and specifically the sermonizing kind, committed to converting listener to a cause or faith, or didactically aimed at instilling imperial moralities and "universal values" (universal for the Eurologocentric *oecumene*, that is). Rather, as both Vico and Heidegger in unrelated if not opposing (as we will see) ways theorized, *the poetic voice is founding, it is the speech of the gods, the principle and the possibility of social coexistence*. I suggest we reconsider Vico's intuition (later proved to be anthropologically, mythographically consistent)[48] concerning the theological myths sung by earliest tribes and clans, what we used to call "primitive" cultures,[49] on the cusp between primate *in-fans* and *homo sapiens loqui*. Yet already by the time Greece reaches its peak cultural splendor and hegemony, by the fifth century BCE, narrative, allegorical poetry is discredited (from Plato onwards), the knowledge its "myths" and "representations" bore in their words were considered vague, imitations of imitations, untenable, certainly not what philosophy, dialectic, logic could now deliver.[50] Further, if you wanted to see, feel, hear the anguished soul of man's being, then you would turn to lyric, epigrams, dithyrambs, eventually to dramatic monologue. But the lyric, contrary

[48] See, for instance, Theodor H. Gaster, "Myth and Story," in Alan Dundes (ed.), *Sacred Narrative: Readings in the Theory of Myth*, 110–36 (Berkeley: University of California Press, 1984), as well as Mircea Eliade, *Myth and Reality*, translated by Willard R. Trask (New York: Harper & Row, 1963).

[49] See Vico, *New Science*, bk 2 ("Poetic Wisdom"), § 1 ("Poetic metaphysics") and 2 ("Poetic Logic"), paras. 34, 375, 383, 741 *et infra*. The key notion here is the appearance of "imaginative general categories" or archetypes in pre-civilized (in the Western sense) societies. These, for Vico, had also *cognitive value* and structured the social patterns and habits of the earliest human cultures.

[50] For this and the rest of the paragraph, see the detailed analyses in my *The Elusive Hermes*, pt. 2, dedicated explicitly to the passage from a mythological to a logothetic understanding of both *kosmos* and the *polis*.

to what Leopardi and his Romantic cohorts believed, comes *after* the founding theological allegories that mark the beginning of clans and rudimentary societies (anthropologically understood). *The lyric* is almost by definition imbued with the rattling and birth pangs of self-consciousness, and in Vico's evolutionary (though cyclical) view, it must a be *a later acquisition*, as it is actually contemporaneous to the rise of rational thinking, with a self-awareness of philosophy itself, and as such represents the earliest challenge to a thinking that has slowly found a way of controlling, through language and symbols, the mysterious powers of nature. To put it in Nietzschean terms, Dionysius is not relinquishing his autochtonous power and energy to the harmonious balanced Apollonian imposition without a fight. In the earliest poetries there was no sense of self (as we understand that word-concept from Saint Augustine through Francis Petrarch to Blaise Pascal and René Descartes) but only a communal speech still very much in awe and terror at the supernatural powers that surrounded the earliest communities. These fantastic, poetic narrations have been lost to the West . . . all attempts at recapturing a presumed contiguity between sign and thing, word and object, speech and image as was still (presumably) retrievable in the pre-Socratics turned out to be, especially after the decline of Greece, elegant soliloquies and wishful thinking.

I am not making a case for a recovery of something "original" in the fetishistic way we have fleshed out this notion by the twentieth century, in literature as in philosophy: originality, Pound's "make it new" sentence, has devolved quickly into a meme at the service of special currents and institutions, especially during the consolidation of monarchies and then nation-states. In the culture, this was followed by a class-anchored fashion market, and it has also turned into a verbal weapon of oppression and intimidation, of latent racism and explicit arrogance.[51] My view is that we should forget trying to be "original" in the West: the avant-gardes took care of that "myth" (in the Roland Barthes sense of the term): first by radicalizing the notion, then exacerbating it, and finally disintegrating and mocking its value.[52] In fact, if the problem of origin still obsesses the critical mind, then perhaps we should train our sights on the new emerging literatures (whether within a given

[51] Think of the differences between William Whitney and Franz Boas, the first arguing for the "superiority" of some languages over others (to the point of attempting to annihilate the languages of the Native Americans), the second for the emphasis on particularism, on the *relation* between a language and a culture. But see the critical literature on dialects, minority English, immigrant speech, bilingualism, to get an idea of the complexity of the issues.

[52] See my book *Prefaces*, ch. 3, and the discussion on who contributed to clarifying this problematic, in particular Hal Foster and Rosalind Krauss. In philosophy, central remains the work of the early Jacques Derrida.

national sphere or in its deterritorialized manifestations),[53] but without constantly comparing them to the many (and convenient) revisions we have of our own. If there is no "original" in a metaphysical sense, then we are simply comparing "worlds," none being prior or better than the other. In this way we would also have the possibility to engage with spiritual, ethical, personal, intellectual, and historical contexts that speak a different tongue, which may not be easily compared and hierarchized vis-à-vis our own canons. It may be that not everyone wants that.[54] Yet it may offer up *hermeneutic possibilities within which to change, or critique, or at best expand our understanding of other cultures.* The key here is that to cross this boundary, it helps to reimagine the nature and role of allegory.

This situation is in our times further complicated by the massive cross-pollination of values and fragmented intromissions of Euro-American modes of speaking, grammars, and preconstituted paths through society, in great part imposed by technological practices and conventions adopted worldwide. The writer and the public of the Native American are exposed to contradictory choices, to imposed strange daily habits, to unforeseen situations, to inexplicable monstrosities. Joy Harjo's poems, for example, speak of the necessity to "Remember" the inextricable connection to the environment, to the suturing power of the imagination as it leaps and relates moon to woman to creation to stages then to cycles and then to the moon once again. It is a call to tune in the flow and the processes, *the interdependence of being and beings*. Life is not conceived like a river with a source and an end but more like a fluid tangible memory that, like the tides of an ocean, lap, splash, and crunch stones, sand, and shells. And return. *As much as an aesthetic artifact, a poem is a healing chant, a thinking of the cosmos.* A poem can thus serve as an inroad into a critique of Western modernist forms of poetry. Another author, Leslie Silko, in the novel *Ceremony*, the main character is caught between several worlds, constantly attempting to regain his original wholeness as taught to him when he was a child on the reservation, but also constantly attempting to understand the horrors of the Second World War and in particular of the atomic bomb. No conclusive "objective" reason can be reached, neither by the West's own logic nor by his

[53] I am using the term "deterritorialized" in the sense of Gilles Deleuze and Felix Guattari's thesis in their *Kafka: Toward a Minor Literature*, translated by Dana Polan (Minneapolis: University of Minnesota Press, 1984), to which we will refer more extensively below.

[54] We may recall here some pages from Dostoievsky's *Notes from Underground*, or Nietzsche's *Dawn*, on people's creation of idols and belief in the "thou shalt" to the point of not being able to think, or ever question what's beneath conventions and moral platitudes.

Amerindian perception of the cycles of nature. Communicating this across the boundary separating the two is apparently impossible. The main character Tayo takes it upon himself to reach a level of consciousness that can embody the aspirations and the failings of *both* cultures. His recourse to a ceremony points to the need to avoid falling prey to the self-destructive logic of the West and to reinstate a communal spirit in an already altered and still changing Amerindian society. Works of this kind speak to the need to reconsider the unsteady and often confusing semantics of interlinguistic, cross-cultural communication. Here the background referents are not stable symbols or icons, but a panoply of mixed, grafted, or inlaid semantemes that have sclerotized if not altogether lost their original signification—and this on both sides, for both cultural/philosophical worldviews—and that require a risky but inescapable hermeneutic participation on the reader/listener's part. This uncertainty, a distinguishing trait of the postmodern condition,[55] is a constant reminder that Platonic Being, if it ever made sense at all (but historically it was made to), is now at best to be understood as a *being-in-becoming*, the voice of a feeling and understanding that highlights its own passing, its transitoriness, its recounting an harmony yet to be attained. It is only in political speeches that Native American Indians speak of repossessing their original lands and live again according to ancient rituals. Objectively, realistically, we all know this is a pipe dream. The Amerindians themselves know this. Yet in their poetry, even after the extermination of the Indian nations, the possibility of being connected to the whole recurs as a background lament, a future memory, a primary yearning.

Allegories of Silence

> When I made it to school
> they thought I didn't
> have a mind in English and if
> you don't have a mind in English
> you have a mind in nothing.
>
> (P. Medina, "Winter of a Rose")[56]

[55] For the broader critical horizon here, see Lyotard, *The Postmodern Condition*; David Harvey, *The Condition of Postmodernity*; Fred Jameson, *Postmodernism, or the Logic of Late Capitalism;* Rosalind Krauss, *The Originality of the Avant-Gardes.*

[56] Cited in Ray Gonzalez (ed.), *Currents from the Dancing River. Contemporary Latino Fiction, Nonfiction, and Poetry* (New York: Harcourt Brace, 1995), 374.

Our most interesting contemporary narratives are those that are deterritorialized, noncanonical, "small" in terms of their audience and acceptance, "long" in terms of their verbal structure. A literature that must be read allegorically because it *speaks-other*, or lets a (previously undisclosed) alterity emerge that does not fit most European models, is that of the Caribbean's. For centuries it was held that the local or regional populations did not and could not have had a Grand Literary Tradition. The critical doxa, already from the eighteenth century, held that they (formerly called "savages") just didn't have the "right elements," such as the "historical record," the monuments, the great deeds—great obviously by "our" standards—the identifiable reassuring and legitimating lofty genealogies. But we eventually realized that it was rather that they didn't have what *we thought* they *should* have had, that is, they spoke—literally and metaphorically—a different language, held different beliefs, had had no significant (again, by "our" standards) evolution of forms, institutions, ways of expressing themselves. A similar phenomenon occurs when we try to interpret francophone or italophone poetry or narratives produced by foreigners or non-natives in the United States who write in French or Italian or Spanish. Expanding the horizon, Ammiel Alcalay has written a very perceptive book on Levantine culture, unknotting the problems surrounding the instances of Jewish writers writing in Arabic, and Arab writers who write in Hebrew.[57]

The necessity to "invent" the meaning, and the social, aesthetic, and/or professional responsibility of this gesture, goes hand in hand with the necessity to allegorize—or should we say, the impossibility of not allegorizing when we interpret, when we write. But this mode of allegorizing is yet to be fully articulated into a theory,[58] because it cannot be leveraged on universals of any sort, it cannot moreover be content to exist and express itself locally (which would be accomplished through indices, signals, orders, commands, instructions, dedicated utterances, and finally, audio reproductions). Moreover, this allegorizing cannot hark back and find refuge in a rehashed Voltairean backyard, and finally it cannot be understood in a demanian, grammatological sense, that is, as basically an intertextual buzzing of metonymically driven transcendental signifiers.[59]

[57] See Ammiel Alcalay, ed., *Keys to the Garden* (San Francisco: City Lights, 1996).

[58] I have attempted some preliminary hypotheses and tested them in my reading of Nietzsche and of D'Annunzio, in the cited *Prefaces to the Diaphora*. See Chapter 3, below, dedicated to an approach to *Thus Spoke Zarathustra*.

[59] See Paul de Man, *Allegories of Reading* (New Haven, CT: Yale University Press, 1979).

The allegory I am attempting to grasp and write about requires a different understanding of the rhetorical, one that has reconnected with ancient but undeveloped possibilities[60] while fully open to the metamorphosis of history. In other words, it is an allegory attuned to, rooted in, and aware of the irrevocable now, the *jetz*-time of the utterance, my Being-in-the-world today and here and in the company of such and such persons and within this specific place (city, town, desert, canyon). Otherwise stated: rhetoric is *both*: always topical because language—poetic or philosophical—is at once an expression of a theory, a quick sketching of a master code, or theorem, or god; *and* it is ever a dynamic construction of a methodics of sort, requiring the act/intention of a selecting and an ordering of the words in the string such that expository patterns are achieved and made to function persuasively. A creative linguistic arrangement called a story, an epic, a long poem, is primordially allegorical in the sense that its telling, its having to be read (possibly aloud) to or by a public (no matter how small) ensures a modicum of concern *for* the other, insofar as the other is a real human being, and assumes that "something" can at any rate be conveyed. *Unlike the lyric, a story may want to say something about something else, other lives, unheard of and often striking jarring experiences, transfigured characters, an alternative geography, a whirring cosmos.* A literary creation should not just entertain or reassure us in our pre-scripted cultural unconscious. It should make one think! Moreover, because it is grounded in the speaking act, the rhetoric of allegory cannot exclude the body, its specificity, its memories, and from that in expanding semantic circles the social, political, and aesthetic facades of conventions and institutions as well. In other words, the allegorical nature of human language is *originary*, a generator of forms and possibilities, of societal and political rites and rituals, of artifacts, in short: of myths, even of theories …

[60] I am thinking of the works listed in the Bibliography by Paul Ricoeur, Ernesto Grassi, Chaïm Perelman, and Paolo Valesio. Though at variance from one another, these thinkers highlight the aporias and theoretical (and political) untenability of the Plato–Aristotle tradition, and invite us to a reconsideration or development of the thought of Chorace, Isocrates, Protagoras, Gorgias, Zeno, and others. Much of my thought in this area, which I develop as an alternative to the long-glorified and dominant pre-Socratic tradition, is contained in my *Elusive Hermes* book. A short chapter titled "No Longer a Paradox: The Sophists as Philosophers of Language and Existence," has appeared in Stefano Arduini (ed.), *Paradoxes*, 61–80 (Rome, Edizioni di Storia e Letteratura, 2012). Available online at www.petercarravetta.com

Provisional Conclusions

As we have seen, historically at least, the allegorical impulse, the figurative power of language-in-action, has been made into reusable allegories with specific stylized values. This has been amply documented, just think of the tradition that begins with allegorical interpretations of Homer and of Scriptures, and more compellingly, through the works of the likes of Dante, Geoffrey Chaucer, Edmund Spenser, John Milton, William Blake, Alfred Lord Tennyson. But throughout, the fundamental rhetoric of human communication and interaction was consistently turned into a system, a tropology, finally a repertoire to manipulate discourse. Only the lyric mode remained as the last bastion, elitist and indifferent to the destiny of the real world, a highly unstable incandescent language of access to a more primal being. For that charge alone, of speaking the *enthusiasmos* and global connectedness and euphoria we associate with a Dionysian moment, we have gladly allowed the lyric a preeminent status, a special ontology for the (s)elected few, ignoring the rest, the non-initiates, the non-visionary. We die alone, so we experience bliss alone. This is fine, but does not do when experience beyond the personal is to be artistically, poetically embodied. In the West this task was taken up by philosophy, by metaphysics, by epistemology, by ethics. The only problem is that this gesture has been consistently predicated upon a set of indemonstrable axioms, the so-called great immutables that go back to Parmenides and Plato. Allegories too have served as the encyclopedias of nations, as generators and legitimators of mythemes, which permitted social organizations and provided codes of values, including aesthetic ones. To clarify, we might say here that the mytheme is to allegory what the episteme is to the philosophy of knowledge.

However, owing to their rhetorical, persuasive, existential, audience-conscious style and simultaneous presence of pathos and theme, allegories retain a necessary differentiating trait, something that marks and both expresses and hides the specificity of its historical occurrence, the pregnancy of its political objectives, the tantalizing prospect of yet another metaphor and with that another worldview. What I am then suggesting is that the allegorical dimension of narration be revalued when confronted with texts from alien, foreign, previously "inexistent" (because suppressed or systematically forgotten, as postcolonial scholarship has been revealing) literatures, or "radically new" aesthetic events and constructs (especially via video art), but without resorting to the tropology and pantheon of overdetermined sclerotized mythemes that can be read as token epistemes, as the "rational" organization of a culture's ways of being, but which inevitably "imposes" an epistemic grid over its results. Think of the work of Claude Lévi-Strauss. The point is to avoid the totalization and ultimate Word that in a way both lyric and metaphysics aspire to.

Today, an allegorical take on these new literatures can alone permit us to venture into their complex worlds and return with a feeling of having experienced a radical sense of difference, of otherness. The jarring *paradoxical tension between fact and saying* enables a *diaphor*, a *differentia*, the *logos* in the abyss (the *Abgrund*) that destabilizes and challenges the blinding arrogance of the Platonic, Enlightenment, and modernist ethos of self-aggrandizement (or self-deprecation, which is the same in a dualistic scheme of things wherein reason parades its ironic side) and hierarchy. What we need in the postmodern epoch is to (re)discover the possibility of a narration *through* clusters of meanings, values and worldviews based not on the fetish of the "word," usually the noun, but on the verb,[61] that is, on *inter*-locutions, on *the rhetoric of a socially codetermined and co-enabling art form*. The founding of our human dwelling through poetry must be understood as *a poetry of relation*, of attempts at *interpreting/participating across one or more boundaries, or limits, or, in factual history, borders*.[62]

To write about what no one has had the idea, or the objective possibility, of writing about: one's silent history, one's non-Eurobourgeois heritage, one's hyperreal border situation, one's social/existential concretization as a living mobile threshold ... which brings us back to the necessity yet again to rethink and invest in allegories, insofar as they are narrative accounts that require and create their own audience, except that here the reader cannot be passive: to register the *other-speaking* (that's the etymology of allegory) there's need for a *focused consciousness*, an *imaginative predisposition*, even a *willingness to give oneself over in some guise or degree to these previously nonexistent values and situations*. In the postmodern epoch, the alternative to the numbing avalanches of images and manipulable data bytes is to sit back, decompress, so to speak, and then listen, actively. Then, after that, to attempt a response for which there is no precedent and there surely is no guarantee. As we will see further

[61] I have explored this problem in my *Elusive Hermes* book, with particular reference to the work of Benveniste and Ricoeur. Of Ricoeur see especially *The Rule of Metaphor: The Creation of Meaning in Language* (London: Routledge, [1975] 2004). I will return to the problem of poetry as being concerned only with the Word in Chapter 3, below.

[62] See the revealing work done by Walter D. Mignolo with his concept of "border thinking," which cannot be developed in this paper but certainly acts as a background alert system. Cf. his *Local Histories/Global Designs* (Princeton, NJ: Princeton University Press, 2012).

down, literature is always place and time bound, like everything else in culture. The notion that meaning is thus "undecidable" has proven to be a fruitless endeavor: we always decide, whether passively or actively. The "peoples" and the "nations" and the "selves" being created-recounted in these new allegories are not of the identitarian, nation-state variety or the Freudian modality. They may evoke, of course, a *réalisme merveilleux*, a characteristic Haitian mode of expression, as in the works of Jacques Stéphen Alexis. Linking the mythical with the historical as a creative positive force, and with the Haitian legacy of the Americas as a whole, Alejo Carpentier finds *lo real maravilloso* "at every step in the lives of men for whom dates are recorded in the history of the Continent … from the seekers of the Fountain of Eternal Youth and the Golden City of Manoa, to certain rebels of the first hour or certain modern heroes of our wars of independence … And the fact is that, because of its virgin landscape, its formation, its ontology; because of the Revelation its recent discovery constituted, the fertile cross-breedings it produced, America is far from having exhausted its wealth of mythologies."[63] Even when the artwork produced discloses even more complicated silences as well as more unsettling reconsiderations on history and the (r)evolutions of societies. The case of Mexico is exemplary.[64]

Whether focused on a primal—and founding—saying at the interface between nature and culture, prompting a chant of unheard (and unpleasant, and unsettling) semantic possibilities; or whether reconfiguring temporalities and exacerbating differences in the clash between worldviews[65]—all of which, incidentally, inscribe and embody the sentient, the aesthetic, and the memorable (as future histories if nothing else)—the reasons for a postmodern understanding of the allegorical are diverse, anti-metaphysical, non-semiotic, and prone to (re)capture something

[63] Barbara J. Webb, *Myth and History in Caribbean Fiction* (Amherst: University of Massachusetts Press, 1992), 18. But see also Michael Dash, *The Other America: Caribbean Literature in a New World Context* (Charlottesville: University of Virginia Press, 1998), and the "Introduction" to Ilan Stavans, gen. ed., *The Norton Anthology of Latino Literature* (New York: Norton, 2011).

[64] See the somber reflection by Richard Rodriguez: "I have come at last to Mexico, the country of my parents' birth. I do not expect to find anything that pertains to me […] Mexico's tragedy is that she has no political idea of herself as rich as her blood" (Richard Rodriguez, "Mixed Blood: Columbus' legacy; A World Made Mestizo," *Harper's Magazine*, November (1991): 47–56, 52). On the different rules for understanding specific cultural icons, and some problems associated with grasping, expressing, representing them, such as the Virgin of Guadalupe, see also Octavio Paz, *The Labyrinth of Solitude* (New York: Grove Press, 1985), who offers, moreover, a compelling portrait of La Malinche in the Mexican cultural unconscious.

[65] This is particularly evident in Native American literature, for example, in Leslie Silko, Sherman Alexei, N. Scott Momaday, and Linda Hogan.

akin to what another generation of critics called consciousness (itself expressed in a language we may not grasp entirely). In this view, which harks to what Edward W. Said called the concrete "generalized condition[s] of homelessness,"[66] the unsteady variable background lends itself not so much to travel writing as to the experience of writing the traveling itself, its meandering through misunderstandings, with flashes of success against constant tripping, tasting aloneness and tasting freedom, dwelling in the familiarity of strangeness, writing about the experience of moving, shifting, and perhaps finding something about oneself, one's ultimate (non-) belongingness. That is, philosophically, the lack of metaphysical foundation as we understand it in Western metaphysics.[67] Increasingly through the twentieth century, in a period that saw our cultures go through the profound alterations to our perception afforded by photography, cinema, video, streaming, electronic composition of music as of texts, this *other-writing* is not faintly attempting to tell us what is being seen or what a given scene or event might actually be, or mean. Ethnography has dispelled that myth.[68] *Knowledge whether scientific or aesthetic is relational.* Without going back to existential phenomenology, even from within a more "Anglo-American" critical context, it is acknowledged that the *episteme* must somehow link up with the *doxa*, disclosing the gap taken up primarily by language itself.[69] But there have been other and very different supporters of this process: Stanley Rosen, Charles Taylor, Cornel West, Edward W. Said, and Stanley Fish have all stressed the cruciality of the *destinataire* of the text, the listener of the utterance, the other of the speaking. To avoid the trap of dualism and facile dichotomies, more agency should be given the receiver, the reader, who is always already within a specific cultural and sociopolitical place, and often with no access to means of production of discourse.[70] Critics from feminism, postcolonial studies, and the many hyphenated literatures that have emerged over the past forty years

[66] See Edward W. Said, "Reflections on Exile," in Stuart Hirschberg, *One World, Many Cultures*, 422–7 (New York: Macmillan, 1992), 424.

[67] Of course, a case has been made that, despite the anti-foundational thinkers we have been mentioning, metaphysics is "doing fine" and not at all declined or *uberwindet*. See the vitality of the discussion in Allegra De Laurentiis and Jeff Edwards, eds., *The Bloomsbury Companion to Hegel* (London: Bloomsbury, 2015).

[68] I am referring mainly to the selected texts in the Bibliography by Renato Rosaldo, Clifford Geertz, and James Clifford to some of which we will return further down.

[69] See Peter J. McCormick, *Modernity, Aesthetics, and the Bounds of Art* (Ithaca, NY: Cornell University Press, 1990), 142–3 *et passim*.

[70] On this, see my *After Identity: Migration, Critique, Italian American Culture* (New York: Bordighera, 2017), ch. 3, on the first major wave of Italian immigrants to the United States, in the period 1890–1914, who had no way of expressing and representing themselves, and so were spoken-*for* and spoken-*about*, but the actual subjects remained unheard.

(see Chapter 4, below) tend to appropriate, analyze, and empower this subaltern subject, giving it voice and making it relevant, often for the very first time in the Western metaphysics/Modernity/Colonial *oecumene*. In this perspective, travel writing too is bound up with the fluctuations of the borderlands, the floating masks and the amorphous constituencies encountered along the way, and the institutions that block certain utterances from going across a semantic vacuum. In a sense, this other-speaking reveals the time-and-place specific concretions of the passages of Hermes, point to his having left the Gods and Heroes of Olympus forever behind in order to reemerge, donning a multitude of novel vestments, as the metamorphosis of language itself, ever coming from elsewhere, ever going somewhere:

> Between the Greek and African pantheon,
> Lost animist, I rechristened trees:
> Caduceus of Hermes: the constrictor round the mangrove.
> Dorade, their golden, mythological dolphin,
> Leapt, flaking light, as once for Arion,
> For the broken archipelago of wave-browed gods.
> Now, the sibyl I honour, mother of memory,
> Bears in her black hand a white frangipani, with berries of blood,
> She gibbers with the cries
> Of the Guinean odyssey.[71]

[71] Derek Walcott, "Origins," in *Collected Poems 1948–1984* (New York: Farrar, Strauss and Giroux, 1986), 12.

Figure 3 "Invention of signs, 1" by Angela Biancofiore.

2

Poetics and Linguistics

Boundaries of Language in F. T. Marinetti and Gertrude Stein

The title I chose for this chapter is a direct echo of Roman Jakobson's revolutionary and influential 1953 essay "Linguistics and Poetics,"[1] which I have always found (since first reading it in the mid-1970s) to undermine the creative impulse of poets, their capacity to expand the limits of human expression. It is all owed to the introduction in the humanities of a rationalistic, scientifically inspired notion of what language is or how it works. Despite its refined architecture, the noted "functions of language," it is philosophically simple: in the chain of communication, the poet's language is basically a swerve from the norm, an exception with regard to the general code. I have contested this as being too simple and reductive, but for different reasons than those of the critics of structuralism who by the 1970s were upending it to a "post-structuralism" or a "deconstruction" of its own inner assumptions and workings. I found it ironic also that this most rationalistic approach was canonized in the 1950s after a near half-century evolution that began actually among the poets. Jakobson in his university years frequented the rambunctious and boundary-busting cubo-futurists and the experimental linguistics proposed by the OPOJAZ group,[2] and the poetics of ZAOUM and nonsense.[3] Thus a case can be made that one of the

1 See Roman Jakobson, *On Language* (Cambridge, MA: Harvard University Press, 1990).

2 The initials mean Society for the Study of Poetic Language, formed by a group of linguists and literary critics in St. Petersburg in 1916. That same year students of Ferdinand de Saussure published his papers posthumously, the landmark *Cours de linguistique générale*. Futurism both in Italy and Russia was already experimenting with the boundaries of language. Young Jakobson grew up in this environment, which included Nikolai Trubetskoy, Viktor Shlovsky, Yury Tynjanov, and Boris Eikhenbaum, shapers of the formalist school as its center relocated to Prague after Stalin took power in Russia.

3 See theoretical writings by Victor Khlebnikov and Alexey Kruchenykh in Mary Ann Caws, ed., *Manifesto: A Century of "isms"* (Lincoln: University of Nebraska Press, 2001), 235–40, considered a starting point for concrete poetry. Khlebnikov definitely influenced the young linguist.

leading theorizers of structuralist poetics in the twentieth century actually got his inspiration from fellow poets experimenting all ways and with all mediums of expression.

Building on earlier studies on these authors, the subtitle points to how two major avant-garde writers, from opposing shores of the Atlantic but sharing Paris for long periods of their respective lives, "pushed language" to its limit, and may serve to open up further the contours of normative linguistics, grammar, and the philosophy of language. I am referring to Filippo T. Marinetti and Gertrude Stein.[4] My view is that for once theories of language ought to take into account what writers themselves have to say about language, since language is the alpha and omega of their very existence and practice. In other words, between the linguists (and/or grammarian, and/or historian of language), and the aestheticians (and/or philosopher of language, whom we know can have varied provenance, such as analytic philosophy, phenomenology, and ontological hermeneutics), we ought from here on make room for the artist's reflection on their own craft, strong in the belief that, as Giambattista Vico remarked, she who does something is more likely to know what that something is.[5]

Consider, then, Marinetti's revolution, beginning with what amounts to a reform of the standard parts of speech.[6] Remove the minor devices of the logical organization of discourse, for example, adverbs, prepositions, conjunctions. In a poem, these are now considered unnecessary. "Free the words," is the battle cry, let them find spontaneous associations or join them together to disclose a new imaginative possibility, a something else not previously possible in the master code and its customary codicils (that is, its having devolved into technical jargons for given disciplines or activities). But what does *that* do to language,

[4] See my articles, in English, "Gertrude Stein," in Walter Beacham (ed.), *Magill's Critical Survey of Poetry*, vol. 8, 2731–41 (Los Angeles: Salem Press, 1982), and a more thorough analytic reading, in Italian, through a Derridian optic, in "Praeludium a Gertrude Stein," in Ettore Bonessio Di Terzet (ed.), *Arte e conoscenza*, 37–85 (Genoa: Università di Genova, 1985). I subsequently integrated these insights in a collection on avant-garde poetics written directly in Italian, Peter Carravetta, *La funzione Proteo: Ragioni della poesia e poetiche della fine* (Rome: Aracne, 2014).

[5] Vico, *The New Science*, δ 330, 374.

[6] See Filippo T. Marinetti, "The Founding and Manifesto of Futurism" (1909) and "Freed Words" (1912, also rendered as "Words in Freedom"), in *Critical Writings*, translated by Doug Thompson (New York: Farrar, Strauss and Giroux, 2006), 11–18 and 120–31, respectively. Excerpts of basic texts contained also in Caws, *Manifesto*, 185–200. Max Jacob also wrote on "words in freedom," in 1915 (Caws, *Manifesto*, 136). For the Italian text, I refer to the widely available Filippo T. Marinetti, *Marinetti e il futurismo*, edited by Luciano De Maria (Milan: Mondadori, 1973; 1981 or other reprints). I am fully aware that Marinetti scholarship in the last twenty plus years has tended to foreground his fascist leanings and deconstructed his misogynistic statements. The fact remains that certain important ideas about language were proposed and promoted by Marinetti. I am concerned with those.

to expressiveness, to semantics, and finally to the power of symbolization of language? To put it briefly, it permits the mind to wander off, unshackle the chain of signification created by the sender (and with that, their literary unconscious), compel the receiver to make their own novel connections, stretch the imagination to allow the new construct to design its own semantic/symbolic continuum, and thus *participate in the construction of meaning*. In Marinetti's own words, for example, "everywhere we tend to suppress the qualifying adjective because it presupposes an arrest in intuition, too minute definition of the noun."[7] For futurists adjectives are like railway signs, semaphors. Verbs should be used in the infinitive, which denies the existence of the traditional normative sentence (with person, mood, the subject-verb-object paradigm, and so on)[8] and prevents style from slowing and stopping at a definitive point.[9] He notes that the infinitive is round like a wheel, whereas the other moods and tenses are triangles or squares, so they impose limits to any free flow.

The point, we recall, is to scatter words as if they were objects into the air, see them in their freedom as if they could fly (an animistic image), whereupon unforeseen new total syntheses are likely, maybe not long lasting but definitely in the actual present of the gestural body. The imagination in short should operate "without strings," without rules. To this clear theoretical (metaphysical) principle, there follows concrete epistemic suggestions, since devising a program, a method to achieve the finality of the principle, one needs to stake out new limits, break old ones, and … create a language. Specifically, without having to rely on coordinating and subjugating conjunctions, without declining the verb, which is the first radical point of departure toward a literature that is *not* of the I, of the EGO, because the pronouns themselves are deemed obsolete.

What we pick up is an awareness of the effective power language, in this reconceptualized way, has over reality. If you change the (rules of the) code, thinking and acting will have to follow a different path. In Marinetti's case, this meant to upend the grammar and rhetoric of dominant institutions, for instance, universities, museums, performance arts schools, and so on. The relevance of this revolution is inestimable, as it informs just about all artistic avant-gardes that flourish at about the same period, from Dada to surrealism, to the Theatre of the Absurd, all the way to the death of the subject in literature, a topic which in

7 Ibid., 101.

8 I am compressing insights from the works of Émile Benveniste, *Problems in General Linguistics*, translated by Mary E. Meek (Coral Gables: University of Miami Press, 1971).

9 Ibid., 103.

philosophy emerges forcefully in the 1960s and 1970s (when even the "author" is deemed dead, irrelevant to our grasp of a or any discourse).

A "freed" image has more possibilities, while it subverts the images that are still strung up and perhaps played like marionettes, pre- and re-coded for established habitual patterns of social behavior. And the words are also liberated! These words break the connections of concepts and, to reconfigure a different semantic cluster, leverage the imagination, that is, let a function of the mind enter freely into the creative process. Let us recall that the Greek word *eidos* is at the root of both, what we understand as idea *and* what generally we call an image, as the work of Edmund Husserl (1859–1938) makes abundantly clear.[10] Thus, in a sense—and contrary to the precepts of idealistic aesthetic of Benedetto Croce (1866–1952), who lambasted the futurists and all avant-garde art—Marinetti brings the poetic text right at the center of the human faculty or gift for conceptualizing, disclosing the capacity for language to suggest, compel, and in the last analysis fire up previously unconceived image-ideas, which is consistent with his overall intention to revolutionize literary and social thinking. Another example: join up two nouns in such a manner as to derail the "normal" or "accepted" range of meaning associated with a particular word, and force the mind of the listener, the receiver at the other end of the linguistic string, to conjure up something that previously did not exist. Examples:

> Summary of Analogies
>
> Defense Adrianapolis passatism minarets of skepticism belly-cupolas of indolence cowardice we'll-handle-it-tomorrow there is no danger it's not possible what's it for …
>
> […] Around Adrianapolis + bombings + orchestra + stroll-of-the-colossus + mechanic shop widen concentric reflexes plagiarism echoes laughter little girls flowers steam-whistles waiting feathers perfumes stink anguish (INFINITE MONOTONOUS PERSUASIVE NOSTALGIC) These weights shims noises smells molecular whirlpools chains nets corridors of analogies competitions and

[10] See Edmund Husserl, *Ideas, I*, translated by Fred Kersten (London: Kluwer Academic Publishers, [1913] 1998). See paragraph 70: "There are reasons by virtue of which in phenomenology, as in all eidetic sciences, presentiations ['representations' in R. Boyce Gibson's version] and, more precisely, *free phantasies* [*fancies*] acquire *a position of primacy over perceptions* … Even where one 'ponders' while looking at [a] figure, the processes of thinking which follow are, with respect to their sensuous substratum, processes of phantasy the results of which fix the new lines in the figure." A crucial passage that concludes: "Thus if one is fond of paradoxical phrases, one can say in strict truth, that *'feigning'/'Fiktion'/makes up the vital element of phenomenology as of every eidetic science*, that feigning is the source from which the cognition of 'eternal truth' is fed" (Husserl, *Ideas, I*, 159–60; emphases in the original).

syncronisms giving-oneself giving-oneself giving-oneself as gift to my friends poets painters musicians and futurist noisemakers **Zang-tumb-tumb-zang-zang-tuumb tatatatatatatata picpac pampacpacpampampe** uuuuuuuuuuu.[11]

Without going into the actual philology of whether Marinetti had been directly influenced by two great precursors, such as Arthur Rimbaud and Friedrich Nietzsche, let us recall that, in general, an alternative to the established range of possible meanings in any one sentence could not be generated if artists (and thinkers) remained within the parameters of normative syntax, of "that's the way, the style, to write or speak in." This is normal convention, which evolves but *does not rupture*. Historically, it can be demonstrated that, despite the substantial shifts brought about by the Romantics and German idealism, the origin of the subjugation of the structure of language and the rules for the arrangement of discourse goes back to the rationalism of the seventeenth century, the Logique de Port Royal and the large-scale standardization of spelling, grammar, and rhetoric over the territory of the specific empire or kingdom (Spain, France, England).[12] We cannot think outside of, or conjure up something as an alternative to, the combined bourgeois and religious order of discourse until we can break that language-use (even in literary writing). The idea of an "establishment" model operating means the creator/sender/user would automatically compel the receiver of the message to think only those meanings sanctioned by the established order, within an acceptable boundary, and with the smallest amount of "noise." But, we argue, in terms of what Roman Jakobson had stated in his 1953 paper, the poetic effect is not simply or solely marked by a "swerve" (*écart*) vis-à-vis a preexistent code (or subcode if within a specialized community).

[11] "Bilancio delle analogie.
[…] (2a SOMMA)
Difesa Adrianopoli passatismo minareti dello scetticismo cupele-ventri dell'indolenza vigliaccheria ci-peneremo-domani non-c'e'-pericolo non-e-possibile a-che-serve …
[…] (4a SOMMA)
Intorno a Adrianopoli + bombardamenti + orchestra + paseaggiata-del-colosso + officina allargarsi concentrici riflessi plagi echi risate bambine fiori fischi-di-vapore attese piume profumi fetori angoscie (INFINITO MONOTONO PERSUASIVO NOSTALGICO) Questi pesi spessori rumori odori turbini molecolari catene reti corridoi di analogie concorrenze e sincronismi offrirsi offrirsi offrirsi offrirsi in dono ai miei amici poeti pittori musicisti e rumoristi futuristi
Zang-tumb-tumb-zang-zang-tuumb tatatatatatatata picpac pampacpacpampampae *uuuuuuuuuuuuu*." Marinetti, *Marinetti e il futurismo*, 322–3.

[12] Another factor that contributed to "standardizing" speech and writing was the translation (or retranslation) of the Bible in the majority of modern European languages. See below, Chapter 8, "Poetics of Translation."

Other writers had faced this problem and attempted a breakthrough. Gabriele D'Annunzio (1863–1937) did it by the relentless coining of new words and the expansion of the syntactical and stylistic possibilities of the Italian language, and doing much to recover the rhetorical inventiveness of the fifteenth-century humanist poets. Stéphane Mallarmé (1842–1898) by breaking language down to its graphic component and bringing it back to mere signs, reminding us of the visual origin of language: the image is at the heart of any coming-into-being, any external concretion, of human language. Giovanni Pascoli (1855–1910) effected his revolution in poetry by endowing the minor parts of speech, onomatopoeias, diacritical marks, exclamations, and foreign words with a semanticity that they did not (and could not) possess before. Indeed, as Gianfranco Contini had pointed out, Pascoli brought poetry to an a-grammatical or non-grammatical level, freeing up new venues for signification that the poetic language from Francis Petrarch through Giosuè Carducci (1835–1907) had not explored and could not have explored by refusing to challenge language itself.[13]

That with futurism language is thus freed to venture into previously uncharted seas of signification is, of course, not something that the established order of society could accept and integrate into the normative, legitimate, "logical" order of discourse.[14] Futurism is, of course, an attack and challenge to the tradition, and the reaction of the representatives of that tradition, with its long entrenched and conformist bourgeois order (we can think of Charles Baudelaire here, and his Salons, all the way up to Marcel Duchamp), was to consider it simply rebellious, marginal, out of step with the mainstream and to reject it as far as it could. We must acknowledge, however, that contained within Marinetti's poetics there is a sketch of a philosophy of language in which semantics, or better, meaning-attribution, and symbolization are not exclusively dependent on grammar and syntax "to make sense," contrary to prevailing academic aesthetics, art can and in fact is endowed with the capacity to yield radically new concepts, in brief,

[13] Gianfranco Contini, *Altri esercizi* (Turin: Einaudi, 1973), originally an Introduction to the Oscar paperback edition of Giovanni Pascoli's *Poesie* (Milan: Mondadori, 1958).

[14] It is unfortunate, as noted above, that in many of his other futurist declamations he went on to say some pretty awful things about human nature, and women in particular, and recent criticism has taken him to task for it. But already in his day, it's not that there was a lack of women involved at such levels or in such communities. See, for example, Mina Loy, *Feminist Manifesto* (1914): "And if you honestly desire to find your level without prejudice – be BRAVE & deny at the outset – that pathetic clap-trap war cry WOMAN IS THE EQUAL OF MAN – for – she is NOT!" (quoted in Caws, *Manifesto*, 611).

that imagination is part *of* thought[15] and therefore a legitimate concern for the philosophy of interpretation. Finally, that criticism ought to take into account, and consider primary, what the artist has to say about their relationship to both language as language and ideas as expressed, as intended, in the work itself.

A similar exploration and rethinking of what language is and can do was effected by Gertrude Stein, another of the great avant-garde figures of the earlier twentieth century without whom a great deal of the poetry of the second half of that century would not have been possible or could have been properly interpreted. In the 1934 lecture, pronounced upon her return to the United States after nearly thirty years in Rue des Fleurus in Paris, and titled "What is English Literature,"[16] Gertrude Stein focused on how literature can become literally dead letter if it is not renewed and reconceptualized by the writer from generation to generation. In looking back over the canon, she comes up with this stirring conclusion:

> One century has words, another century chooses words, another century uses words, and another century using words no longer has them.[17]

Her argument runs along these lines: in Shakespeare's time—in Dante's time, by analogy—a national literature had all the possible words it can ever use at its disposal, so it is almost impossible not to be creative. Traditionally called the "fathers" of their national tongue, they created the words (the works) for the tribe, and what they said/wrote stood the test of time, which despite highs and lows became canonical. But the following century, or epoch, poets already must *elect* from among the range of words (and associated concepts) available in the *langue*, or the ordinary speech of a given community or country. A succeeding generation *uses* the words, which means has established a more circumscribed and perhaps more normalized, standardized deployment of the lexicon of the tribe than before. We might say this coincides with the rise of a bourgeois society, at least in Euro-America, with journalism, with growing access to public education. This would be what in a more broad characterization can be called the age of prose, which is basically the eighteenth century and part of the nineteenth. But then this same unstopping process of standardization and conformity to normative grammars and logic and stock expressions basically

[15] On the relation between thinking and the imagination, see the exploration by Edward Casey, *Imagining: A Phenomenological Study* (Bloomington: Indiana University Press, 1976).

[16] See Gertrude Stein, *Writings and Lectures 1909–1945*, edited by Patricia Meyerowitz (Baltimore: Penguin Books, 1974). All citations are from this edition.

[17] Ibid., 41.

drains the words of any life, makes the linguistic sign an empty signifier, and the newness, freshness, and magic of language vanishes: thus, and we can be certain Gertrude Stein was referring to the late nineteenth century—that is, to realism, naturalism, and descriptivism against which the avant-gardes in general rose—the community "uses the words but no longer has them."[18]

What does the artificer, the creator/manipulator of language who is the poet, do in this uninviting literary panorama? Start from scratch, rethink the expressive possibilities of language basically as actually used by people, and push the boundaries further out. In another lecture of the same period, titled "Poetry and Grammar," she addresses this problem head on. Starting where she left off in the previous essay, she notes: "It is extraordinary how it is impossible that a vocabulary does not make sense." Juxtaposing this to the conclusion she had reached in another essay concerning what is prose (I will come back to that in a second), she observes:

> But that is natural, indeed inevitable because a vocabulary is that by definition, and so because this is so the vocabulary in respect to prose is less important than the parts of speech, and the internal balance and the movement within a given space.[19]

In brief, "Poetry has to do with vocabulary just as prose has not." But now, how does the artificer work with words and attempt to give them back life, so that they are not "empty shells?" Gertrude Stein recounts her earliest experiences listening to and learning poetry and admits that it took her a long time to figure out where the problem lay. She determines that *poetry is essentially a question of nouns*: "Poetry is concerned with using with abusing, with losing with wanting, with denying with avoiding with adoring with replacing the noun."[20] Looking at this analytically, and summing up how she came to this determination, the author states that the relationship between words and things is so gratuitous and, Ferdinand de Saussure would say, so arbitrary that naming something by its established name is not really saying anything new or different. She

[18] Compare to Ezra Pound's *The ABC of Reading* (New York: New Directions, [1934] 2010), ch. 4, where he states: "You still charge words with meaning mainly in three ways, called phanopoeia, melopoeia, logopoeia. You use a word to throw a visual image on to the reader's imagination, or you charge it by sound, or you use groups of words to do this" (37).

[19] Ibid., 138.

[20] Ibid.

introduces notions such as feeling, excitement, pleasure, and choice, which is an intrinsically intellectual act. She says:

> Think what you do when you do do that when you love the name of anything really love its name. Inevitably you express yourself in that way, in the way poetry expresses itself that is in short lines in repeating what you began in order to do it again. Think of how you talk to anything whose name is new to you a lover a baby or a dog or a new land or any part of it. Do you not inevitably repeat what you call out and is that calling out not of necessity in short lines … So as I say poetry is essentially the discovery, the love, the passion for the name of anything.[21]

This passage shows how a phenomenological process works, while it seems to guide thought by the hand. It leads one to a *poetics of the word*, as she would say in another text. But perhaps it is important that she uses the words "name" instead of "noun" interchangeably: "I discovered everything then and its name, discovered it and its name … I repeat nouns are poetry."[22] The task is "altering or replacing of the nouns."[23]

Here we run into a problem: on the one hand, to (re)energize the word (noun/name), one has to stop "using it" to refer to something else, and then repeat it and sing it and play with it until it resonates with an emotionality, a sense of existing that had vanished in the background noise; on the other, there's recognition of a cohabilitating function of the mind, which involves choosing the words, basically determining which words will be poetic: "Language as a real thing is not an imitation either of sounds or colors or emotions it is *an intellectual recreation* and there is no possible doubt about it."[24] Here we seem to be in line with both poetry as linguistic recreation at a distance and poetry as feeling total with the very appearance of the word that it predates and even precludes a meaning, what it says or might say (about something else). I would not call this a "contradiction:" it is not a question of looking at this poetic and asserting that it self-negates. It is more in the spirit of wanting to grasp how poetry must venture on the edge of un/intelligibility, of un/speakability, of being-*langage*, pure utterance. We are compelled to remove all the critical

[21] Ibid., 140.
[22] Ibid., 141.
[23] Ibid., 145.
[24] Ibid., 142; my emphasis.

vocabularies that get in the way. Some of this can be achieved by pruning the very rules that govern normative speech. Significantly, Stein writes that periods acquire a life of their own, that sentences are not emotional but paragraphs are, that adjectives are not interesting, verbs can make mistakes, as in erring (which I find intriguing). But *movement* is entailed at all times. Prepositions are the preferred, non-semantic part of speech. Agreeing in this with linguistic theory, prepositions are basically switching modules, relays, fixtures, they are like an enzyme: they permit meaning to be created by linking the appropriate parts of the sentence one way or another, without having to be a *sememe* in the chain. Conjunctions are workhorses, and it is consistent that Stein's writing is marked by parataxis, by polysyndeton. Interesting coda to her reframed grammar for writers is the characterization of the pronouns, which "are not as bad nouns because in the first place practically they cannot have adjectives go with them … they represent someone but they are not this or his name. In not being his or her name they already have a greater possibility of being something than if they were as a noun is the name of anything."[25] According to the great linguist Émile Benveniste, pronouns do not constitute a unitary class, some are merely formal markers, while others partake in and are determining in "instances of discourse," that is, "the discrete and always unique acts by which the language is actualized in speech by a speaker."[26] But they also basically set up the primacy of the "I/you" relation. The fact that the pronoun can exist and serve both domains, that of language *qua* language and of language *as-spoken-to-others*, gives them a particularly fundamental role in understanding where the limits of language may lie, and how poets and philosophers grappled with this problem. As pronouns, moreover, denote the *person* or actual speaker in a primordial way, is there a subterranean subjectivity present in Gertrude Stein's theorizing? She had already stated as much when reflecting on her acquisition of words: "I had always known it and its name but all the same I did discover it."[27] A consciousness is here present, at least presupposed. Writers, poets, think about what they want to do, they make cognitive decisions. It is not all "inspiration" (though restoring a certain dignity to the expression wouldn't be so bad).

25 Ibid., 128.

26 See Benveniste, "The Nature of Pronouns" and "Subjectivity in Language," in *Problems*, 217–22 and 223–30, respectively.

27 Ibid., 141.

Gertrude Stein pursues this line of inquiry in "Portraits and Repetition."[28] She writes that "Succeeding and failing is repetition because you are always either succeeding or failing but any two moments of thinking it over is not repetition."[29] Repetition is not of the concept, of the referent, let's say, about a real "rose" in the case of the line "a rose is a rose is a rose." The repetition is rather a trigger for the embodiment of an emotion, a pulsion of being-*in-itself*, a vital force, something dear to us as when we repeat the name of something we love, as we saw above. It's really as subjectivistic as continental philosophers have been saying is the case all along, and that implies there is a leveraging a sort of transcendental subjectivity that claims to be non-referential, not self-centering.

Is this the way to restore a freshness, maybe even a bare sayability, a *dicibilité*, to the words that no longer mean anything? Is emotion everything? Something is awry here.

The other aspect of this poetic theory that is problematic concerns the fuller possibilities afforded by discourse *tout court*. It is consistent with Gertrude Stein's practice as a poet/writer that her production includes works that are theatrical, musical, elementary in the sense for children, filled with "natural" rhythms. At the same time, her more "formal" presentations and writings show only variations of tone with respect to the style used in her creative works. Her writings are not delimited by reigning definitions of genre, the distinction between prose, poetry, drama, formal address, or metapoetical musing disappears. And yet again, by her lights critical, philosophical, scientific discourse is *ab initio* alienated, detached, arbitrary, common, uninteresting, even boring!

The historical avant-garde gave the century two models for revitalizing the language of the society through aggressive reforms in the practice of poetizing and in the theoretical implications for a deeper understanding of the fundamental apparatus of humans: language itself. Poetics should become a legitimate field of inquiry with linguistics and philosophy being two collateral arenas that can furnish concepts and tools to the interpreter of the poetic process.

[28] Gertrude Stein, "Portraits and Repetition," in *Writings and Lectures*, 99–124.

[29] Ibid., 117.

Figure 4 "Invention of signs, 2" by Angela Biancofiore.

3

Poetics of Paradox

An Approach to *Thus Spoke Zarathustra*

My answer: the subject as a multiplicity.
Friedrich Nietzsche, *Dawn*

One way to interpret the epigraph is to start out from locations in the critical field that emerged after the end of the postmodern epoch, that is, to begin within the preoccupations with decentered or, alternatively, ec-centric, thought. Begin with the subject, the poetical "I," the psychological ego, the philosophical transcendental ego, the Absolute Consciousness at the time when cultural discourse, in the panoply of disciplines (such as continental philosophy, postcolonial studies, gender studies, post-humanism, and bioethics), was already submitting novel critical configurations that explore *heterotopias* (Michel Foucault), on the one hand, and on the other, the haunting disclosures and challenges of possible *syntheses of the heterogeneous* (Paul Ricoeur). From these *loci*, which have already accepted the decline of metaphysics, and with that the lack of an ontological foundation, in a universe of beings tossed about in the persistent mutability of forms and meanings: how can we broach the question: exactly what was Zarathustra trying to say? How can we possibly interpret, transmit, or teach this text?

The questions presuppose that somewhere, somehow, after deliberate inquiry, we might come up with a clear answer, a straight (though partisan) univocal response. But we know that is impossible: Nietzsche himself cautioned us against taking this road. How can we decode a text, a speaking, which like Hermes, is capable of taking on countless semblances and is by definition always on the road? How can we pretend to speak about, and therefore convey, *any* sense when everywhere the prophet tells us we should not accept *formulae*, kneel to the *aurea mediocritas*, summon the will and courage to (symbolically I take it) kill the fathers, our teachers in particular, and with that subvert grammar, liberate thought, embrace again the emanations, the expressions, of the senses?

And what can we say about history, already considered a thorny and near intractable ideology, or philosophy, in the 1874 essay "On the Usefulness and Damage of History for Life"? Yet, do we not know that, whatever it is, history became one of Nietzsche's battlegrounds as he combats with the tragedians, Socrates, Jesus, the grand allegorists, Georg Wilhelm Friedrich Hegel, Arthur Schopenhauer, Richard Wagner, *le monde entier*! Each time wearing a different mask: think of what precedes the Zarathustra poem (*Dawn, Twilight, Gay Science*), and what follows it (the *Genealogy*, the labyrinthine *Nachlass* that was supposed to make up the unfinished *Der Wille Zur Macht*).

The "turn"—or "swerve" or "écart"—in Nietzsche's thought as represented by *Thus Spoke Zarathustra* is one involving our understanding of the past. The *Zarathustra* tells us that to understand history we must understand it allegorically, and that, indeed, the book is an *allegoresis of social consciousness* replete with symbols and icons that refer to possibilities, to meaningful social concretions, to ideas rooted in the subject's capacity to transcend itself.

The subject: we know Nietzsche's implacable critique of the subject, both in its scientific and in its idealistic guises. We know that he de-grounded it, humiliated it to render it more humble, returning it at the same time to its chthonic pulse, its physiological reality, something that between Christianity and the rise of the bourgeoisie had been missing from our lives.

But then, what kind of subjectivity is propounded in the *Zarathustra*? How can the *Über-Mensch* overcome—*überwindet*—the Platonic-Cartesian-Kantian subject and still pretend it can speak from a *locus* where a consciousness is present, where a human actually addresses another human, where one chooses to live with, or through, Dionysian pulsions? How do we make such a strange, elusive person/persona speak?

The transfiguration of the past is a known contested *topos* explored by philosophers, historians, and poets. Just to be clear, recall that in *Poetics* 1451a–b, Aristotle makes a distinction between historian and poet: the first tells of what actually happened, the second what might have happened (or, alternatively, what should have happened). For this reason the case has been made that poetry is the more scientific (i.e., philosophical) because it aims at general truths, while history gives particular facts. What is foregrounded as a problem lying in wait in this canonical *topos* is the articulation or the means of representation. In Aristotle's time, both history and "science" could be put in verse, without making of Homer a scientist and of Empedocles a poet. As we saw above in Chapters 1 and 2, the issue is debated well into the twentieth century, but there are some significant developments. With refinements, in fact, this distinction carries through Isidore of Seville (560–636), who distinguishes between *fabula*, fable ("so that through an imaginary story a true meaning may be applied to the story's action"), and *historia*, "a narration of deeds accomplished; though it what occurred in the past is sorted out," to arrive at a "plausible narration" (*argumentum*).[1] With Jean Bodin (1530–1596) we are at the dawn of modernity, and his partial reframing will be very influential: of History … the true narration of things, there are three kinds: human, natural, and divine. The first concerns man, the second concerns nature, the third the Father of nature. One depicts the acts of man while leading his life in the midst of society. The second reveals causes hidden in nature and explains their development from earliest beginnings. The last records the strength and power of Almighty God. This leads, philosophically, to three divisions: "[knowledge of/through history] is probable, inevitable, and holy. And the same number of virtues are associated with it, that is to say, prudence, knowledge, and faith." This articulation is pretty much shared by Francis Bacon and later by Giambattista Vico. Though Vico will not discount Providence, it is the *relation between knowledge and judgment*, the unquestioned and the probable, that most interests him. Furthermore, when it comes to society's "memory," we can only know the first one, the probable, because we built it ourselves: humans can only know what humans invent and construct. Nietzsche will be struggling mightily to deconstruct this triad. Of course, this problematization of the past spurs reflection on the future, the problem now being: since we cannot speak of absolutes (of utopias), what is the status of knowledge, the terrain for judgments, the horizon to plan ahead, what values in our postmodern era, our globalized, mediatized, cybernetic lives. Further, whether by contrast, by spontaneous reflex, we can speak of a future at all.[2]

We could easily open up a sidebar here and list many who have already declared that the future is gone,[3] that the future is simply an expanded present, that in the hum of the quanta that now defines us, the notion of a future makes absolutely *no* sense! Staying our course, if history can be reduced to or, better

1 On *argumentum*, which I read as *topos*, see Ernst R. Curtius, *European Literature and the Latin Middle Ages* (Princeton, NJ: Princeton University Press, 1953), 452–5.

2 The "crisis" straddles the millennium: see Jean Baudrillard, *The Illusion of the End*, translated by Chris Turner (Stanford, CA: Stanford University Press, 1992), and Slavoj Žižek, *Living in the End of Times* (London: Verso, 2011).

3 See Jean Paul Russo, *The Future without a Past: The Humanities in a Technological Society* (Columbia, MO: University of Missouri Press, 2005).

yet, be transformed into a genealogy of morals, how can we today face the deeply ethical challenges raised by the human genome project: is it enough to jettison all previously accumulated, interlocking, and too often conflictual notions of morality, the *thou shalt* imposed to the herd, while we are at the same time witnessing the disruptive yet influential presence of moralities linked to nativism, exceptionalism, xenophobia in the secular and creationism and anti-science in the religious realms? While some of my colleagues address such haunting problems raised by bioethics, ecology, and the post-human, the not-so-silent near majority speaks of species-fixity and rereads Charles Darwin to see where it agrees with the Old Testament, and specifically with the conviction that everything is already contained in "Genesis."[4]

So, how do we entreat our fellow humans to renew themselves, to abandon (or at least minimize, make it a personal affair) religions and all other ontotheologies, to distrust the almighty *logos* and refurbish instead the *logoi* of the individuals who walk the planet and seek not only to survive but also to live (in part, or not altogether suppress) their Dionysian impulses? How can we tell students in Rimini and Lisbon and New York that a thinker who has consistently attacked any notion of Truth and the will to truth and reoriented himself toward a *will to art*, a will to self-empowerment, to seek a principle of continuous self-elevation and self-transfiguration, without falling back into those same discursive formations that have annihilated him, that have, paradoxically, killed that same God held to be the savior of us all? How can we trust someone who believes that literature—that art in general—is always one step ahead of life, and that to live life like a work of art is perfectly coherent and comprehensible? Is it still possible? And is it something we want to do?

The three themes I propose to get into this network, and into *Thus Spoke Zarathustra*, are: *person*, *persuasion*, *paradox*. They are everywhere present in the book, and they can serve as hermeneutic checkpoints for the questions just raised. First of all, *person* does not exist other than as a partial realization of predetermined ideals: the person is never fully realized, fleshed out. This incomplete being—decades later on developed as "l'existence come quelque chose que manqué"—is found to be the power, the engine behind the drive to achieve a unity, to attribute to itself an identity. The "true" person accepts from

4 This is the notion that humans are authorized to master and subject nature, animals included, to their needs; see Genesis 1:26–30, and in the "other" beginning, Genesis 2:8, where nature is made *for* man, not to speak of the asymmetrical relation between man and woman.

the very start the condition of having to live by means of mediation, of the type constructed on the syntactic of *as if* (Ger.: *als ob*; It: *come se*)[5] linguistic/conceptual elements (presuppositions, "pretend") that mark what elsewhere I demonstrate are essential constituents of interpersonal discourse.[6] Essentially this means accepting that things can be transfigured in language, or that language can "configure" or "re-configure" them as meaningful entities. Thus the subject emerges as a *perennial fiction*, an *impersonification*, even at times as an *im-posture*, but certainly as something that is *other than* what it portrays. Or at least there is an *otherness* that is not manifested. It is, in short, a ruse, a stratagem, better: a mask.

If this is the case, there is the need to accept the surface, the *monstrum*, and in the real world of humans, this means, rather, *the many masks allowed by the varying articulations*. No need therefore for essential being: as the later exegete Martin Heidegger would conclude, we have forgotten Being. I would add: we could not ever even have it to begin with. *What we can approach is what has actually existed*, and what we have a record of, historically, is a long procession of masks, an interminable catalog of representations, some iconic, some less emblematic, but always fictions of what we think ourselves to be.[7] Pushing this a bit further, the mask is then all we have of the person, in fact we can say that the mask equals the person (as a look at the etymology suggests). An individual can then be described as a crucible of different persons, each time necessarily wearing a different mask, according to the different accepted usages of the noun "person" in a variety of syntactical/rhetorical contexts. The ontology of man can

5 See on this *Kant Studien* founder Hans Vahinger (1852–1933), who authored *Die Philosophie des Als Ob* (1911); see Hans Vahinger, *The Philosophy of "As If": A System of the Theoretical, Practical and Religious Fictions of Mankind*, translated by C. K. Ogden (London: Routledge & Kegan Paul, [1924] 1965). Vahinger deserves more attention. One of the first serious critics of Nietzsche, he bends Kantianism to accept Schopenhauer and Darwin, challenges pragmatism and some of the grand assumptions of Western metaphysics and epistemology. In recent decades his influence has been more in literary and psychology studies, associated with "modelling." But he has also been called a "hermeneutic fictionalist" on the basis of his basic claim that we imagine how things work when we can't see or record them, and use these fictions to figure out traits and consequences. His examples based on then nascent subatomic physics are enlightening, and foreground Chapter 7, below, on the role of metaphor in science.

6 Mostly in *The Elusive Hermes*, but also throughout this book.

7 Most major literatures I have explored over the years have in their canon the disrupters, the anti-establishment writers, the great satirists, from Rome to the early Modern, figures such as Giovanni Boccaccio, Ludovico Ariosto, François Rabelais, Miguel de Cervantes, Laurence Sterne, and Jonathan Swift. Kick-started by Romanticism, the whole of the twentieth century has seen the growing critique and dismantling of the Judeo-Christian/Greek-Roman canon, as it culminates in Erich Auerbach, the last nostalgic. See Chapter 8, below, on canons.

only be gleaned through the plurality of masks. Playwrights from Sophocles to William Shakespeare to Luigi Pirandello always knew that.

Now this can give the shivers to Platonists and Cartesians, and Catholics and Calvinists all at once. But is this necessarily a bad thing? Do we have to throw away the baby with the bathwater? Keeping *Beyond Good and Evil* in mind, Harold Alderman suggests that, according to Nietzsche, the work of a thinker is always hidden behind two types of masks.[8] The first is the one that the thinker consciously introduces in his work, the second is borne out of the always false interpretation of every word, or step, or sign of life. The interpreter dons a mask often unawares that they in turn are introducing another one in their own work as exegete. "Thus the thinker, recognizing that in an absolute sense he is always ahead of his times, of his operating, in his needs to hide his thoughts through metaphors and allegories, in the hope that the reader would be led beyond the exoteric masks to the esoteric ones."[9] The point here is that the thinker must face up to a situation in which communication is intrinsically difficult, at the least something not to be trusted, but also that cannot be circumvented. There is something behind the metaphors and the allegories. What is it? The thinker needs to look at the language itself, as used. For without the language, the masks themselves cannot come into being.

I must now draw on an earlier research of mine concerning Nietzsche and language, and specifically on the transition from the aphoristic style to allegory.[10] Intrinsically, allegorical speech requires an audience, it is the most primordial discursive form, dating back to the very foundations of social coexistence when, as Vico first intuited,[11] the hunter-gatherers stopped their marauding and settled in the *locus*, establishing the three main tenets of any human societial group or clan: the burial of the dead, the incest taboo, and the recognition of the supernatural through the *invention* of the godhead.[12]

Now this godhead was a mysterious power, and how else to speak about what doesn't have a name, or is unknown, being made up of tectonic tremblors, and

[8] Harold Alderman, *Nietzsche's Gift* (Athens: Ohio University Press, 1977).

[9] Ibid.

[10] See the chapter "Before *Zarathustra*: Nietzsche through the Rhetoric of the Aphorism," in *Prefaces*, 13–78. A few years ago there appeared Joel Westerdale, *Nietzsche's Aphoristic Challenge* (Berlin: de Gruyter, 2013), which follows a different itinerary, adopts a different idea of rhetoric, and comes to slightly different conclusions. He probably did not know of my chapter.

[11] See Vico, *The New Science*. The next two sentences encapsulate concepts I develop from Vico.

[12] This primordial wiring of humans living and thriving coextensively has found, directly or indirectly, confirmation in the twentieth century, in thinkers ranging from Sigmund Freud to Bronisław Malinowski to Clifford Geertz.

lightening, and eruptions from the gut of the earth? The clan is the archetype of the plebs, and whether from above (the warrior king, the high priest) or laterally, among themselves, an individual always speaks *to* the others, or rephrasing that: one speaks to the *others*, by way of fables, wild imaginings, eventually theological accounts. The real problem, as I argued in Chapters 1 and 2, is that, historically, we run into the Platonic *niet* of the Homeric tradition, and the Aristotelean dualisms or constructions of binaries that have besieged Western thought for the past 2,400 years. That is why we think it is natural to see things as *either* good *or* bad (evil), proper or improper, true or false, one or the undefined or excluded other, and so on. What is remarkable about allegorical thinking, before it too fell prey to what I have described as the semiotic version of allegoresis—practiced from Philo through Dante on until Alfred Lord Tennyson and Gabriele D'Annunzio—is that it can carry *at least* two meanings at once, express or reference two or more distinct worlds equally and contemporaneously, that of the putative social referent, and the one of the complete availability of another voice—*allo-agourai*, other-speaking—that of the fiction itself, the envisioned, proposed, alluded to world of the imagination. This does not contest some of the more empirical or sociohistorical studies on Nietzsche's polylogic mind, and where language itself is the fulcrum of the interpretation. Here I intend to add to those perspectives.[13]

Nietzsche accepts the mask as that which allows the possibility of self-representation of the living person, but that does not mean that all masks that have ever existed through history need to be accepted. In other words, he claims as a condition of life what the Eurologocentric Immutables[14] deny, that perhaps—May God forgive us!!—we are *not* all equal! The argument goes: We have convinced ourselves, and have historically acted upon such a credence, that yes, *before the law we are all equal*, a necessary axiom to allow for the manageable emergence of complex societies when the *polis*, the city-state, slowly becomes empire and nation-state. But *there will always be others*, marginals, foreigners,

[13] See, for instance, interventions in Bernd Magnus and Kathleen Higgins, eds., *The Cambridge Companion to Nietzsche* (Cambridge: Cambridge University Press, 1996).

[14] I am using the word-concept "Immutable" (as applies to Being, Nothingness, Destiny, Necessity) inspired by Italian philosopher Emanuele Severino (1929–2020), who used it in his readings of Parmenides and Plato and found their persistence in the entire Western tradition. Besides some untranslated books such as *Gli abitatori del tempo* (1978), and *Technē: La radici della violenza* (1979), see now in English his most engaging work, *The Essence of Nihilism* (London: Verso Books, 2016). For a general background, see interventions collected in Silvia Benso and Brian Schroeder, eds., *Contemporary Italian Philosophy* (Albany: State University of New York Press, 2007).

special cases, possible undiscovered peoples, hybrids, creators, and madmen, call them what you will, but still human lives, existences, persons, who may not want to be part of the herd, who may not care to march in step with *los demas*, who may find any one identity too tight, too unreal, too much to bear for an individual who, in some instances, is or might be also *polytropos*, capable of different articulations, imbued with a just as mysterious link between language and mind.

What I am suggesting here is that there is a living-being who is actually a becoming-being, a *being-in-becoming*, that can be imagined as a living moving bridge, a transfer, a meta-function *between* the powerful archetypes—Dionysius and Apollo, Socrates and Jesus, *and* Immanuel Kant and Hegel, Schopenhauer and Søren Kierkegaard—but existing *there*, in the trans-phase, in the in-between stage, ready to don the veils and the shields that connect meaningfully once through the opposing herms.

This being-in-becoming is what is announced by Zarathustra.[15] Further, it would be the man of the beyond (not, obviously, as some living dead or horror-show infantile concoction), that is, the person who overcomes himself fully aware that there is no other he could become. This man takes quite a while to leave his community behind to enter a community of the elect. But these elect are not comparable to the aristocrats or the *haute bourgeois* Nietzsche despised. However, if we read *Thus Spoke Zarathustra* as the fiction, the narration, of the second rebirth, the allegory of the re-creation of humanity, then perhaps we can grasp what the eternal present may signify. Kathleen Higgins shows how, for example, the character Zarathustra repeatedly gets lost in subjective layers or possibilities in the second book, how he then detaches himself from his mission, and how in the end he returns, much like another famous pilgrim, to the right path.[16] The reading is rigorous and stimulating, but it does essay to prove, in the end, that Zarathustra's wanderings have a coherent mission. My own reading is trying to see where perhaps we can go beyond.

In other words, we must effect a close reading of some of the masks that Zarathustra wears when he addresses different groups, and focus on what is the

[15] All references are to the English translation of *Thus Spoke Zarathustra* contained in Friedrich Nietzsche, *The Portable* Nietzsche, edited by Walter Kaufmann (New York: Viking, [1954] 1982), 115–439.

[16] See Kathleen Higgins, *Nietzsche's Zarathustra* (New York: Lexington Books, 2010). I have also learned much from the extensive commentary and critique by Laurence Lampert, *Nietzsche's Teaching Teaching: An Interpretation of "Thus Spoke Zarathustra"* (New Haven, CT: Yale University Press, 1986).

dominant semantics in the different arguments, or *topoi*, all the while asking ourselves: what is he talking about? Well, the typology is well documented, though typically penned in ironic or parodistic, when not altogether sarcastic, tones. Our prophet speaks to those who live in the world behind the world, to the flies at the marketplace, or to the friend, or lambasts the so-called fundamental virtues as "gift" to the compassionate, then also champions the difficulty of overcoming of oneself, and so on. Focusing on the language, we realize that the allegorizing is that typical of the fable, for the Z book is an intellectual parable. But now consider: *this speaking of something other* is markedly different from the allegorizing of Homer, Dante, Spenser or Tennyson or Victor Hugo. The reason is that what is missing is a *specific cultural referent* wherein and for which this otherness emerges from the parables. The *Zarathustra* allows this *otherness to speak without being determined by, or chained to, a specific mythology, an external geohistorical context: it is myth without mythology, so it becomes the expression of genus, Myth*. This bears its own set of problems.

Zarathustra accepts right from the opening pages that there is such a thing as the eternal recurrence of the itself, not of the same, which would suggest the recurrence of a mirror image.[17] See for example "the child with the mirror." Rather, that itself speaks of the dynamics and the perspective of existing, the anxiety of seeking the past (which comforts us) in the future, in the yet-to-be, the future of the myth of one's proper origin.

Yet his rejection of Plato and Hegel compel him to construct a notion of dialectic that is peculiar and that can be explained as being closer to a persuasive rhetoric than an expository method. Let us recall that Nietzsche had rejected Plato's kind of writing and that after *The Birth of Tragedy* did not succeed in writing what we call an organic book, one with a thesis, a series of logical demonstrations, and a conclusion. His own rhetoric turns upon the strategy of macrosyntheses, of philosophy briefs, of the aphorism, the brilliant revelation, the sentential.

In the *Zarathustra* the prophet's voice does set up some neat oppositions, almost like epistemic dyads, such as dialectic of redemption/desperation, depth/height, darkness/light, being tossed in an abyss of light in which time stands still. Here we are introduced to the "high noon," the *nunc stans* of the atemporal

[17] I have benefited much from a remarkable commentary by Giangiorgio Pasqualotto to the Italian edition, in Friedrich Nietzsche, *Così parlò Zarathustra*, translated by Sossio Giametta, 365–546 (Milan: Einaudi, 1985).

and the eternal. Does this mean that Nietzsche is, after all, a product of his time and therefore inescapably imprisoned in the dualisms of positivism, or of the tradition in general? Not really: rather than despairing at the assumption or better *revelation that being that is, is being in becoming*, and that the eternal return of things smacks of nihilism, he envisions in this "man of the afterwards" (through the semantization of a morphological particle, the "über") the joy of freedom precisely embodied in the things that are, and have always been, in a circle of *ex*-istence, whereas the great passions generated by wars and resentment can now be seen along a straight line that extends from the unknown of the past toward the infinite of the future.

The discovery of this *circulus vitiosus deus* on Nietzsche's part constitutes, according to Karl Löwith, the discovery of an escape from two thousand years of falsehoods, that is, from Christianity. For the latter ideology invented and propagated a progressive idea of history based on an absolute principle of consummation and redemption at the end. Think of the idea of Providence and God's manifestation through history. As a matter of fact, history is understood as the Judgment of God over time, a thesis that extends from Augustine through Karl Barth, in short, history based on a *theology of history* that must perforce include the barbarism of civilization and progress.[18]

The man of which Zarathustra gives announcement—the man who "returns," much like Quaetzcoatl after an ancestral prefiguration—is above all the man intent on how to find the Self, in a Jungian way cleansed of all the "I's" of everyman and their obsession and petty pursuits.[19] Nietzsche the person had effected this on himself, as can be gleaned through the two volumes of *Human, All Too Human*. Furthermore, this Self does not legitimate itself as a power that transcends man but rather is given as ex-pression, ex-istence of a given person, of a singular unrepeatable individual. It thus becomes a sort of mainspring for human action fully conscious that it must bear good *and* evil, construction *and* destruction, joy *and* suffering, what most logical-minded people call contradiction—counterargument!—and I insist it should be seen rather as *paradox*, that is, "para," next to, by, and "doxa," opinion, public speech, linguistic

[18] This does not mean that there weren't counter-histories or revisionist theories of history, from Dante through Lorenzo Valla, Pico della Mirandola, Jean Bodin, Hugo Grotius, and so on. Nietzsche is interrogating the general will, so to speak, the dominant views over the several epochs, the adaptation of Christian beliefs to bourgeois legitimation.

[19] See C. G. Jung's *Seminar on Nietzsche's "Zarathustra,"* edited by James L. Jarrett (Princeton, NJ: Princeton University Press, [1934–1939] 1998).

or mental habit but that together, as a the word paradox (in most Western countries), has come to mean "contrary to public knowledge, extravagant."

Zarathustra teaches not to feel guilt for this condition, as it affects most of humanity. Further, he offers no apology, but also no hope of escaping the circle. Yet there emanates a full awareness that life has meaning precisely because one *must* constantly elevate oneself, attain the Great Health that is at once spirit of self-conservation and self-transcending.

We should also bear in mind *when* the Zarathustra book was written: this is the Victorian age, the age of Bismarck, the age of great anthropological discoveries, of Darwin, of the circulation, within less than half a century, of a spate of major allegories on the human condition —such as we have from Hugo, Tennyson, Wagner, Henry Wadsworth Longfellow, Fyodor Dostoievsky, Robert Browning—of sweeping socially conscious panoramas, such as naturalism, verism, realism, of the contemporaneous yearning for a perfect world—consider the number of utopias being written during this time and the concrete efforts to build religious or socialist communities—and the ultimate effort to master what was still somehow unknown on this earth: the scramble for Africa (Brussels and Berlin treaties of 1878 and 1884–5) and decisive incursions into Siberia, the Amazon, preparations to reach the South Pole, cutting of isthmuses, first Suez and then Panama, the arrival of electricity and the laying of cable across the Atlantic. Indeed there was much euphoria in the second half of the nineteenth century, so much so that a scientist declared, as the century was waning, that "we invented everything: there is nothing left for us to do!"

In this climate, there arise discussions on the meaning of history. On the one hand, much of it was swept into the Hegelian fires of nationalism and nation-building: Greece, Italy, Germany, most of South America, and heavy rumblings within the Austro-Hungarian Empire. On the other, the philologists piecing together an even deeper past. Many were the lives of Jesus published at this time. When in Sils Maria the incendiary vision of the poem surfaces, all these contexts constitute a veritable crowd of suffocating claims, harangues, politicking, presumptuousness, unfounded optimism, and justified self-serving violence. Nietzsche had survived all this, the white-hot prose of *Beyond Good and Evil* had cleansed him of the paralysis beneath the skepticism, he needed one ulterior major flight *out*. Suddenly, the blasts of aphorisms shot into the unspecified throngs, basically into nothingness, cease. What happens at the level of the author's rhetoric is remarkable, for how could he shift gears so abruptly, so radically, so inexplicably?

My response is that *allegoresis was inevitable.*[20] Specifically, *the aphorisms—the dispersed lapilli of his earlier books—are now placed within dialogical exchanges.* We see and hear interlocutors who exchange experiences and concepts, give advice, effect self-critiques, mention delusions, utter corrections of previous beliefs, and there are shards of discourse that refer explicitly to concrete (though not localized, or geohistorically determined) realities. In brief, *a community is presupposed,* a thus a plurality of selves is summoned to register and take into account the vicissitudes of the prophet and his symbolic tales. All the assertions made about the life, being, and virtues of the new man are told in *dialogic exchanges*, and we witness an effective maturation or evolution of the character Zarathustra himself, a trait that one is tempted to compare to Odysseus or the pilgrim Dante. But closer scrutiny would also reveal something of Gilgamesh or the Bhagavad Gita.

The first self-transformation of the character defined by the little stories that Z recounts concern the acceptance of the limits of one's own animality, which is required to attain a more sober, or less paranoid or hysteric, relation with the world. Z leads us to think that the continuous meeting with/bumping into the things of the world, with what comes and goes, is the very heart of the pleasure principle, it means a saying yes to life, to eternity itself. Rising early in the morning, at the very onset, Z declares: "O great star, what would your happiness mean, had you not those for whom you shine?" (Z, Prologue). What is the world without humanity? What's the point of the world if it doesn't mean anything, if it makes no sense? The thought leads to the most ancestral of myths, the worship of the sun, true to the historical Zoroaster, as Rudolf Steiner writes:

> In such a way Z's disciples saw and truly felt in each single person a reproduction of what the world presents us with on the outside. Not in the theories, the concepts or the ideas, as much as in the living feeling which pervades the human being, setting him before the universe in a way that he could tell himself: I am a little world, but as such I bear within me the trace of the great universe, I am in its image. And as man, I bear in my bosom a principle that tends toward the good, and a principle which stands in its way, much like in the great universe we find Ormuzd and Arimane facing each other.[21]

[20] I have explored this pattern in papers I read on authors such as William Wordsworth, William Blake, Giuseppe Ungaretti, Gabriele D'Annunzio, Salvatore Quasimodo, Pier Paolo Pasolini, and Garcia Marquez.

[21] Rudolf Steiner, *Zarathustra, Ermete, Buddha*, translated by L. Schwartz (Rome: Basaia, [1911–1934] 1987), 21.

A bit theological, this view, and still somewhat informed by a dichotomy, the dualism of contrary forces. Yes, Nietzsche was a great estimator of Heraclitus, hard to escape that pull. But we are interested in something else here, and that is, to put it in existentialist terms, *the necessary copresence of the other*: living and self-transcending will soon disclose the enabling condition of co-participation, a potential lodged within the being-in-itself to become being-for-itself and begin the ulterior process of being-for-others.[22] This will be developed separately.

Let's look at this from another vantage point. I must, says Z, *decline*, as the people among whom I will descend say. But the word *Untergehen* in German is used also with reference to when a ship goes under, when it sinks. After ten years in isolation (and not forty days like Jesus), a willed, not imposed, isolation, Z has no doubt about what he intends to say. However, he must embody it, and this occurs through the *logoi*, which he will utter and usher upon his interlocutors. He will have to speak this message to the various constituencies, so that they can know and think about what is being said, and here he must undertake a journey.

Will there be a "return"? Is there anything resembling *Ulysses* in this? No, there is no Ithaca, no returning from this journey, as he consciously undertakes to bring forth the message of the overman. Z descends from the mountain and roams the valley to shine forth the torch, he has Promethean features. This "going under" in fact reminds us of other myths, the descent into Hades, which traditionally signifies touching the very base, the ultimate base of earthly and bodily matters, their annihilation, and their transformation into shades, into nonentities. So even before there commences the ascent to noble pursuits, to the peaks where only eagles soar, one must go through, and live, a *catabasis* and experience what it means to be a snake or a cock or a camel or a priest. Not even poets fare well in this massacre of one's unexamined preconceptions, the individual's pretense that there is an essence behind the mask that, alas, remains just another mask.

Finally, after the long tortuous journey, we reach the overman (Z II, 12), which you may recall, begins by questioning the great Judeo-Christian and Greek ideal: the Will to Truth, inextricably linked to a will to power:

> You still want to create the world before which you can kneel: that is your ultimate hope and intoxication … your will and your valuations you have placed

[22] I am simplifying terms from Jean-Paul Sartre's *Being and Nothingness*, translated by Hazel Barnes (New York: Philosophical Library, 1956).

> on the river of becoming; and what the people believe to be good and evil, that betrays to me an ancient will to power.[23]

The paradox, the drama, here is that what the self-overcoming requires is a going-through, or a sinking into, this dilemma, which *can only be expressed, or articulated, by means of a language that is already tainted, already marked and overdetermined semantically and symbolically, indeed historically.* The wisest have placed the people on the bark that accepts good and evil as something that exists in history, stabilizing the premises for what Jean-François Lyotard would call a *grand recit* such as emancipation or progress, a "better future," all attainable through "your dominant will." But now the little ship moves further away from the shore and cannot but carry this load of people and their belief system, their trust in the will to achieve and justify these values: "it avails nothing that the broken wave foams and angrily opposes the keel."

Yet beyond all this, the real problem, Z says, is not the notion of good and evil, but the will itself, the will to power, the will to life.[24] How can we solve this apparent riddle, since elsewhere we gather that the will is necessary to self-transcending? Here we read:

> I pursued the living; I walked the widest and the narrowest paths that I might know its nature. With a hundredfold mirror I still caught its glance when its mouth was closed, so that its eyes might speak to me. And its eyes spoke to me.
> But wherever I found the living, there I heard also the speech on obedience. Whoever lives, obeys.
> And this is the second point: he who cannot obey himself is commanded. That is the nature of the living.
> Where I found the living, there I found will to power; and even in the will of those who serve I found the will to master.[25]

The rest of the passage speaks of the relation of smaller to larger, weaker to stronger, perhaps consuming a tradition that goes from Aristotle through Hegel and is found also in what at the time was on everyone's lips, namely *The Origin of Species*. But the passage continues stressing that underneath the struggle about values, there is a deeper drive, a *prerational will to power, which can translate into self-affirmation, and sense of completeness,* and this we can only grasp *through* the masks paraded by a long string of theories about what is good and strong,

[23] Nietzsche, *The Portable Nietzsche*, 225.
[24] Ibid., 226.
[25] Ibid.

and what is evil or weak. The will to power must translate itself in language, speak from the gust, so to speak: "what does not exist cannot will: but what is in existence, how could that still want existence?" It's a self-consuming tautology, an illogical axiom. Rather, "only where there is life is there also will: not will to life but, thus I teach you, will to power." Thus life sacrifices itself in the name of power. A power that always overcomes itself and that must find a language to exoress this, to pretend that it is some sort of great philosophical revelation.[26]

Let's step back a moment. We have ascertained that any action in the name of values is an act of violence, we might say a distorted manifestation of the will to power: "you do violence when you value." But we also read, on the same page, that "a more violent force and a new overcoming grow out of your values and break egg and eggshell." Is Nietzsche not talking about an historical dynamics at play here? A dynamics that acts upon societies over time and yet is no longer recognized as such? Isn't Z suggesting, given the originary ontological presence of the will to power, which we may easily translate into what is commonly called a drive, a pulsion, an instinct to not be sidestepped by the associations with the word-concept "power," through allegorical indirection that:

1. when we value (i.e., evaluate) we do violence, but we cannot not do violence, so therefore our values have to continuously change;
2. that changing—that is, breaking—the egg, means breaking the eggshell, or the container or support of the essential value (the yolk), and
3. is not this eggshell, metonymically, a mask? A mask *also,* I should add, since the essential egg is a condensation, an icon, therefore again a mask of the belief system we happen to be living in.

Let me take another step back and try to fathom this in another way, bringing into the fray the earlier considerations on the "last man," the "representative" human, the typical person, who is not wholly integrated, who has forgotten Being, who is said to be *animale rationale*, and who exists between the physical—*ta fisika*—and the ratio of the non- or super-sensible, the metaphysical—*meta ta fisika.* The last man appeared already in the second *Untimely Meditation*, the one about the usefulness and damage of history for life, where we learn that next to the pride of modern man there stands the self-irony of his condition. This will become the *Blinzeln*—winking, nodding in assent, "ammiccare" in Italian—of *the last man in Z, whose condition is that of having to live in the crepuscule and*

[26] Ibid., 227.

where beings historicize themselves continuously in the great agony of not being able to change anything about the past.

As things have unfolded in a particular way, you might say on the basis of a dominant script, a stylized, sclerotized allegory—as we saw: Christianity, Progress, Equality, etc.—so it must be forever, so there arises the necessary Thou Shalt, the moral imperative. However, this triggers the rise of the spirit of Vengeance, which we as a civilization also masked under the more acceptable notion of "punishment." Did not European society claim it wanted to end suffering? To effect that, we proceeded to punish those whom we believe are causing suffering. In brief, the last man of late modernity can only be defined negatively: man is the animal who is not yet precisely determined: "Das noch nicht festgestellte Tier."[27]

Let me acknowledge how this echoes somehow Giovanni Pico della Mirandola's (1463–1494) *Oration on the Dignity of Man*, where he states, as the Lord is about to speak to Adam, that Man is "a work of indeterminate form" (*indiscretae opus imaginis*) and therefore a work to be built by one's own free will.[28] This ties in with the will to power. But, says Z, man is "a rope tied between beast and overman" and for all intents and purposes, he is not yet born, so he hovers over the abyss. He is, rather, an *ongoing project*, where becoming now is seen not as becoming according to the mythologemes of our past but a becoming in tune with the chthonic and instinctual forces that fuel the drive, the power, to ex-sistere, to ex-perience, to tune in, literally, as the word rhythm harks back to its common origin with the word-concept form: rhythm, *rhusmos*, which shapes forces, movements, prayers, the logos itself. It is the way to calm down the gods, the route for the very vibrations of the body to emerge, and dance and music were of crucial relevance to Nietzsche's understanding of the human condition.

My synthesis of the overman, the man of tomorrow, requires that I understand the construction of history not as a rearward-looking refabulation, not as critiqued, for example, by Walter Benjamin, but in view of what I wish would happen in the future, fully aware of the constraints that make most of us "last men."[29] If I cannot live in the full disclosure of the ever-renewing moment, in the dawn (as opposed to the crepuscle) of a locus that creates its own light

[27] Friedrich Nietzsche, *Sämtliche Werke: Kritische Studienausgabe in 15 Bänden*, edited by Giorgio Colli and Martino Montinari (Berlin: de Gruyter, 1977), 2:623.

[28] Cf. Giovanni Pico della Mirandola, *On the Dignity of Man, On Being and the One, Heptaplus* (Indianapolis, IN: Bobbs-Merrill, 1965), 4.

[29] For Benjamin's critique, see Walter Benjamin, *Illuminations* (New York: Harper, 1996), 253–63.

(*locus a non-lucendo*), a Dionysian *Lichtung*, or *life as a work of art*, for the rest of us mere mortals the lesson to be learned from the grand allegory is that the human being/person is a paradox that dwells in the constant need to persuade their interlocutors, the rest of humanity, that as a marginally free spirit they may cultivate the gift-giving virtue even before the chaos represented potentially by love, by creators, by those who aim at being *an-arché* (obviously not necessarily anarchists in the way some of his bomb-throwing contemporaries were: the contested *arché* is that of the bourgeois idealists and historicists).

To want to live life fully is an ideal, but can we still get closer to this indeterminate person, the overman, in a real world, in the concreteness of empiria? The message here is that acknowledging the pull of the pleasure principle is not automatically tantamount to exercising negation of duties or prevention of a virtuous life. Maybe it is a question of rhetoric, of what persuasion I stir up in those about and around me. If wherever I found life I also found will to power, perhaps that is where I have to look and determine the language of those masks to understand how and why certain facts occurred the way they did and not otherwise. The way to do so is to *understand* human existence, not to convalidate an *a priori* axiom or theologheme. Those megamyths have been written and inscribed in our cultural memory, they constitutes the history that the young Nietzsche rejected as damaging to the free exercise of our faculties. The Frankfurt School and the Parisian in our century spoke of libidinal history, then biopolitics, and various forms of repressed sexuality (all of which can be traced to book X of the *Republic*, with the fourth-century Christian church giving it full ethical legitimation: sex only for procreation). In the unfolding of the human condition through time, however, there is no linearity, there is chance, risk, playfulness, mystery. The will to achieve precedes representation, and so we must learn to read the existing, present-day allegories as the *paidea* of the last man. The idea is to seek life through its ever-recurring movements and pattern and cycles. The third part of Zarathustra opens with a section on "The Wanderer":

> I am a wanderer and a mountain climber … and whatever may yet come to me as a destiny and experience will include some wandering and some mountain climbing; in the end, one experiences only oneself … what returns, what finally comes back home to me, is my own self and what of myself has long been in strange lands and scattered among all things and accidents.

The fact that he also goes on to say "what can happen to me which is not properly mine" has led some to postulate an immanent determinism in Nietzsche, but that is incorrect, since already Christianity had worked out the paradox of divine predestination and individual choice. Attempting to rewrite or, better, reconfigure the past means ordering our discourse *as a function of whoever we wish to speak to*, masks notwithstanding or, better yet, precisely because we must speak about, and to, the masks. This is achieved by telling fables. But there is a multitude of stories, of actions anyone can understand, anywhere. The truth of the overman can be said as myth. As such, it needs to be interpreted, absorbed. Maybe codified (when there will be a Chair dedicated to him!).

But in the allegorical tales, there persist that unavoidable tension or intention to want to persuade someone else, you tell those metamorphoses to a group or community precisely because you want your listeners, who can now finally understand (better than they could the aphorisms) to act and think in a particular way, to transcend themselves—after all, is that not what teachers, politicians, prophets do? We implicitly teach how not to be afraid of death and make the best of *this* lifetime. The eternal recurrence of the same, which can lead to a negative nihilism unless one lives entirely like an artist, in (though sublimated) Dionysian *ivresse*, can also be understood as the regular recurrence of *a* difference, one which is my—yours, his, hers—per-version of how I retell the tale of the last man to my progeny, and of how I can live with the paradox *nihil sub soli novis* while my own singularity is unique and irreplaceable.

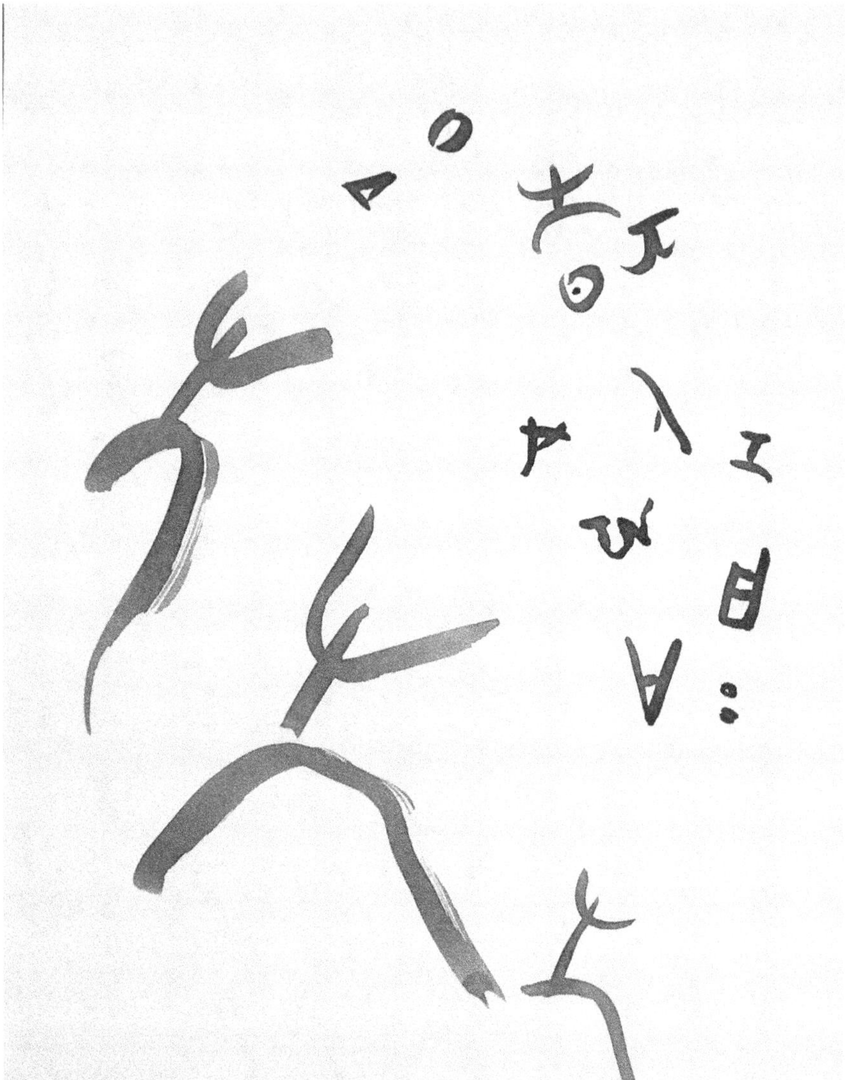

Figure 5 "Invention of language, 1" by Angela Biancofiore.

4

Poetics of the Manifold and the Hybrid

Poets between Cultures

The characteristics of poetry flow necessarily
from the nature of language and
the active function of poetry
in relation to society, man and reality.
Christopher Caudwell

Thinking Poetry and Language

The *I* is the principle and destination, the absolute self-reference of its utterance, wrote Émile Benveniste, and before it, the world an inchoate, undefinable infinite flux.[1] There is a sense in which the I and the world are, from inception, two separate things. It turns out another human being is part of this external-to-my-body reality, this inchoate flux. Thus a human soon discovers the great *otherness*, what we call the world, and within that, an other. Further background to my ongoing critique of the idea of language as merely an expressive, neurological tool to get by in the world is the following reality check, again by Benveniste:

> To speak of an instrument is to put man and nature in opposition. The pick, the arrow, and the wheel are not in nature. They are fabrications. Language is in the nature of man, and he did not fabricate it. We are always inclined to that naïve concept of a primordial period in which a complete man discovered another one, equally complete, and between the two of them language was worked out

1 Cf. Benveniste, *Problems in General Linguistics*, 195–204 *et infra*. But see also for general background to discussion here and further down on antiquity, as well as the anthropological relevance of language-use, his *Le Vocabulaire des institutions indo-européennes*, 2 volumes (Paris: Minuit, 1969).

> little by little. This is pure fiction. We can never get back to man separated from language and we shall never see him inventing it. We shall never get back to man reduced to himself and exercising his wits to conceive of the existence of another. It is a speaking man whom we find in the world, a man speaking to another man, and language provides the very definition of man.[2]

This sparks the very auto-creation of the Self: "A language without the expression of person cannot be imagined."[3] Thus, from the start there is the need of a language to bring these two together: "It is in and through language that man constitutes himself as a subject, because language alone establishes the concept of 'ego' in reality, in its reality which is that of the being."[4]

But at the same time, *can* the *ego sum* exist without the *ergo tibi*?

Let me switch register momentarily and rephrase this preface with reference to certain well-known *discursive formations*[5] that have taken place from the Romantics to the end of the twentieth century. There is a complicated field of critical foreboding in a swath of literature that goes from Giacomo Leopardi, Gérard de Nerval, John Keats, Arthur Schopenhauer, Søren Kierkegaard, Fyodor Dostoievsky to the early Friedrich Nietzsche, Luigi Pirandello, Franz Kafka, Eugenio Montale, Miguel de Unamuno, Martin Heidegger, Karl Jaspers, Samuel Beckett, Claude Lévi-Strauss, and Gianni Vattimo. It is the tradition of nihilism. Within that resides the possibility that being is essentially non-being, and that no-thing, non-sense, entropy reign supreme. On this ontology, nothing has spoken more eloquently than lyric poetry: nothing has more signally emblematized the demise of the tragic, the proliferation of masks, the fear of what may lie behind the mask and the tormented efforts of philosophy

[2] Benveniste, *Problems in General Linguistics*, 223–4.

[3] Benveniste, *Problems in General Linguistics*, 225.

[4] Ibid., 224.

[5] I am using the critical expression "discursive formations" in the sense theorized by Michel Foucault in *The Archaeology of Language and Discourse on Language* (New York: Harper & Row, [1969] 1976). To recall the basics, discursive formations are constituted according to how statements are organized, which can be in one of four ways: (1) how different expressions *define* a given object or form of expression; (2) the form and type of their connection, which is revealed *by a certain style*, or as *trope*; (3) how they determine the conceptual *systems underlying statements* and how they are *dispersed* in the culture, where lodged and given normative meaning for all of them (sort of metaphysical absolutes and their grounding a number of these concepts); and (4) "*regroup* statements" on the basis of *unitary forms and their strategic choices*, such as "themes" (or what I call *topoi*) that persist, referential "spheres" (Foucault, *The Archaeology of Language*, 32–5). In the pages that follow I occasionally look at how in poetics a variety of statements meet, cross-breed, and will change over a generation or two. But the concern is still how the poetic act is understood amidst so many boundaries of language, that is, in the junctures among any of these four characteristics of discursive formations.

at furnishing an answer. Retrospectively, we know what happened. Science and philosophy progressively isolated what was called knowledge from what was called aesthetic, or poetic.[6] It is an epochal turn in a dialectic that began when Plato out-talked the sophists to cultural death in the *Phaedrus*, imposing his master paradigm. Knowledge was to be obtained methodically, through the use of a dialogical dialectic, deductive mostly, in terms of some ultimate aim or value, the forms, which serve as principle and end of the enterprise.

You may notice I used the same expression as I did just above concerning the lyric. Am I confusing something here? Not really, if we consider that the *fundamentum inconcussum* to both knowledge and poetry, to ideas and reality, is the fact that they are both linguistic, rhetorical acts, and that both poetry and philosophy are, according to Aristotle, the product of wonder. In short, we will have to posit an anthropological *Grund* here: it is really existing human beings who produce poems, something about the materiality of their ex-pression must be accounted for.

There is also another field of meanings that marks, more than anything else, at the linguistic, rhetorical level, the evolution of the modern poetry as represented by the lyric. This line actually explodes hyperbolically the possibility that language may contain the ultimate secret of life itself, of a total and totalizing purpose. I am thinking of Poe's "Poetic Principle," and the correlated "Philosophy of Composition," which break the linguistic sign in half, concentrate on the pure signifier, and in which reality turns up as a *phoneme*, which bears instantly on the coming-into-being of *sememes*, or basic units for signification, for meaning, but that was not important. This is the first most powerful, paradigm shifting affirmation of what was later to be called the "poetics of the autonomy of art,"[7] of *l'art pour l'art*, of the high points of symbolism (mediated through Baudelaire) reaching the rarefied heights of an obscuring clarity, a blinding light of mystery and revelation with Stéphane Mallarmé and Paul Valéry, with the avant-gardes, with Filippo T. Marinetti, with Dada, surrealism, and at the other end of the arc with Gertrude Stein's *Poetry and Grammar*.

And then there is the tradition, also rooted in Romanticism, of lyric poetry as precisely an ontological pursuit, a philosophical questing, the ultimate exploration. Again going through the pivotal figure of Baudelaire, this poetic

6 See Chapter 6, on "Poetics of Science."

7 See the phenomenological poetics of Luciano Anceschi, *Autonomia ed eteronomia dell'arte*, and my synthesis in English in "Luciano Anceschi," cit.

might comprise Friedrich Hölderlin, Gottfried Benn, Stefan George, Rainer Maria Rilke, aspects of the younger Ezra Pound, the younger Giuseppe Ungaretti, Montale, Salvatore Quasimodo, with Wallace Stevens, with Juan Ramon Jimenez and Pedro Salinas, Antonio Machado, and Federico García Lorca. This is lyric as the expression of various forms of disenchantment, a song to the desperate (because useless) practice of singing. This poetic nihilism (which parallels the nihilism of the thinkers and writers mentioned above) finds different stylistic registers in the various poets, but it has abdicated reality, it has—shocking revelation, which we will pick up in a moment—found that language does not communicate, in fact, cannot communicate anything.

If we refer back once again to the still valid general assessment made by Hugo Friedrich in *The Structure of the Modern Lyric,* we can say that the continuity of the lyric model can be characterized as follows: *Lyric poetry does not need the world and deletes all links with reality*. It is the common destiny of *both* traditions, the formal lyrical poem *and* the avant-garde pure-signifying machine, to inhabit a space that negates existence, and where the linguistic expression turns upon itself, constantly denouncing the impossibility of speaking, telling mini-stories of the chasm between history and occurrence. It prompts above all an unstoppable growth of *logoi* in ironic, self-ironic, mock-ironic, parodistic, and ultimately satirical attitudes. In addition, as we have seen in the above chapters, *Modern lyric is depersonalized, and as such it can be read as a general telling of the incubus or the labyrinth, an obsessive plunging into and purification of the national literary tradition.* In order to focus on a more restricted environment, consider an assessment made by Randall Jarrell in the key 1942 essay "The End of the Line,"[8] in which after delineating some relevant differences between Romantic and modernist/avant-gardist poetry, he sketches the general characteristics of modernist poetry:

1. A pronounced experimentalism, originality being everyone's aim.
2. External formlessness, internal disorganization.
3. Heightened emotional intensivity, violence of all sorts.
4. Obscurity, inaccessibility, illogical structure and texture.

However, writes Jarrell, there is a social-cultural fallout from this: "without this for a ground the masses of the illogical or a-logical lose much of their

[8] See for those years Randall Jarrell, *Poetry and the Age* (Gainesville: University Press of Florida, [1953] 2001).

effectiveness." Because of his insight, or erudition, the poet's audience shrinks, only the few really understand. In fact, he concludes, the poet is a specialist like everyone else." We can intercalate at this juncture: the lyrical poet has become a member of an elite, which claims for itself a millennia-old tradition of prestige and emulation. If we consider the remaining three characteristics of modernist poetry, of *lyrical poetry as individualist*, as pure ego talk, with its great emphasis on parts, not wholes ("the rare narrative or expository poem is a half-fortuitous collocation of lyric details"), *obsessed*, in the best tradition of Romanticism, *with sensation, perception, nuances*, and displaying "*irony of every type*," we cannot but conclude once again that *the lyric is a profoundly metaphysical utterance, veined by a melancholic (pre)disposition, haunted by its proximity to nihilism.*

In Jarrell as in Barrett Watten, in John Crowe Ransom as in Charles Olson, we learn the poet is riddled with insurmountable paradoxes (others still say "contradictions"). Though the poet may write about ordinary life of the times, or even tragic situations, they are also keenly aware of the fact that they are removed from them, that their *relation to* ordinary life, to reality, is highly specialized, requiring highly tuned antennae (as Pound called them), which of course pick up peculiar or specific aspects of that reality. In short, lyric poetry began to lose its former, grand, universalist rhetoric, rhetoric of the ultimate metaphysical questions: why life, why death, wither the Good, why the tragic irony, and so on. Lyric poetry during and after the Second World War experienced and expressed the plight of isolation, alienation, hyper-individuation. Though this generation of poets exploited their difference to the hilt, and stepped in to demolish the mythologies surrounding science and technology and "progress," they also turned their gaze inward, making the poetic enterprise personal, even theological.

This is the conception of the poetic lyric, which as I argued in Chapter 1, I think we should no longer consider the queen of the arts, the most profound human expression, as we saw with Leopardi above. This is a lyric that cannot obtain in the postmodern, technological worldview, where alienation reigns supreme. Its implied metaphysics not only rejects the possibility of a non-Western mindset or alternate mode of philosophizing, but within it the social, real, contingent, the very *ex-istere* is secondary to a higher and more formal pursuit of general rules and principles, normative values, and reassuring beliefs. The contingent, however, is the spark of history and change, of communication, of the possibility of communication.

Rehabilitating Rhetoric

It is evident at this juncture that we might have to rethink the very nature of language, the rhetorical premises themselves of any act of communication. First of all, our postmodernity requires that we be both more sweeping across the globe and more humble about our pretense to explain everything away our way. In his book *Border Crossings* Henry Giroux advises, "to take up the relationship between language and the issues of knowledge and power on the one hand, and to re-theorize language within a broader politics of democracy, culture, and pedagogy on the other."[9] This is as sound a self-conscious hermeneutic attitude as you are able to hear in these times, an hermeneutic that does not forget its materialist component. It is certainly a problem we all face, professionally: a willingness to instill in students, to teach them (whatever that might turn out to mean), and above all to show them (we learn through *mimesis* primarily!!) that besides lecturing on what we know, we can also listen to what we don't know or cannot immediately place into our own complex but ultimately circumscribed Western European worldview. How do we teach non-European literature (if we are neither born nor trained in a non-European country)? Is the fact that it may originate in another tongue than the national idiom we speak a fact of major or minor consequence? Of course, since we can only hear the music but not understand the words, how do we go about establishing, broadly speaking, the referents, the symbols, the scapes that are inevitably present? With Giroux I agree that we must take advantage of forms of criticism that give high priority to topics such as postcolonialism, feminism, critique of the state, relationship of language to power, aesthetic and politic, and that our activity should become a sort of "transformative politics." I am not so sure I want to do it in terms of an oppositional ideology or through a play of antithetical paradigms. As I have explored and partly demonstrated elsewhere, to critique by counter-foisting one logical argument against another has led, in the West, to a notion that you can prove who's right and who's wrong on the basis of semiotic conventions, not really based on reality, especially when that reality has not yet entered into our symbolic order or cultural unconscious. I believe the retheorization of language (the *diaphoristic* rhetoric I am seeking) includes also the possibility that language may not be communicating anything

9 Cf. Henri Giroux, *Border Crossings: Cultural Workers and the Politics of Education* (London: Routledge, 2007), 21.

at all, that paradoxically, the lyric may have understood this before all other forms of linguistic articulation, before the philosophers of language.

Consider, for instance, that with Plato and Aristotle we have secured a notion of language as representational of an order or dimension called reality, that through its most influential version in Western culture we have elaborated systems of science and explanation based on the idea of a correspondence of some sort between reality and idea, between what I think and what actually is. But then why do Nietzsche, Heidegger, and a great many of their exegetes speak of rethinking language and being, expression and experience, the mystery and power of poetic language, with reference to the pre-Socratics, to those thinkers who sought in the utterance and the coming-into-being of the *logos* the quintessential founding gesture, the coincidence of being and being-there, the revelation of the unity of all things. From the early 1930s on Heidegger approaches the poets as the guardians of Being by virtue of their voice, their founding saying, their capacity of staking out for us a disclosure, a *Lichtung*, which alone shines of its own light (it is not reflected, as in modern philosophy and science, where knowledge and the world are always reflected, or we might say mediated, through a formal system of signs).

Before the Eleatics, rhetoric is broadly understood as based on two cooperating factors, expression and reception. The first may be actually called persuasion, the second hermeneutics.[10] In the fifth century BCE, Gorgias introduced a thesis that can be summarized as follows: (1) nothing exists; (2) even if anything existed, it would be incomprehensible to humans; and (3) even if man understood that nothing, he would not be able either to express it or communicate it to others.

Let's analyze this. Concerning (1), "exists" is a fact oflanguage, is a word, and as it is possible with language to speak about anything, even of what is and what is not, there is no internal criterion to tell them apart, that is, whether something "is" or "is not" has nothing to do with the reality or truth of whether something exists or not! Concerning (2), if language is not reality, then reality is not contained in the words, and once again we cannot express in words what distinguishes the real from

[10] I have since spent more time in this area, and my understanding of the rhetorical has been influenced by my reading of the Sophists, whom I consider bona fide philosophers of language and of ethics. See Carravetta, *The Elusive Hermes*, pt. 2, § 1; Carravetta, "Paradoxes: The Sophists as Philosophers of Language and Existence," in Stefano Arduini (ed.), *Paradoxes*, 61–80 (Rome: Edizioni di Storia e letteratua, 2011). Available online: http://www.petercarravetta.com/wp-content/uploads/2015/01/The-Sophists-as-Philosophers-of-Language-Cover-TOC.pdf (accessed October 7, 2020). For the references that follow, see Rosamond Kent Sprague, ed., *The Older Sophists* (Indianapolis, IN: Hackett Publishing, 1972).

the non-real. A depressing thesis, but a very serious one. When we now reconsider (3), we better grasp how this paradoxical rhetoric of noncommunication actually serves as a mainspring to a very concrete, necessarily committed interpretive practice. In the *The Encomium of Helen* (50–64) we read that Helen of Troy was typically considered an exemplary case of catastrophic seduction—a metaphor for an attitude, which the community that knew Homer as the encyclopedia, as the Tradition, judged to have such and such a moral value. But by examining the premises upon which Helen is judged and condemned, Gorgias not only justifies her behavior and actions but also goes on to praise it highly! Above and beyond the fact that he demonstrates, before Socrates came on the scene, the technique of arguing by counterargument, what matters here is that he demonstrates the third point, namely, that language does not communicate anything "above" itself (as a form, an axiom, a god) except through a coordination of signifieds (or meanings) already acquired, given in the local public unconsciousness, or proposed to them. That's where myth and primordial allegory enter the scene of language. Speaking "rhetorically" if anything convinces the audience because it exercises a mild (per) suasive attunement that is nearly physical, that transcends meaning as such. The sense of the discourse rests on the affect, the emotive charge given to the communicative event.

This theory of language as de-linking raises the stakes in both the sender—the speaker/writer—who must be willing to admit that a certain misunderstanding, a certain amount of what they will say will inevitably be lost, and on the part of the receiver—the reader/listener—who must now sharpen their hermeneutic skills, aware of the fact that meaning is basically a construction, generated *ex novo* each time, and that they will never know what the sender was thinking, or intended, at least not 100 percent. A theory of language according to which meaning is constituted by the abyss or rupture or asymmetry between sender and receiver has been picked up in the twentieth century by Karl Bühler. *Auslosung*, "scatenamento" in Italian, or in English "de-linking," implies that the speaker provokes an effect that is different in each of its listeners, because different is their preparation, linguistic competence, sympathy for the argument, etc, which ultimately influences their understanding of the meaning they think is being conveyed.

This problem has been faced by many philosophers of language in the twentieth century, most emblematically by Ludwig Wittgenstein, whose parabola from 1920 to 1950 is living proof of the possibility that there is something always missing, something residual, something extra perhaps, in any act of communication and that, therefore, to pretend to find truth, or reality, in and through language, is at most an approximation, a "being in the area of," in *limitrophy*, an ethical necessity yet, and at worst an hallucination of reason, a tragic illusion. Writing about Thomas Berhard and the crisis and dissolution of what he called the Austrian episteme, Aldo Gargani (1933–2007) notes that even to talk about Wittgenstein's dilemma with language proved to be impossible.[11] At one point, he cites Berhard: "Everything is so different. Everything is always so entirely different. It is impossible to make oneself understood [Sich verstandlich machen ist unmoglich]."[12] And elsewhere, "I speak a language which I alone and no one else understands, much the way in which everyone understands only their own language... So that everyone, whoever he might be and no matter what he may do, is always pushed back into himself, everyone is always a nightmare to oneself."[13]

Poetics of Noncommunication

To go back to the realm of poetics from which we began, Allen Tate had remarked, in his 1938 essay "Tension in poetry," that ideally we should entertain the notion of a "Poetry as the embodiment of the fallacy of communication: it is a poetry that communicates the affective state, which (in terms of language) results from the irresponsible denotations of words." A huge statement, the first part of which may compel reflection on a fundamental aspect of the linguistic art: language does not (allow us to) communicate? Really? But the second claim is untenable as well, as there is no such thing as an "irresponsible denotation of words": I have long argued that poets *do know* that even the denotative aspect of words used in a poem does not prevent them from generating strings of association through their being simultaneously connotative, layered with past meanings, and so on. Especially in a poem. In particular, if the poem is a "long poem," discursive and allegorical, as perforce it must be, by virtue of its discursive construction.

With the allegorical conceived as the very foundation of language, the public speech and storytelling about *experiences and images organized for the collective to hear (read)* and which inscribe thus a group memory; and with an

[11] Cf. Aldo Gargani, *La frase infinita* (Milan: Feltinelli, 1976), 12. Gargani also wrote a book in 1972 titled *Il sapere senza fondamenti* (Foundationless Knowledge), which anticipates many of the ideas we find in Paul Fayeraband, Joseph Margolis, and Richard Rorty.

[12] Gargani, *Frase infinita*, 12.

[13] Ibid., 13.

understanding of *the allegorical as a weakened metaphysic*, as a circumstantial and sociohistorically determined context for the very possibility for that discourse to exist; then we may be able to face the great challenge of writings whose symbolic systems and frames of reference alert us, immediately, that we are at a loss, that we may be threatened in a way, that these stories are "foreign." The point here is to move toward a greater poetic-hermeneutic investment, with playfulness, at least in a non-obsessive, nonrestrictive (nondogmatic) use of our own traditions. It is conceivable we can make headway into a conversation, a dialogue with a voice/s that speak/s from beyond the masks, but we can surmise with Viconian certainty that *it is from a somewhere*, it is real, just another place (perhaps unknown to me), voicing an other or others with a twist because their languages and literary memories and past social history are to us or to me unknown.

Consider finally that with allegory as thus briefly reframed we can still entertain a valid, fruitful critical and pedagogical experience, even in the face of the demise of the lyric and the critical deflating of metaphysics. We can finally respond to forms of writing that are *not* rooted in Western Being, in Plato, in subjectivity as we know them from Saint Augustine to René Descartes to G. W. F. Hegel to Edmund Husserl.

This writing advocated for here is foreign writing, in an ontological way: being estranged from oneself, as we learned from early existentialism: we are already ex-istent, isn't the fear that we may be estranged to ourselves one of the reasons we place so much emphasis on identity? On grounding our own, first and universally, as opposed to that other out there intruding. Advocated is a language of reference, that points to the lived world of the living-interpreting subjects (before they are defined by race, gender, nationality, and so on, which would constitute their ontic reality). This divestment, let's call it border writing, writing between (often several) worlds, the narration of exile, of journeying, the allegory of the itinerary: though some of this writing was chronologically born in those years, it has nothing to do with Modernism as Western bourgeois literary and artistic institutions floating among studios, galleries, famous publishers, museums, galas, and libertine parties.

Modernism subsumes so many different poetics that it is becoming increasingly difficult to find the generalities underlying them. For in truth what do Ezra Pound, Gertrude Stein, Luis Zukofsky, and William Carlos Williams have in common? Just think: one re-semanticizes history, myth, and messages, overloads the signifieds; the second de-semanticizes and breaks down the logic of grammar, banalizes reference, brings language to the level of children's song, aspires to achieving the pure signifier.[14] Zukofsky works at the level of the isolated lexeme and often morpheme and grapheme, whereas Williams most humbly collects the evidence from everyday parlance, from the stock routine designations, bureaucratic records, citations, the detritus of the already said and done, making poems that would suit Walter Benjamin's image of looking from the last wagon of a train, everything you can see is already gone!

> Ya, selva oscura, but hell now
> Is not exterior, is not to be got out of, is
> The coat of your own self, the beasts
> Emblazoned on you.
>
> (Charles Olson, "In Cold Hell, in Thicket")

Names, Journeys, Experiences

Among the most essential tasks of a poet is that of polishing and fine-tuning the language of a society, ensuring that its words, and their capacity to interest and innovate, do not degenerate into automatic ready-made phrases, endlessly repeatable until they lose their range, richness, their predisposition to be more than univocal messages or, worse, signals. In this view, the poets who attack long-encrusted locutions or splinter everyday words or word-clusters would be automatically avant-gardists, convinced as they are that the province of poetry is the word, actually the noun, the *lexis*, the *onoma*, essaying to shock it out of its torpor, and recharging it with political, symbolic, visual, enigmatic allusions.

Though this line of inquiry can yield revealing results, there is another approach to poetry as the realm of the word, and this consists in reworking the part of speech in terms of another of its fundamental functions, namely, that of naming reality (or whatever reality is under consideration). From the Bible and Homer and down through Aristotle, Vico, Nietzsche, and Heidegger, the poetic word has also been conceived and experimented with in terms of its *founding* capacity, or its somehow "magical" power to invent or devise a "world" of sorts. This poetry by and large focuses on the possibility/eventuality *that* it

[14] See Chapter 2, above.

can and does create with words a "world," no matter how feeble and fleeting. We can call this *ontological poetry*. Wallace Stevens would be representative of this mode.

At other times, the poetic word has been looked at in terms of *what* it brought out, what it highlighted amidst the noise and the silence of language, of the world borne out of language. This type of poetic has a political soul markedly at variance from that of the avant-gardists. For a poetry in which isolating, touching, lighting up the naming function of the word is *a poetry* intrinsically *concerned with naming the world*, pointing toward reality, and a sociohistorical symbolic *life-world* at that. We can call this a *gnostic* or *cognitive* poetry. To name something corresponds not merely to mentioning a word-that-refers-to-something the first time, in a casual sequence of "new" words or things we discover. To name something is to bring it into existence from the void or nullity of non-Being; it is very much like creating or inventing an idea or feeling or psychohistorical knot. This is intrinsically a question of identity because if I mention the proper noun (and a name) "France," or refer to a cluster of critical problems as somehow related to France, I have already excluded all other possible nations or ethnic or cultural backgrounds, and that effects and pre- or co-determines the sense of the ensuing reading.[15]

Finally, we should consider *a poetics of the phrastic or the narrative*, grounded upon a time-and-place bound expression that, like ancient allegories, like modern long-poems, do not bank on the utterance of the word *only* but rely *also* most heavily on *what is being talked about with specific, contextual frames*, a poem that intends to tell, according to the author's style and interests, something about something else, a poetry of the verb as opposed to a poetry of instantaneous magical (albeit founding) word.

In other words, from Heidegger we must move on to Vico: here language is also founding, but it is stories, *fabulas*, not words in isolation, that give shape and direction to the society:

> You cannot write a single line w/out a cosmology
> a cosmogony
> laid out, before your eyes.
>
> (Diana di Prima, "Rant")

[15] This is a major tenet in Lyotard's *Le Différend* (Paris: Minuit, 1983). See my interpretation in Carravetta, *Prefaces*, 191–212.

Notes on Other Fields Disclosed

There is always the danger
The facts will fall and part

Repeat what cannot be altered
Infinite and misunderstood
[…]
This innocent yet compelling
Permanence.

(Andrew Levy, "Don't Forget to Breathe")

In the anthology *Artifice and Indeterminacy*, Christopher Beach makes use of the expression "Postmodern avant-garde,"[16] which complicates unnecessarily the field of poetics if for no other reasons than historiographic and critical clarity: the avant-garde is one thing, the postmodern is an entirely different kettle of fish.[17] Yes, there are avant-garde aspects to post-Second World War poetics, and we need go no further than the Beat generation, or American expressionist painting, to realize that, but the climate had changed, and the stakes were higher. To the continuity—implied in saying we are still the grandchildren of modernists—one must juxtapose the discontinuities, the breaks, the different questions asked and the different horizons where the founding and the recalling were to be occur. Further confusion was created by Paul Hoover's *Postmodern American Poetry* (1994). It includes 120 poets! It includes everybody who has published more than two or three books and appeared in the magazines. But what do John Cage, Diane di Prima, Charles Bernstein, Robert Kelly, Lorenzo Thomas, David Shapiro, and Miguel Algarin have in common to place them under the aegis of the postmodern? Other than the fact that they are poets?[18] Such an anthology contributes to canon formation,[19] but it dilutes the very field it is meant to represent and codify.

Following another critic, Douglas Messerli, it is important to distinguish between schools if only to circumscribe a field of inquiry, to distinguish whether

16 Christopher Beach, ed., *Artifice and Indeterminacy: An Anthology of New Poetics* (Tuscaloosa: University of Alabama Press, 1998), ix.

17 Cf. Beach, *Artifice and Indeterminacy*. On the often confused but fundamental differences between avant-gardist poetics and postmodernism, see Peter Carravetta, *Prefaces*, 133–62, and *Del postmoderno*, 51–127.

18 Cf. Paul Hoover, ed., *Postmodern American Poetry* (New York: Norton, 1994).

19 See Chapter 8, below, on canon formation.

they are out there to found a new world, to refer to a specific world, to recover something lost, or whether instead they believe, against all odds (like Ernst Block) that in these dystopic times we actually need utopias.

Overall the panorama of poetics had shifted in the 1980s, as some of the currents that followed the Beat generation, really orphaned, did not know what to do, and having relinquished history, allegory, representation, and reference in poetry, they found solace within enclaves (around magazines or metropolitan outlets) and ruminated a self-centered, ego-boasting/bashing, emotion laden/purged pale imagism or pointism. There was present, also, a diffused feeling that, in some aspects, poetry could still be political, it could change something.[20] But the gist was: I am not going to subject my language-poetry search to the ravages of advertising, bureaucracy, clichés, sentimentalism, and the like. The gesture of refusal, the very fact that the poet would not engage the world because what counted was purifying the inner relationships of language, meant that what was deemed political was the constant subversion of preconceived forms (we can think here of Ron Silliman, Clark Coolidge, Bern Porter) and the opening up of spaces of signification that were ultimately highly charged and, yes, the maligned word, NEW. Somehow, though, this approach did not reach out to establish that *measure* in the world of beings, the fallen or suffering human beings in this circumscribed splinter of the world, in this precise historical-geographical location called the United States, this specific corner called New York, or San Francisco, or Miami, and within that, the persons who, as Gertrude Stein had noted, having the words, did not know what they meant.

That being said, as the culture becomes a wasteland, efforts were made nevertheless to restore the mighty word. Though not on the six o'clock news, or cited in the halls of power, poets were gathering up the pieces after the utter fragmentation and alienation of the lyric and concurrent dissolution of the avant-gardes. We can list, in shorthand:

1. The Naropa Institute and "disembodied poetics."[21]
2. The parabola of *LANGUAGE poetry* (Bernstein, Silliman, Barrett Watten, Bob Perelman, John Davidson).
3. The innovations in diction and reference of *performance poetry* (Jerome Rothenberg).

[20] Cf. Charles Bernstein, ed., *The Politics of Poetic Form* (New York: Roof, [1993] 2008).

[21] Cf. Anne Waldman and Marilyn Webb, eds., *Talking Poetics from Naropa Institute*, 2 volumes (Boulder, CO: Shambhala, 1978).

4. Objectivist and post-ojectivist poetics, which follow upon Pound's imagist poetics, and who work with the detritus of everyday language and engage myth, history, and politics.
5. A grouping that can be labeled *New York poetics*, focused on the Self, the construction of groups and affiliations, the metropolitan landscape, and greater participation in the visual arts.[22]
6. A grouping that persists in believing in a reader, one that can entertain a focus on the language-content itself, also seeking adepts and comrades; this includes much poetry produced by feminists and other marginal(ized) groups, such as queer and lesbian, gay, bisexual, and transgender (LGBT), as well as writers who delve into trauma of various origins.
7. There are poetics that overrride the limits of the text (as traditionally understood, bound to a page) and become *multimedial*, and performance oriented, as in the work of Laurie Anderson and Ishmael Reed, or Richard Foreman.
8. There exists a multicultural poetics, which opens up to a vary magmatic writing in a multicultural, multilinguistic universe; this might be also termed *poetics of dislocation*,[23] *migration poetry*, or *transnational poetics.*
9. Finally, there is what I am provisionally calling *hyphenated poetry*, and which usually groups poets marked for national provenance or ethnicity: Hispanic American or Latinx, Greek American, Italian American, Native American Indian, and so on. In these poetics, I feel there are certain constants, or *topoi*, which can be subsumed under the labels of *identity*, *place*, and *reference*, and assign them a confrontational, critical role vis-à-vis the sociopolitical reality of America at the beginning of the millennium.

[22] A New York poetics, much like an Angelino poetry and others marked by a place (a city, a region), has complicated roots and ramifications. The starting point is still Ron Padgett and David Shapiro, eds., *An Anthology of New York Poets*, 1970. Noteworthy as the new millennium unfolds is the activity surrounding the *Lost and Found* project launched by Ammiel Alcalay in New York in 2009, at the CUNY/Graduate center, a unique publishing, public, and pedagogical endeavor that also serves as a venue to train graduate students in archival research, the presentation of textual scholarship, the interaction with heirs, estates, and artistic circles. *Lost & Found* 's approach to keeping poetry alive is to gather a grouping of researched, edited, annotated rare or "lost" works from collections of correspondence to journals, transcriptions of talks or lectures. The collective has uncovered the curricular materials of poets such as Toni Cade Bambara, June Jordan, Audre Lorde, and Adrienne Rich. Another approach—extremely responsive to a world-level place like New York—is to valorize the writings by visual artists, particularly those who are also critics and writers, and who like the poets operate under the constant threat of the capitalistic advertising machine of the Post-Orwellian Warp. See for example the publications of Edgewise Press, founded by Richard Milazzo in 1995.

[23] See Meena Alexander, *Poetics of Dislocation* (Ann Arbor: University of Michigan Press, 2012); and Jahan Ramazani, "A Transnational Poetics," in *American Literary History*, 18 (2) (Summer 2006): 332–59.

These are poets who have been trying to work away from reflex essentialism, vague universalism, and pithy individualism, poets who believe that there is a specific concrete world *outside the text* and therefore are struggling to rethink the use of language as minimally deictical, inevitably symbolic, and most assuredly content laden. The problem is, we cannot read them directly nor can we methodically unfurl a set of symbolism we are familiar with and then try to weave a series of connections, attributing a pretty accurate interpretation. The problem is akin to what Edouard Glissant calls the "opacity" of the material expression of this alterity, something we cannot avoid confronting because it goes with the poetic act being essentially a relation between an "I" and a set of intersecating worlds (worlds-in-language, conflicting discursive formations, but despite which a poietic, creative/critical value must emerge: remember that *poiēsis* implies *technē*).[24]

Much of this comes through in authors who have a multilingual, multicultural background, or with poets who choose to live outside the United States. Their verse rings with a subtext or an otherness that speaks indirectly—namely, as other-speaking—to a more stratified, more interlaced social reality where all attempts at homogenization, simplification, and stupidification of the American psyche are blasted asunder or sketched out in patterns reminiscent of the most committed neo-avant-guardism of the 1950s and 60s. I found this to be the case with the production of Safiya Henderson-Homes, Jimmy Santiago Baca, Joy Harjo (*How We Became Human*), Emilia Paredes, Maria Mazziotti Gillan, Kyoko Mori, Myung Mi Kim (*Under Flag*), and Mei-Mei Berssenbrugge.[25]

Let us look up close. In *Red Beans*, Jimmy Santiago Baca writes: "Migration is the story of my body, it is the condition of this age." In *Panoramas*, in the poem "The Lower East Side of Manhattan" he writes:

By the East River
Of Manhattan Island
Where once the Iroquois
Canoed in Style …
Now the jumping
Stretch of Avenue D
Housing Projects.

[24] See Chapter 6, below, on "Poetics of Science."

[25] For a quick critical panorama as the millennium ends, and to grasp the complexity of what followed, see Peter Carravetta, "Vital Crossings and Histories: Recent Tendencies in American Poetry," *Poetry NZ*, 18 (1999): 76–82.

At the end of the book, we find another poem about this specific context that ends thus: "Como fue que las montanas desaparecieron / En las maletas las frutas de su memoria."

And after a singular historico-ethnico description of who actually escaped from Europe to the Lower East Side, and what it has become in the multilayered brutal exchanges of "signos y vidas" in New York, it appears now as: "Hasta el rio / El Rio Este." Throughout we note the marvelous phonetics of bringing the two languages to mirror each other.

Consider now a different poet, Myang Mi Kim, in *Under Flag*:

> Along the meadow
> The Wander's gypsum shoes
> Crossing and Bearings
> Steadily pernicious
>
> She could not talk without first looking at other's mouths (which language?) (pushed into) crevice a bluegill might lodge in.

This uprooted, out-of-place condition of the poet is recounted by other authors, for instance, by Victor Hernández Cruz:

> The earth is migration, everything is moving, changing interchanging, appearing disappearing. National languages melt, sail into each other; languages are made of fragments, like bodies are made of fragments of something in the something ... Old geography lingers in the languages of the conquistadores: names of rivers and fruits. Our Spanish—which has Latin and Italian—has Taino, Siboney, Chichimeca. It has sounds coming out of it that amaze it and over the years it has been spiced, making it a rich instrument full of our history, our adventures, our desires, ourselves. The Caribbean is a place of great convergence: it mixes and uniforms diversities; it is a march of rhythms and style.

This kind of poetry between worlds, between languages, compels one to modify Charles Olson's view that the energy dedicated to content should be kept out of the energy that goes into form. Consciousness is crucial to poetry writing, even as we just sloop over form, word, image, cadence, and rhythm. I am not sure that, though ever conscious of their individual word choices, these poets can consciously detach the energy of the form from the power of the content (whatever it might be, and wherever it may occur, as a concrete act: there is always the component brought to the poem by the reader/critic).

In fact, and going back to the confusion of the postmodern age, it cannot be denied that some of the most piercing and revealing literary and cultural criticism during the past quarter of a century came by way of anthologies, scholarly articles, and monographs dedicated to, for example, black writers, black women's writings, Asian American literature, Caribbean writers, Chicano writers, Chicana poetry, literature by Latinas of the United States.

This is especially detectable if we focus on the necessity, on the part of poets, to play up to the paradigms imposed by newfangled institutional agendas and missions (creative writing majors, composition courses, news media, public founded organizations, etc., needed for "survival"), while protecting their kin in whichever way—preferring certain tropes to others, pursuing newly configured ideologies, or inventing a particular style. This sets the premises for the creation of an *archipelago* of localized, often barely visible subcultures that, however, permitted poetry as a threatened species to survive.

Coda: Homage to John Cage

What Remains Is Not the Absence[26]

Versions they **W**ere of bodies and signs
Brilliant game of **H**eraklitos the obscure
Allusions **A**nd never gratuitous
For kabbalahs **T**roubling and cliques of all sorts
Whether studied **R**ecycled unhinged up and down
His name a trap a fram**E**work a friendly smile
Deeply conte**M**plated paths yet trickster's delight
Erring discourse **A**nxious groping
Deviously poetrarch**I**tecting pseudocreations
Wanting to have fu**N** but ever saying otherwise
Recasting pheme**S** and themes and memes
The truth an as**I**de it was clear and echo

[26] In 2011, I was contacted by Daniele Poletti, who directs the small press Dia-phoria (http://www.diaforia.org/diaforiablog/info/), to contribute to a John Cage memorial of his birth (1912–2012). One hundred guests from the world of culture participated. In a Cagean way, the editor put an arbitrary limit of 1,001 words (the poem is 987 words–spaces) to say something about this question: what is that you miss the most, and what remains, of John Cage? This was my contribution, imitating/emulating the master by writing a mesostic, in which I embodied (I hope) my thoughts on what John Cage means symbolically and philosophically to the evolution of the arts in the twentieth century.

Of a refrain of drum**S** and pipes often sad
Unflinchingly desce**N**ds into the self the gods
A threat to sophists ge**O**meters Manichean antiheroes
Unfathomably mul**T**ifarious and prolific
In/famous **T**ext of his poetics
To minds a c**H**allenge and to knowledge
He Orpheus Herm**E**s and Prometheus
He ever the or**A**cle the sphinx
The emptiness that **B**ends feeble certainties
As we will **S**urely gather up in his trail
Diasporic agnostics m**E**sostics prognoses
Matrixes cou**N**terfactuals
Even the **C**artographies
Of John Cag**E** the chameleon.

Figure 6 "Invention of language, 2" by Angela Biancofiore.

5

Poetica Cosmographica

An American Poet in Taiwan

Take your pick: ferocious iconoclast, perennial avant-gardist, implacable innovator, obsessive writer, transdisciplinary voyager at the limits of (mortal) comprehension, mind-bending researcher of (im)possible cosmographies. The list of critical epithets or of guiding threads could be expanded, perhaps it already has been at the hands of more daring interpreters, but expat poet Madison Morrison (1940–2013)[1] is not to be contained within any, however supple the theorem of literary art. His writing, for the last twenty years of his life, from faraway Taiwan and other countries in Southeast Asia requires that we expand our critical reach to cover many regions of the globe. To give an idea of what this author was up to, let me cite from a study of Frank Stevenson dedicated to his entire project (as was complete by 2005):

> *Sentence of the Gods*, MMs lifelong project, his life-text (epic, human-cosmic) world-text, in its projected grammatical totality represents a single "sentence" uttered by the gods; the life force of the text is the ongoing construction of the sentence and also its carrying-out, for this is the singular book that Morrison, in effect, has "sentenced" himself to write … each name represents a separate "book" of the entire utterance. SOL, LUNA, ARES, HERMES, HERA, APHRODITE,

[1] For general information about the author, see MM's Web (n.d. Available online: http://www.madisonmorrison.com/ [accessed October 8, 2020]). All of the twenty-six books that make up his world opus, *Sentence of the Gods*, are available. For a critical introduction, see Ron Phelps, "The Sentence of Madison Morrison" (MM's Web, n.d. Available online: http://www.madisonmorrison.com/sentenceofthegods/the-sentence-of-madison-morrison.html [accessed October 8, 2020]), which contains several commentaries on specific books. For a biographical sketch, see also Find a Grave, "James Madison Morrison" (June 22, 2013. Available online: https://www.findagrave.com/memorial/112736291/james-madison-morrison [accessed October 8, 2020]). This article was originally written in 2003–2006.

> EL. And thus the sentence becomes also a self-reflection and self-repetition (as in prayer and mantra).[2]

But in order to enter Morrison's labyrinth, we must momentarily take stock of the entry point, what was happening to Euro-America at the beginning of the twenty-first century.

The overall scenario was not reassuring. At all levels. Some of us, some of my colleagues, some of them poets, had most recently renounced the very possibility of an art form or, better, of an artistic practice that would yet disclose—ah, the dreamers!—unimaginable images, unthinkable thoughts, unwritable scripts. As if with the end of the Cold War, with all that buzz about the end of modernity (and with that, necessarily, of the avant-gardes), artists had to moor and mothball their sloops, corral their vaticinations, museumficate their ever-challenging per-versions, and yield to the digitized channels of untrammeled videocapitalism.[3] In one dominant version of (literary) history, with the passing of (chronological) time, the present becomes past, the new becomes old, and what was revolutionary yesteryear is transformed into conservative tradition, at best an ever-present yet convenient procedure or strategy, at worst an unseen unrecognized habitus, knee-jerk responses. The avant-gardes of yesteryears won Pyrrhic victories: from Man Ray to Salvador Dali to Jackson Pollock to Richard Kostelanetz, obsession with a-referentiality, with the play of pure signifiers (color, line, endless juxtapositions and cross-pollination of genres and styles and phonemes) have held sway, and ironically can now be seen and heard daily, tons and tons of them, in advertising. Aesthetic *Entfremdung* has severed the links between forms and contents, with the adulation of the former at the expense of latter.

Wozu dichter? Why do we have poets in these days of obsessive serial recycling and free marketing of several millennia of icons and images and tenuous yet durable encapsulations of … what? Grand values? The "Immutables" of Western thought? Kostelanetz once wrote that

> Modern art at its best deals not in the manipulation of conventions but their conspicuous neglect, because familiar forms are the most common counters of

[2] Frank W. Stevenson, *Chaos and Cosmos in Morrison's "Sentence of the Gods"* (Bangalore: St. Joseph's Press, 2005), 55. In an email dated December 23, 2003, Morrison wrote to me that "Sentence of the Gods is a global (or universal or cosmological) epic, which attempts to revive allegory in a modern context. Its subject is 'The Life of Man.'"

[3] See Barrett Watten, *The Constructivist Moment: From Material Text to Cultural Poetics* (Middletown, CT: Wesleyan University Press, 2003), 46–7 *et infra*.

commerce; one test of genuine innovation in art, even today, is its resistance to an immediate sale.[4]

Like most writers shaped by that generation, Morrison certainly manipulated conventions, especially in his earlier work, but we might say *that* was the mode of research and expression for a writer whose only overarching characteristic can be subsumed under the aegis of *graphology*. To this day, he has progressively gotten more and more difficult, complex, definitely not someone up for "an immediate sale." It doesn't matter that he is "difficult": again, in the great tradition of the avant-gardes, may "the plain reader be damned," as the magazine *Transition* announced way back in 1927. Art ought *to not go* out to the reader: everything in our society seems to want to do that, every sales pitch, each political rally, all human intercourse: coax, coopt, steal, glorify. But at the same time, no one is advocating total detachment from the reader: Morrison is no lyric poet! Rather, what counts is a shift in emphasis, of the type advocated a few years before by Ron Silliman, Don Wellman, Lyn Hejinian, and others who worked with *O.Ars/Toward a New Poetics*.[5] Morrison seems to believe we have to make the effort to *go to* the artwork. From here emerges one of the traits of his poetics (as can be expunged from later works such as *Engendering*[6] and *Realization*[7]): if art is sacred, if art is cosmological, then one must accept the rituals, the trials and tribulations of the journeys, the sense of wonder and discovery that emanates from this dynamics of the mind, this expurgation of the habituated social unconscious, the catatonics of our self-reassuring selves. Madison Morrison spares no one, he takes no prisoners. He is attempting nothing less than the grand epic! But in a contemporary form, a *post*-avant-garde, *post*-modernist creation, something for which there is no one precursor or lineage, for as we saw above (Chapter 1), the epic was sunk by the beginning of the twentieth century. From the very beginning, Morrison is off on the scriptural charts of the endless search.

* * *

4 Richard Kostelanetz, *Autobiographies* (Santa Barbara, CA: Mudborn Press, [1975] 1980), 222.

5 See for example *O.ARS/1*, "Coherence" (Cambridge, MA, 1981); *O.ARS/2*, "Perception" (Cambridge, MA, 1982); *Ironwood 20* (Tucson, AZ, 1982); and other special issues of poetry and poetics journals from the mid- to late-1980s that grappled with the issue of what constitutes an audience or a community in the face of, on the one hand, the splintering of the poetic *parole*, and on the other the issue of the role and relevance of poetry among the other arts in the advanced stages of electronic and media-driven performance arts.

6 Madison Morrison, *Engendering* (Norman, OK: Poetry Around, 1990).

7 Madison Morrison, *Realization* (Verona: Anterem Edizioni, 1996).

Let us look at *Revolution*.[8] Originally written by two authors,[9] it deals with two young college coeds, their experiences and relationships, a married professor, and a grid of oblique exchanges. Narratological techniques include citing from diaries, transcriptions of phone calls, reproduction of the French texts the characters utilize, direct translations, scenes wherein characters drink, party, extol or question or reminisce about what they are reading. The style is cut and dry, descriptive, a sort of *école du regard* approach. But it also displays the characteristics of a post-Pirandello post-Beckett somber exposition. Certain topics are teased in different locales or situations, for example, the problem of noncommunication (between mother and son, with a clerk, within the couple[10]), or the relevance of dreams, which are as important as actual conscious memories of bygone experiences. The prose makes us go from dream to reality to newer projection effortlessly. One begins to get the sense that according to Morrison there is no ONE life, one identity, or a single unifying *logos* or *ratio* that can hold all these interlocking vicissitudes together. This is not seen as a crisis but rather as a challenge, an opportunity. The multiple identities are not necessarily to be equated with clinical schizophrenia. Rather, it would appear that we have a possibility to reconnect or interweave somehow all the strands of our thoughts, as many pulsions from the imaginary as may occur to us during the act or process of reading (or experiencing). This allows for the reinstating of the present. The technique of reproducing journal entries in *tempo reale*, in the *jetz-zeit* of the act-of-writing does not so much intrude into the narratological realms created/explored along the way, it just simply reminds us, or maybe even warns us, that this is a writer writing a story. This technique allows for historical reconstructions, and since the line between story and history has long been crisscrossed and often erased,[11] *Revolution* may be understood not only as a major turn in the writer's journeying toward a

[8] Madison Morrison and Dan Boord, *Revolution* (Taipei: Bookman Books, 1985).

[9] When it was republished years later, it contained only Morrison's chapters from the 1985 edition, and retitled: *MM's Revolution: A Menippean Satire*, with a Chinese translation (East & West, 1998). No indication of place of publication is indicated.

[10] Morrison and Boord, *Revolution*, 58, 67–8, 138, respectively.

[11] See on this the theoretical work of Paul Ricoeur, principally *Time and Narrative*, vol. 1, translated by Kathleen McLaughlin and David Pellauer (Chicago: University of Chicago Press, 1990). The issue has been at the center of many debates in postcolonial and cultural studies in the United States for the past forty years at least. Writers on both sides of the Atlantic have long raided official histories and used their "fiction" in variously motivated attempts at rewriting history, or the national allegories of emerging sovereign states, or in the cases of diasporic cultures seeking some sort of homogeneous or coherent sense of identity.

new kind of *geohistorical narrative* but also as representative of the theoretical juggernaut of the boundaries between genres and among disciplines.

Let's look closer. For instance, in chapter 6: "A Chinaman Looks at Paris" (which reconnects with chapter 2): who is to say that the "outsider's" experience of Paris is not as important as Voltaire's or Michelet's version of what Paris is, or was? One can read/hear a battery of voices: From conscience? An alter ego? A phantasm? A friend? A citation from Roussel? Or Napoleon? A "heavenly maiden"? It feels like a slide into a dream and from there into history.[12] The narrator meets a "guide" (is it an Enkidu? a Virgil? an angel Gabriel?) who takes him through the Louvre, synecdoche of the Western Understanding of (the) Art(s). The two undergraduates Elizabeth and Kathy reemerge from time to time in the economy of the narratological domain. They mull over grand philosophemes, occasionally from a non-Euro-American culture: "All life is sorrow. All sorrow is due to desire. Sorrow can only be stopped by stopping desire."[13] Does anyone believe in this stuff anymore? But realism was never an enemy, and Morrison will go on in subsequent books to question, explore, and reframe the question as actually heard or likely to have been heard by him in real life. For *that* is what people say, and *that* is what he records. So, his characters' occasional leanings toward idealism and dialectic are no longer suspicious.[14] Narration moves on to history according to Tu Fu. We haven't even begun to think the ancient Chinese way, characters say. But the notion of history as/is adventure is a great leap forward. Roussel: the undying, the primordial belief in the power of literature.[15]

Revolution survived, in my mind, the intratextual topicality, as well as the external context of its genesis. The Cold War is over, the avant-gardes have been defanged and subjected to the laws of media commerce, some experimental and committed literature is beginning to sound "dated," but not this text, not at all. It was already full of its own self-transcendence, it made a cogent case for the immanence of *allography*, as Genette calls it in his recent book,[16] the writing of the *other-place*, the writing as *placing-elsewhere*. To be able to write in such a continually transformative manner, some well-oiled if not ageless techniques are set into play. In a sequence in chapter 7, "Storming the Bastille," we have

[12] Morrison and Boord, *Revolution*, 141–2.
[13] Ibid., 165.
[14] Ibid., 234.
[15] Ibid., 167.
[16] Gerald Genette, *L'Oeuvre de l'Art: Immanence et transcendance* (Paris: Minuit, 1993).

the following rhetorical crossings: The narrator's story alights upon an episode beginning with a journal entry, in which a character, Deflue, enters *from within* an imaginary historical consciousness, introduces in turn Governor de Launey, who in turn exists solely within Elizabeth's dream, which now is nested within the story of the highly circumstantial taking of the Bastille, which it is made plain exists now only within the textual dimension (engagement with a Reader is assumed), which exists within a merchandise object called a book, which existed in the mind/hands of two authors for several months perhaps, one of whom is a person called Madison Morrison who of course may have several "biographies" or life stories going on somewhere on the Eastern hemisphere, in the end trouncing the very question of authorial intentions, of historical causality, and of semiotic or logical primacies, closing with the equivalent of a punch in the eye: who fired the first shot? The soldiers or the crowd?[17]

* * *

The collection of poems *Soluna*[18] affords another possibility of entering Madison Morrison's cosmos in a near chronological fashion. Already, his trademark acrostic, following the frontispiece but preceding the table of contents, alerts us that we are about to embark on a rich journey. The key Figuras are arranged in the tradition of visual poetry. These are: the Sun, the Moon, the deities Ares, the messenger or bearer of communication and all exchanges par excellence Hermes, then the earth-mother Hera, the über-symbol of femininity Aphrodite, ending with El, which in the Old Testament stood for God. If anyone looks for the ganglia of Morrison's pluriverse, then here we have some minimal frames of reference, or "constants." *Soluna* is a search for "sense" at that fatidic *mezzo cammin*: "you're an extraordinary thirty-three. / Some say you're not typical. Your demeanor says / otherwise. You have squeezed until it hurts / but found nothing in the middle."[19] In other words, the narrator ponders what he is all about, juxtaposing the external image he is recognized by with what he feels is his inner perception or attitude. Wringing the knot further, he finds there is nothing there on which to rest his soul or psycho-assumptions. Unlike many a poet confronted with these often tacitly Neoplatonic dilemmas, he is not

[17] Morrison and Boord, *Revolution*, 148.

[18] Madison Morrison, *SOLUNA Collected Earlier Poems* (New Delhi: Sterling Publishers, 1989).

[19] Ibid., 13.

satisfied with self-irony and social parody. Morrison will not wallow in self-indulgent defeatism. He will look outside, further out, further into something that might contain both his body/soul and the "sense" of life, of society, indeed of the universe. Here then commences the endless journey. So, he begins his experimental/experiential quest in allegorical terms. "A Triptych of Anapocrypha" attempts to meld opposites.[20] Then, he turns to the figura of the "guide."[21] Further down, in "The Blinding of Homer,"[22] he pushes the envelope: "Is there really any choice?" somewhat perplexed that there exists a circularity to the questing after the great (Western) metaphysical questions. The narrator becomes a witness, both passive and participatory, processing the pulsions, reckoning with the recurrence of beginnings-and-ends, and then we edge into that geography of the cultural (un)conscious that will become his trademark. The sequence "O"[23] is a minimalist *elenchos* of specific flashes whose only claim is to have been raised by the narrator's consciousness, where word, image, and place represent an unseen, unsayable sequence of feeling, image, idea. In the sequence "Light"[24] the poetic voice, or persona, grows and conquers longer linguistic structures, deploying cinematographic techniques, two to three stresses per line, still short and swift. The next poem "U"[25] returns to an externalized, and therefore sign-dependent ego, so the poet can narrate in realist terms what one may see of one's self from the outside, as it were. Here nature, quotidian events, and the "others," can be catalysts for self-knowledge without the pre-assumptions and liabilities of the all-knowing Platonic or Cartesian Self. "Need"[26] moves in another direction, exhibiting a pseudo-epic function, but in style and tone it wraps along its interplay of tetrameter and pentameter the entire English tradition, from medieval quest narrative through Ariosto-like extra-diegetic reminders to the reader, the pedagogic neoclassical tale, so blatantly evoking the quest narrative staying just inside irony and parody, in a way allowing a philosophical (re)search for transhistorical *topoi*. Let us stop here for a moment.

For one thing, the geographies are now a plethora of inner struggles,[27] inscribing a horizon with "endless trajectories, equilibria and schisms." Some

[20] Ibid., 25.
[21] Ibid., 28.
[22] Ibid., 40.
[23] Ibid., 51–83.
[24] Ibid., 87–158.
[25] Ibid., 161–85.
[26] Ibid., 189–213.
[27] Ibid., 189.

palpable evidence that the greater understanding of one's many selves must occur with/through a woman. This entails, as we gather from some of the shorter pieces at the end of the collection, dealing with the exacerbation of the schism between word and thing, between person and the naming of the person,[28] the ubiquity of the tags and names of the lived-life, the traces of having-lived reduced to a restaurant check. *Soluna* is at one and the same time the transition from the "end" of the experimental avant-gardism of Western poetry and the beginning of a different, cosmographic, planetary approach to the writing art.

* * *

Reading Madison Morrison, I have often felt I was reading a long-projected but never realized version of my own poetic autobiography. That's when I ran back to Richard Kostelanetz' *Autobiographies*[29] for some clarifications. I learned about an in-progress textuality that abhors any prescribed poetic or work dynamics. A forever stalled project, the very moment one is aware that programming is *de rigoeur*. I don't think there is a return possible from Morrison's exile, as a peek at the books written to complete *The Sentence of the Gods* will reveal. I have to use word-concepts such as extra-tension(al), rhizomatic cross-breeding, the *inter-esse* that cantilevers the super-vigilant self-awareness, as when he says "the present author," "in front of me," and so on, against intercalated descriptions and citations from learned books. What counts is *the interrelation without either beginning or end.*

We can expound upon this perspective by bringing in to bear several quotations from Martin Heidegger. In *Was heisst Denken*[30] we read that what needs to be thought is *sage*, that is, myth understood as *saying*, as that articulation (writing, say) that speaks to the thought-provoking (*das Bedenkliche*). There is no outside to this cosmos, but at least there is no longer a beginning or an end. Elaborating upon Friedrich Nietzsche, Heidegger did clear up the introspective self-consciousness of the twentieth-century understanding of the human being.

[28] Cf. "Faculty Exchange Envelope," ibid., 222–4.

[29] I also spontaneously associated Morrison to works by Paul Vangelisti (for example, his early *Portfolio*, partly reproduced with selections from his other books in *Embarrassment of Survival Selected Poems 1970–2000* [New York: Marsilio, 2001]) or many pages from Thomas Pynchon, and some artists published in the journals the French journal *Dock(s)* and the Italian neo-avant-garde publication *Carte Segrete*.

[30] Martin Heidegger, *What is Called Thinking?*, translated by J. Glenn Gray (New York: Harper & Row, 1968).

But did he go "beyond"? Perhaps. In his effort to transcend the silent strictures of Western metaphysics, Heidegger speaks of the Event, the Happening, *das Ereignis* as the sole *locus* where a meaningful enchantment, or unveiling, or even entrapment of/by the *Lichtung* is possible. Madison Morrison seems to have made of these Radiating Clearings (my version of *Lichtung*) a way of life, extending them horizontally (across cultures, geohistoric sites) but also vertically (as Being-in-such-and-(only)such-a-place). Now Heidegger goes on to repeat that what must be retained in this process is memory, a sort of *mare nostrum* wherein *Andenken* (recalling) can happen. In Morrison, geohistory is the operating realm for this recalling.

Heidegger remains within Western *logology*, Madison Morrison chooses to exercise his quest for a divine disclosure in the *heterology* of non- or extra-Western mythologies and philosophies. He could rightly be called a planetary writer. His cosmology will provocatively look to the divinities of other peoples, of differently compressed or expanded historical frames, and introduce a sense of temporality that we cannot clearly identify or describe. Morrison dedicated separate books to "places" that embody and reveal complex discourses, stories, worldviews, such as Sweden, Paris, Arizona, India, Thailand, China, and in each has incorporated the mythologies of those societies, including from the Upanishads to the Bhagavad Gita. But these reflections, which are a rewriting and condensation of the wisdom of the sages, are constantly interrupted by the almost manic recording of things-as-seen or felt, transcribing the very movement of his body, or practical information. In some cases, entire sections are made up of journal entries, as in *Revolution*.

In a long essay on "Allegory in the Western Epic,"[31] Morrison discounts allegory insofar as it designates a genre that works with a stock of mythemes, from Achilles to Odysseus to Satan, from personifications of Greed or Courage or Revenge. All Western epics, he claims, are allegorical.[32] He seems to follow on Erich Auerbach's footsteps, and his notion of seeing in poetry the coincidence of the universal and the particular is still leveraged on a dualistic universe. He finds this to be the case in Homer, Ovid, Dante Alighieri, Torquato Tasso, and John Milton. With Torquato Tasso (1544–1595) in particular, he finds

[31] Madison Morrison, *Particular and Universal: Essays in Asian, European and American Literature* (New Delhi: Crane Publishing, 1999). The collection includes a subtle analysis of the importance of Eastern thought in the works of Ezra Pound, T. S. Eliot, and W. B. Yeats, and a study of poetry and philosophy in Lao Tzu.

[32] Ibid., 95.

that the poet's striving to ensure that his "narrative is substance, not just rhetoric; decorum ethical, not just stylistic," leads to an "even more imaginative transformation of Aristotle [on the basis of which] allegory [is] *the verisimilar imitation of the universal*."[33] As often with visionary poets, the distinctions posed by philosophers and critics cannot be superimposed on the poet's declarations about their work. Thus, there seems nothing wrong with encapsulating Platonic ideals at the same time: "The higher Truth toward which the epic poet strives is the truth of Universals ... *Imitation* becomes the representation of merely external realities, for allegory alone, says Tasso, can represent the internal, ethical life of man. Allegory takes over at the point where the literal, or historical, leaves off, where *Imagination*, that is, begins."[34] Is this not a deeply philosophical concern: how to reach, express, and understand higher values, elusive processes, essential questions? And had he not stated, just earlier in the same essay, that with allegory, "interpretive responsibility ... falls upon the reader's shoulders?"[35]

That's what we have been saying all along: the allegorical work is not self-contained, it is from inception primed for letting an other-speaking reach and circulate in a community, a region, a "people." One hears its voice across space-time, across the abyss of self-isolation and containment; and one will respond in some guise. Perhaps besides saying, which we saw as the hallmark of the lyric and the aphorism, allegories also involve explaining or translating, the other two components of the ancient word *hermeneuin*?[36] Morrison's strategy is to make his sentences (phrases, labels, numbers, minor parts of speech, idiomatic expressions from other languages) reverberate by juxtaposing them to most diverse registers of expression, or apparently irreconcilable semantic fields, cutting up or, better, "interrupting" phrases such that the whole does not seem to have any logical or commonsensical continuity:

> *Words to be spoken when Osiris cometh to the first Arit in Amenda.* I am eleven. "I am the mighty one who createth his own light." In the summer, to help with the flower beds, my mother hires a two-hundred-eighty-pound defensive lineman from the High School football team. "I have come unto thee, O Osiris, and,

[33] Ibid., 112–13, emphasis in original.
[34] Ibid., 113.
[35] Ibid., 106.
[36] See Chapter 1, above, reference to Richard E. Palmer's *Hermeneutics*.

> purified from that which defileth thee, I adore thee." He digs in two hours what would have taken my father a day. "Lead on." Midway through the morning he asks for a drink of water. "Name not the name of Re-stau unto me." My mother brings him a glass. "Homage to thee, O Osiris, in thy might and in thy strength in Re-stau." He sends her back for a two-quart jar.[37]

Note the active space disclosed between phrases, from deadpan *nouveau roman* description to authoritative grand symbolism of a civilization: it's as if brain and mind were having a conversation in which they consistently missed each other and yet recognized they were both "there"—as in Being-*there*, *Da*-sein— at the same time, *relating to each other nonetheless.* Or consider this other clip from *Engendering*:

> Community Extra-Curriculum: *Rule a big country.* "Relaxation." *As you'd fry small fish.* "For the mind and body." (*Without poking them*). Kundalini Yoga. *He who rules the world.* And Meditation. *In accord with Tao.* (Sarb Jit Kaur Khalsa). *Will find.* Hatha Yoga. *That the spirits.* (Kathleen Harrington). *Lose their power.*[38]

The writer who pens down meticulously, almost obsessively the interweaving of these clusters of discourse is spontaneously unfurling a cosmology. Cosmology is a tricky business. It is preferably lodged in-between physics and metaphysics. In his *Philosophia rationalis* (1744), Christian Wolff (1679–1754) writes "*Cosmologia est scientia mundi qua talis*" (cosmology is the science of the world as such) and deals with the world on the basis of the parts that constitute it: matter and form, movement and rest, quantity and quality, image and thought are from the beginning *co-related.* But what of the language to express that? Morrison's *Realization* and *Happening*, in a processual fusion of disparate long narratives, exhibits the diverse temporalities of the writing-act, the reclaiming of a temporal prophetic saying, and since the cosmology can only come into being as writing, then we must call Morrison's work a *cosmography.*

The poet here can be called an *allographic* author, the convener in his scene of writing, of textualities, of semantics, and more broadly of images (or ideologies) that rub sharply against one another, yet engages by sequencing frames (*Gestell*) according to accessible juxtapositions, alternatively by resonance, by metaphoric affinity, by metonymic linking, by microsemiotic abductions.

[37] Madison Morrison, *Magic* (Memphis, TN: Working Week Press, 2000), 28. Later parts of this book engage the allotrope Hermes, with excerpts directly from the *Corpus hermeticum.*

[38] Madison Morrison, *Engendering*, bilingual edition (Taipei: Cosmos Culture, 2002), 107.

One might here suppose that through the epic journey undertaken, Madison Morrison ultimately wishes to reconcile (without *ri-legare*) the undaunted *différends*[39] of existence, the torts contained in the expression "distortion."[40] During this journey, the protector is not Jupiter, nor Yahway or Osiris, but the interconnecting, transnational, unstable *polylogoi*-speaking of Hermes,[41] which take up six of the twenty-six volumes of *The Sentence of the Gods*.

[39] Conflict or contest of phrases (of meanings, therefore, and of referents) as elaborated by Jean-François Lyotard in *Le Différend*.

[40] We should remember that in critical theory and hermeneutics, during the second half of the twentieth century, the fundamental distortion present in communication (which makes any rational or logical search for an Absolute merely a restricted intellectual exercise) has been a key in the thought of thinkers as dissimilar as Jacques Derrida, Stanley Fish, Gianni Vattimo, and others.

[41] On the plurality of masks and functions of the figure of Hermes, see my *The Elusive Hermes*, esp. 363–72.

Figure 7 "Communication, 1" by Angela Biancofiore.

6

Poetics of Science

Poiēsis, technē, logos

Premises

I want to situate my lecture between two broad conceptual horizons or institutional fields, namely, that of the humanities and that of the sciences. The fact that there are three overdetermined word-concepts in the subtitle of this intervention should suggest, almost preemptively, that the discussion about the relation between poetry and science are vitiated from the start by a false dualism—poetry *and* science? Or, more commonly: poetry *vs* science? My intention here is to overcome such facile oppositions, if we are to understand how the two are *not* at all in opposition to, or mutually exclusive of, each other. In fact, I will argue that each activity can and indeed has illuminated the definition, task, and perspective of the other. These are cogent issues: science and its handmaiden technology, have taken over the running of our society, of our thinking even, and poetry—which in this lecture will also stand as a synecdoche for the humanities—has been relegated to the cellar, become the disinherited relative, a troublesome engagement with language that does not easily play and fit into the paradigm and prospect of a utilitarian, market-driven, and profit-oriented *Zeitgeist*.[1] The topics to be treated being so broad and interconnected, in order to begin to understand the relationship, I will have to be less than poetical and attempt to map out, through a series of frames, what the problems are and what some resolutions might look like. I am sketching here only four possible frames or scapes.

[1] Cf. in this context Emily Grosholz, "Poetry and Science in America," in Kurt Brown (ed.), *The Measured Word: On Poetry and Science* (Athens: University of Georgia Press, 2001), 69–89.

After Being

In the famous essay *Wozu Dichter?*,[2] written while the world was still recoiling from the slaughter of 55 million people, Martin Heidegger picks up a line from Friedrich Hölderlin's *Bread and Wine* and asks the Socratic question: "What are poets for in a destitute time?" A time when "the world's Night is spreading its darkness," the gods have fled and "divine radiance has become extinguished in the world's history." In the essay, the thinker looks to the poets as the beings who can sing about the traces left behind, who can lead us to the Open (*Lichtung*) where man, the human being, essentially dwells, and perhaps point us toward a recovery of the *fourfold*—earth, sky, divinities, and mortals.[3] For Heidegger, the essential being of mortals is locked in language, which is our *domus*, our dwelling, the place (*Raum* as opposed to *Ort*), in another locution the "templum," where we can best experience the letting be of the world's *is*, being, where the building itself is to ensure that place becomes the *locus* of our song and connect with what we are above and beyond or, better, before other aspects of our humanity that inevitably take over our being in the world. The poets are the ones delegated to found the community wherein humans dwell in contact with earth, sky, divinities, and other mortals. At a time when it is all too evident that we *ab*use the earth, can't see the sky, have lost the divinities that allowed us to gather up in wedding feasts of humans and gods, and mortals have forgotten Being in favor of beings, of entities, the task of the poet is even more daunting: alone before their mortality, the poet seeks the light through the only means possible: language, which is what fundamentally marks us as "special," as privileged custodians of Being.

Characteristic of humanity is that it ventures out into the world, it faces and confronts Nature, and when matters are not propitious, humans pre-posit or confer a meaning, a role, to their mortal selves. "Man sets up the world toward himself, and delivers Nature over to himself."[4] "Man produces new things where they are lacking in him. Man transposes things that are in his way."[5] We begin to

[2] Martin Heidegger, "What Are Poets For?," in *Poetry Language Thought*, translated by Alfred Hofstadter (New York: Harper & Row, 1975), 89–142. Originally included in the *Holzwege* (Frankfurt: Klostermann, 1950), it was written on the twentieth anniversary of Rainer Maria Rilke's death, in 1946.

[3] Ibid., 149.

[4] Ibid., 110.

[5] Ibid.

see a deep distancing between man and the fourfold developing here, for man interposes something between himself and the whole. "The Open becomes an object," Heidegger writes, and the world itself is brought to stand and into a position, ready for production and reproduction, in short, to be mastered. This leads to the recognition that another basic trait of Western man is the ability *to will* things. Willing, as theorized by Friedrich Nietzsche, changes humans into subjects whose capacity for self-assertion permeates the drive to dominate:

> To such a willing, everything, beforehand and thus subsequently, turns irresistibly into material for self-assertion. The earth and its atmosphere become raw materials. Man becomes human material, which is disposed of with a view to propose goals.[6]

From here the step into the contemporary worldview is short, for this process reveals the grip that modern technology has on humanity: "Not only are living things technically objectivated in stock-breeding and exploitation; the attack of atomic physics on the phenomena of living matter as such is in full swing. At bottom, the essence of life is supposed to yield itself to technical production."[7] This condition discloses another danger, relevant to our discourse here: "The inherent power of technology shows itself further in the attempts that are being made, in adjacent areas so to speak, to *master technology with the help of traditional values*."[8] Further, here is where the thinker must turn to the poet. He begins with an excerpt from Hölderlin's "Bread and Wine":

> One thing stands firm: whether it be near noon
> Or close to midnight, a *measure* ever endures
> Common to all; yet to each his own is allotted, too,
> Each of us goes toward and reaches the place that he can.[9]

The key word is measure, *metron*, a projecting/delimiting, a capacity that makes humans relate and compare/contrast not only how close or far we are from the gods, but also negotiate the material world, this world of entities. I will argue that poetics is an attempt to de-limit, circumscribe or at any rate identify the creating *words-as-worlds*, "as each of us goes toward the place that he can."

6 Ibid., 111.
7 Ibid., 113.
8 Ibid., 113; my emphasis.
9 Ibid., 95; my emphasis.

But the means employed to carry this out are not external forms, Heidegger writes. That is to say, interpolating for the sake of brevity, it is not, or it is not any longer, that we merely make use of instruments as aides or props to facilitate our mortal lives, as was thought for several centuries from the time of the Scientific Revolution to the high point of positivism, whereby mechanization and eventually more sophisticated technologies were conceived as an extension of our bodies: a lever to give us more strength, a steam engine to allow us to pull more freight, and so on. Putting a slight Hegelian twist to this, technology is really the completion of a process that begins in theology, becomes philosophy, then science, and finally matures in the later centuries of the second millennium as the basic "Enframing," the *Gestell*, of our world.

A few years later, in 1949, Heidegger gave four lectures in Bremen, one of which was titled "The Enframing." He later expanded and read it again in Munich, in 1955, with the title: "The Question Concerning Technology."[10] I'd like to gloss a few notions from this landmark essay in order to set the stage for the remaining three frames of this inquiry. The philosopher begins by stating that technology, properly understood, is not the equivalent of the essence of technology. It is not of the domain of the *instrumentum*, though that is what everyone readily sees and relates it to. In fact, starting from this perception, we quickly see that the technical is what allows us to gain control over the world, as means to an end. But now we must move on to question what means and end actually signify. Simply put, a means "is that whereby something is effected and thus attained."[11] What is effected, however, must have a cause, something that set it into motion.

To work out of this quandary, Heidegger goes back to established philosophical wisdom, which is basically Aristotle's distinction of four kinds of causes:

1. *causa materialis*, i.e., the silver out of which a chalice is made;
2. *causa formalis*, or the shape or form into which the material enters (a chalice and not a bottle);
3. *causa finalis*, its intended purpose, the sacrificial rite in relation to which the chalice is required in such a form and in such a material; and
4. *causa efficiens*, which is what brings about the effect or realization of the chalice, namely the silversmith.

[10] Martin Heidegger, *The Question Concerning Technology and Other Essays*, translated by William Lovitt (New York: Harper & Row, 1977).

[11] Ibid., 6.

Heidegger had already stated that technology displays the fourfold nature of causality. But then he asks: why four causes? Where do they come from? And is it possible they hide something else? The questioning now turns to the nature of causality itself. Causality, *causa*, we learn, belongs to the verb *cadere*, to fall, "and means that which brings it about that something falls out as a result in such and such a way."[12] Yet what Latin and modern thought interpret as causality has nothing to do with bringing about and effecting. Cause—Ger. *Ursuche*, It. *causa*—"is called *aition* by the Greeks, which means that to which something is indebted." In brief, the four causes, all belonging to one another, are simply the *ways of being responsible for something else*. From his explication of the four concepts through the example of the chalice, I'll gloss two in particular. First, the final cause, *causa finalis*, Heidegger writes, that of consecration and bestowal, circumscribes a particular space, therefore speaks of *boundaries*, which in Greek is *telos*, but once again, it is *not* telos as aim or purpose, as we normally understand this term, but rather as that which is responsible for what as *matter* and what as *aspect* are together co-responsible for the sacrificial vessel. Quite a different conceptual universe. A similar explication concerns the *causa efficiciens*. Heidegger holds that the silversmith, for example, is not simply or merely the person who, because of the physical work of realizing the chalice, is the final actor in the process. The artisan is the person who considers carefully and gathers together the three aforementioned ways of being responsible and indebted. He writes, "to consider carefully is in Greek *legein, logos. Legein* is rooted in *apophainesthai*, to bring forward into appearance."[13] We can see the third term of our title emerging, but we have to be patient before we can get fully into it.

The emphasis here is on the human who, gathering and embodying the first three causes, is "co-responsible as that from whence the sacrificial vessel's bringing forth and resting-in-self take and retain their first departure," and the "pondering" of the artisan is part and parcel with the concrete *how* and *what* of his production. The emphasis now shifts to the *presencing*, the bringing-forth into appearance, that which is marked by the "starting something toward its arrival." Thus to be realized, to become what is, in the sense of embodying an essence of something, in this case the chalice, the being responsible is occasioning or inducing this going forward, the real cause implied in *aitia* is

[12] Ibid., 7.
[13] Ibid., 8.

what occasions a more inclusive meaning, bringing us closer to the real essence of causality. The concerted interplay of the four ways of occasioning are what allows something to come into *presencing*, into being. Here emerges the first word-concept of out title: citing a line from Plato's *Symposium*, the sense of bringing into presencing can be grasped as *poiesis*: "Every occasion for whatever passes over and goes forward into presencing from that which is not presencing is *poiesis*, is a bringing-forth [*Her-vor-bringen*]."[14] Otherwise said, it is not only handcraft or manufacture, and not only artistic bringing into appearance and concrete imagery that is involved in the bringing-forth, as *poiesis*, but "*Physis* also, that is to say, the arising of something out of itself. *Physus* is indeed *poiesis* in the highest sense," he adds. Most of us would call this process creation.

Here I must point out a distinction that will allow me later on, if I can still hold your attention until the fourth frame, to part company from Heidegger. Consistent with his avoidance of anthropomorphic speech and scientific metalanguage, the thinker underscores this bringing-forth as almost a *causa sui*, a magical (not his word) happening, the bursting of a blossom into bloom, in itself. But then, he adds, "In contrast, what is brought forth by the artisan or the artist, e.g., the silver chalice, has the bursting open belonging to bringing-forth not in itself, but in another (*en alloi*), in the craftsman or artist."[15] The question for me resides precisely in this distinction between what, in Sartrean terms, we could characterize as the *for itself* and the *for others*. Let us go over this again.

Reiterating that this bringing-forth occurs in the province of unconcealment, or *alētheia*—truth—we now move on to the essence of technology, whose elementary characterization is also that of a revealing. Introducing the second term of our title, *technikon* is a Greek term meaning "that which belongs to *technē*." In this context, a further observation makes us aware that "*techne* is the name not only for the activities and skills of the craftsman but also for the arts of the mind and the fine arts. *Technē* belongs to bringing-forth, to *poiēsis*, it is something poietic."[16] At this point we can see *the common origin of both technology*

[14] Ibid., 10. Plato, *Symposium*, in *The Collected Dialogues*, 557. For context, we are in that part of Plato's dialogue where they are trying to define Love of what is beautiful, compare it to the good, and then debate about its universality. In Michael Joyce's 1935 translation, here is the sequence: Diotima: "what we have been doing is to give the name of Love to what is only one single aspect of it: we make just the same mistake, you know, with a lot of other names." Socrates: "For instance?" Diotima: "For instance poetry. You'll agree that there is more than one kind of poetry in the true sense of the word – that is to say, *calling something into existence that was not there before, so that every kind of artistic creation is poetry*, and every artist is a poet" (Plato, *Symposium* 205b; my emphasis).

[15] Heidegger, *Question Concerning Technology*, 10–11.

[16] Ibid., 13.

and poetry. But as to why they parted company for the past two thousand years, the reason resides in the fact that, once again scouring the etymology of ancient Greek, *technē* is linked with *epistēmē*: "both words are names for knowing in the widest sense. They mean to be entirely at home in something, to understand and be expert in it."[17] Further analysis tells us that with Aristotle *technē* acquires the sense of revealing what is not yet before us but could disclose itself one way or another. We will later see how this is a basic precept in modern biology. Whoever builds a house, for example, reveals what is to come forth according to the four modes of occasioning. Yet this revealing

> gathers together in advance the aspect and the matter of the ship or house, with a view to the finished thing *envisioned* as completed, and from this gathering determines the manner of its construction. Thus what is decisive in *techne* does not lie at all in the making and manipulating nor in the using of the means, but rather in the aforementioned revealing. It is as a revealing, and not as manufacturing, that *technē* is a bringing forth.[18]

A page later, we read that, as a consequence of this, "modern physics, as experimental, is dependent upon technical apparatus and upon progress in the building of the apparatus."[19] The question next is: what is it about technology that it puts modern physics to its service? Notice the reversal of the two terms: most of us would think of technology as deriving from physics or being a visible, practical emanation of it. The answer lies in what elsewhere Heidegger characterized as the forgetting of the essential nature of Being, the tendency evidenced throughout history to ignore (whether willfully or unconsciously) the connection between *technē* and *poiēsis*. In brief, we have interpreted the revealing that rules modern technology as a challenging (*Herausfordern*), "which puts to nature the unreasonable demand that it supply energy that can be extracted and stored as such."[20] To the predictable question, "does not this hold true for the old windmill as well?" the answer is a flat no: "its sails do indeed turn in the wind; they are left entirely to the wind's blowing. But the windmill does not unlock energy from the air currents in order to store it."[21]

[17] Ibid.
[18] Ibid., 13, emphasis added.
[19] Ibid., 14.
[20] Ibid.
[21] Ibid.

From this point on the essay follows with a few quick remarks on the obsession with extracting and storing energy and supplies for our lives, the assessment that through technology we have constructed a world bent on furthering something else, namely, a stockpile of resources in which we trap the sun's energy at maximum efficiency and at minimum expense (what we call cost-effective). We need to have it on call, obeying the laws of the *instrumentum*. The nature of technology as a constant challenging has disclosed a propensity, indeed a necessity, of setting-upon and standing-reserve, which in turn require ordering (in both senses of the word.). Thus:

> That challenging happens in that the energy concealed in nature is unlocked, what is unlocked is transformed, what is transformed is stored up, what is stored up is, in turn, distributed, and what is distributed is switched about ever anew. Unlocking, transforming, storing, distributing, and switching are ways of revealing. But the revealing never simply comes to an end. Neither does it run off into the indeterminate. The revealing reveals to itself its own manifoldly interlocking paths, through regulating their course. This regulating itself is, for its part, everywhere secured. Regulating and securing even become the chief characteristics of the challenging revealing.[22]

One may easily translate this into another metalanguage, that of Marxism, and see the demon of accumulation as the driving force of modern societies. The conclusion here is that this pattern culminates in the standing-reserve, the *Ge-stell*, or Enframing.[23] The word has the sense of apparatus and of skeleton. What we have before us is a condition of beings that is not at all technological, though it seems condemned to recognize that objects, parts of assemblies, pistons and gauges and so on are part of this technological exteriority. A dark downside of this condition is that the Enframing, in holding sway, posits itself as a destining:

> Since destining at any given time starts man on a way of revealing, man, thus under way, is continually approaching the brink of possibility of pursuing and pushing forward nothing but what is revealed in ordering, and of deriving all his standards on this basis.[24]

This is the supreme danger. In brief, man himself becomes part of the standing-reserve,[25] a condition that can be background to a grasp of the structure

22 Ibid., 16.
23 Ibid., 26.
24 Ibid.
25 Ibid., 27.

and function of camps and gulags. In terms of political economy, it may point to the growing disregard for the needs of millions who have become expendable sources or resources for low-wage labor. The problem remains that there is no demon in the machine, so to speak, and there remains the mystery of its essence. We are threatened with the possibility that we may be denied entry into a more original revealing and experience the call of a more primal truth. The attempt Heidegger makes near the end of the essay, to say that in destining there is a granting that may yet offer us hope—inspired by two lines of Hölderlin's that say: "But where danger is, grow / the saving power also"[26]—is not convincing, though he does go back to the common origin, for art as for science in the word *technē* as an expression or, better, as the possibility of *poiēsis*.

Now, we do recall that in another paper Heidegger does call on the poets as the founders of the community. This founding is rooted in the word, the *logos* itself. Returning to our first essay, written within earshot of the thunder of the atomic bomb over Hiroshima and the eerie silences of Auschwitz, thinking and poetizing had not simply found themselves on the brink of the abyss but also were falling headlong into what during the same period he theorized as the *Ab-grund*, the groundlessness of the human condition: "In the age of the world's night, the abyss of the world must be experienced and endured. But for this it is necessary that there be those who reach into the abyss."[27]

To conclude this part, what we have, then, is a strict correspondence between *poiesis*, *technē*, and *logos*. We will now take them up in two different contexts: history and language.

Between Rhetoric and Reason

Returning to standard English and more approachable concerns, we can begin with an observation, made half a century after Heidegger's, by a keen observer of the poetic scene in the United States, Dana Gioia. In answering the question of the title of his book *Can Poetry Matter?*[28] the response is that, whether the times are "destitute" or not, poets are facing different sorts of obstacles, namely,

[26] Ibid., 28.
[27] Heidegger, "What Are Poets For?," 92.
[28] Dana Gioia, *Can Poetry Matter? Essays on Poetry and American Culture* (St. Paul, MN: Greywolf Press, 2002) (based on a 1991 feature in *The Atlantic*).

a society that has no time for them and a profession that, while cataloging them, is at a loss to find a place, or a purpose, for poetry. If in 1946 the role of the poet appears to be to "attend, singing, to the trace of the fugitive gods," in the 1990s the "bestowing" and the new "beginning" for poets who "reach into the abyss" may concern the exploration of the hypothesis: whether there are yet gods out there whose word has not been heard and, in fact, could not be heard because we have been attuned to, or detuned by, the onslaught of mass media, technologically driven performance, marketability, and the evident devaluation of politically committed art. Leafing through some issues of *Poetry* magazine or the *Norton Anthology of Postmodern Poetry* will easily confirm this situation. Topically, it is back to mulling over isolation, alienation, loss of possible worlds, celebrating the miniscule epiphanies. Moreover, the super-specializations in the natural sciences and the forbidding mathematics and technological hardware and software that go with advanced scientific projects have pretty much left the poets, not to say the rest of us mortals, out in the cold. At best, we can comment on the technological world picture *from the outside*, on the basis of its concretizations in society, responding both to the advances but mostly the failures, and abuses or misuses, of science. This is not an end-of-the-world scenario: social scientists, historians, linguists, and philosophers have long learned to work back from effects, tangible facts, *à rebours*, to retrace origins, causes, and possible motivations. Maybe even an Aristotelean cause. But the misunderstandings, or noncommunication, if not enmity, between poets and scientists is almost a common place, it needs no introduction, no explanation, no excuses.

But have things always been this way? I rather think not, as the gloomy picture I sketched is a relatively recent development, historically speaking, less than two centuries in fact. Further, I submit that the assumed superiority of the sciences is strictly tied to extra-scientific forces and interests, not to anything intrinsic to science. Let us go through a quick, external history of the probable origin of this problem, where before it became science as we know it, it was called first philosophy in general and then in Middle Ages and early modernity natural philosophy. In Plato the distinction between science and the humanities is not yet clear-cut, and he struggled mightily to find a way to establish a new *epistēmē*, create a different conception of knowledge, by attacking and denigrating his competitors, which included the Milesian school, the Pythagoreans, and above all the Sophists. In his maturity, he broke with the Homeric tradition, which up to that point embodied the basic knowledge of the people in the *polis*. It was the poets who handed down the encyclopedia of notions, values, habits, codes of behavior from generation to generation. Moreover, poets spoke through allegories, and what was needed, Plato argued, were more direct and precise ways of referring to what is to be known. With the flowering of Athens in the fifth and fourth centuries BCE, a new paradigm was sought, though dialectic was still available to both philosophers and writers.[29] Perhaps owing to the growth and popularity of the lyric, the dithyramb, new forces and voices were heard on the proscenium. In book III of the *Republic*, "some forms" of poetry were barred from the ideal state, though in book X, where the ancient *diaphora* is explored and critiqued, the contest between poetry and philosophy is won by philosophy.[30] Too many have overlooked the fact that it was not all poetry that was debarred, only the rhapsodes, the lyricists, the partisans of a style of expression that touched tellurian depths, that summoned *eros*, and as a Dionysiac principle, that bore with it *chaos*, something which would tear asunder the new perfect order Plato envisioned. But it is significant that what was permitted were fables, children's songs, and pedagogical tales apt at instilling the values of the guardian and the worker, the ruler, and the gods. This exception or opening for poets had a long and successful history.

Aristotle on his part also acknowledged that both poetry and philosophy are born from wonder, but there is in Aristotle a first major break between the two, namely, philosophy will be concerned with the true on the basis of formal logic and metaphysical axioms, whereas the realm of poetry will properly be that of the verisimilar. The domain of emotions, where dream and plausibility, memory and desire dwell, was the province of poetry, in all its forms. Actual knowledge, on the other hand, was the province of syllogisms, geometry, and arithmetic. Still, the role of the poets was central in social life, and poets were expected not only to know as much as any cultured person about the basics of science but also to teach it. They were as respected as the philosophers, the astronomers, the consuls, and the engineers, the more successful ones served as court intellectuals. This is made emblematic a few centuries later when, in Rome, Lucretius wrote his opus, *De rerum natura* (On the Nature of Things), which was the first modern scientific encyclopedia written in verse. Lucretius tackled everything, from the creation of the universe to the structure of time and space, the atoms and their

29 For a more detailed and technical exploration of these points, see my *The Elusive Hermes*, pt. 2.

30 On this, see Rosen, *The Quarrel between Philosophy and Poetry*. Here we read: "The quarrel between philosophy and poetry is in the first instance political or moral. Stated in terms less exaggerated than those of the *Republic*, the quarrel amounts to this: poetry encourages desire, and hence the will" (13).

movement, reproduction, the soul, mortality and how they are all interwoven. A staunch Epicurean, his poem is at once a political treatise—aiming at freeing people from the superstitions of religion—a treatise in metaphysics—he speaks of being and nothingness—and a treatise in cosmology.[31] Many scholars see here already concepts that sit well with twentieth-century physics:

> The whole universe is always in ceaseless motion
> It does not matter in what regions of the universe
> You set yourself: the fact is that from whatever spot
> Anyone may occupy, the universe is left stretching
> equally unbounded in every direction.

The imagination of the poet works with what it has at hand from a given encyclopedia or what interests her at that particular juncture in time. If we skip to the Middle Ages, we find that, outside of the logicians proper, anything that can be discussed at all (politics, science, history, religion) was entrusted to poets, chroniclers, and literati, as much as by any other doctor or jurist or theologian. Dante Alighieri is the grand example of this, among whose early books there is one titled *Acque e caelo*, and whose knowledge of medicine, astronomy, and what today we would call psychology stands as the benchmark of the times.[32]

Matters start to get a bit more complex during the sixteenth century. Recall, by broad strokes, the following: the crisis of Christianity, brewing from within and exploding with the Reformation, and then Counter-Reformation; the opening up of the Atlantic and the concurrent felt need for new instruments, new categories, new answers to advances in astronomy and mathematics. By the beginning of the seventeenth century we have what can now be actually called science, with names that became symbols such as Copernicus, Galileo Galilei, Francis Bacon, René Descartes, and finally, Isaac Newton. Some tried to incorporate aspects of ancient learning, but most had no use for it, and they would have dashed God himself were it not for the strident politics of the Counter-Reformation, the religious wars, and the instinct of survival to keep on working.

[31] See Stephen Greenblatt, *The Swerve: How the World became Modern* (New York: Norton, 2011).

[32] The scholarship on Dante is immense. But one can start with the work of Teodolinda Barolini and Robert Durling. For a specific study, see Simon Gilson, "Medieval Science in Dante's *Commedia*: Past Approaches and Future Directions," *Reading Medieval Studies*, 27 (2001): 39–77 (Available online: http://centaur.reading.ac.uk/84398/1/RMS-2001-02_S._Gilson%2C_Medieval_Science_in_Dante%27s_Commedia.pdf [accessed October 8, 2020]).

Poetry reacted to the multifarious cultural tribulations in the most diverse ways: some, for instance Torquato Tasso and John Milton, still sung in epic swirls the glories of Christianity, although scholars believe the latter used the Ptolemaic system for structural reasons (he acknowledges Galileo and the new worlds revealed by his telescope in *Paradise Lost* [1667]). Tommaso Campanella and Giordano Bruno, both great philosophers, wrote poems and plays in which the new learning is everywhere, as did John Donne in his "metaphysical" poetry.[33] As the acute observers of man and nature that they were, the poets could not but be interested in the ongoing series of discoveries in geography, hydrology, and mechanics. Thus, they knew of and learned from new reports of strange people and animals and plants in faraway places over the globe, to the worlds opened by better telescopes, microscopes, hygrometers, clocks, mechanical devices, toys, and so on. When Newton appeared during the later decades of the seventeenth century, modern science was born.[34] Inventor of calculus and a host of mathematical theories, his studies on light, motion, and astronomy established him as the premier genius of his age. *The Principia Mathematica* (1687), in which he develops the three universal laws of motion, is still the foundation of non-relativistic physics. His influence was extensive and set a solid foundation for Enlightenment ideas about a trust in reason that were developing around him and elsewhere on the continent.[35]

The poets stood in awe, but did not retreat, and in fact took on with ardor the possibilities disclosed by these overlapping fields of knowledge, the new worldviews. There is an extensive corpus of poetry that is either dedicated to or inspired by Newton's discoveries. Poets such as Henry More, Abraham Cowley,

[33] See among many fine studies, Alison Hawthorne Deming, "Science and Poetry: A View from the Divide," in Kurt Brown (ed.), *The Measured Word*, 181–97 (Athens: University Press of Georgia, 2001), which glosses Donne's *Anatomy of the World* (1611), where the poet was coming to terms with the epochal, and devastating knowledge introduced by Galileo the year prior: "The universe suddenly had been peppered with ten times the stars that had been there before. The perception of the Earth's place in that expanded (though not yet expanding) universe had been thrown into metaphysical revolution … [and citing Donne]. And new philosophy calls all in doubt / The element of fire is quite put out; / The sun is lost, and th'earth, and no man's wit, / Can well direct him where to look for it / […] / 'Tis all in pieces, all coherence gone'" (181). Her final word is that "the challenge today is to reach an audience not comprised solely of members of one's own tribe. A poet finds voice by holding some sense of audience in mind during the process of composition" (193). Since elsewhere I hold that poets are always, often their own poetics notwithstanding, in tune with their times, perhaps we should read them outside of English departments, as torches in the dark outlooks coming from psychology, anthropology, social theory, and history in particular.

[34] Cf. Edward Dolnick, *The Clockwork Universe: Isaac Newton, the Royal Society, and the Birth of the Modern World* (New York: Harper, 2011).

[35] We also know he wrote about alchemy, theology, did a literal interpretation of the Bible, and sent John Locke a treatise disputing the existence of God, which was—perhaps wisely—never published.

in part John Dryden, Edward Young, William Thompson, William Broome, and Elisabeth Carter all penned poems that were either didactic or celebratory of the new scientific verbum, even as they struggled to handle the question of the role of God in this expanded universe, or the even more wondrous visual and conceptual worlds revealed by microscopes. In 1721 Aaron Hill writes *The Judgment Day* in which, acknowledging "Sir Isaac Newton's vast improvements," he lets his fancy loose on this frightful topic, but not before showing how well he understood the new science:

> Millions of countless miles are lost between,
> And sick'ning thought grows tir'd, to stretch so far!
> How vast the concave spheres, which, hence, are seen!
> Th'enormous vaulkts, with wheeling worlds glow round!
> Rolling, sublime, they slide oblique, yet none their paths
> Confound![36]

Poems were also written, however, to show the *limitations* of the new sciences, and one can find illuminating critiques in the work of Christopher Smart, Matthew Prior, Thomas Hobson, and others. Smart, for example, in a 1752 collection titled the *Omniscience of the Supreme Being*, treats the theme of the futility of sciences, basically on the grounds that they still did not know what instinct is, and he refers to the migrating nightingale that uses no science for navigation: "but instinct knows / What Newton, or not sought, or sought in vain."[37] The skepticism from the religious camp is only a step away from outright satire, and here one can look into Thomas Shadwell, Henry Fielding, Samuel Garth (*The Dispensary* [1699]), which probably influenced Alexander Pope's *The Rape of the Lock*. *The Dispensary* also foreshadows Jonathan Swift's *Mechanical Operations of the Spirit*, and the masterpiece of the genre, *Gulliver's Travels*, where we recall the scientists of Laputa maneuvering the Flying Island on magnetic principles but who were so absorbed in speculation they had to be reminded of the simplest of daily chores.

In general though, the poet as the master chiseler of words and spinner of metaphors and images, found in science new raw materials to expand their visions and perceptions, and were it not for our critical biases and the filters of generations between us and the seventeenth century, we would be rewarded

[36] Cited in W. Powell Jones, *Rhetoric of Science: A Study of Scientific Ideas and Imagery in Eighteen-Century English Poetry* (London: Routledge & Kegan Paul, 1966), 51.

[37] Ibid.

with countless surprises and ultimately some fine explications of complex and now forgotten mechanical issues and their place in society. From several sources I learned that each new science or subfield of it, as it was coming into its own, became a preeminent topic of discussion in elite circles, but it became a choice *topos* for the poets as well. New discoveries were announced and discussed in this early stage of public media, in the growing number of periodicals, encyclopedias, and learned societies and academies. As a curiosity, in the early 1700s the greatest interest was in astronomy, by 1740 the crown goes to microbiology, by the 1760s botany takes center stage, and by the 1780s geology emerges as the most intriguing field of learning. One figure who had an incredible influence on literature at the end of the century is Erasmus Darwin (1731–1802; Charles' grandfather), whose achievements are legion and whose books were well known to pre-Romantics as well as Romantics and idealists. His most famous poetical effort, titled *The Botanic Garden* (in which for the first time in modern history we see the words oxygen, hydrogen, and azote [nitrogen]), is made up of sections published separately and dedicated to *The Economy of Vegetation* (1792) and *The Love of Plants* (1789). Here we read lines such as:

The whirling Sun this ponderous planet hurled
And gave the astonished void another world.

A proponent of the theory of evolution decades before his grandson made it popular,[38] he also worked with the likes of James Watt, Henry Cavendish, and Joseph Priestly,[39] and foretold the future use of steam:

Soon shall thy arm, Unconquere'd Steam, afar
Drag the slow barge, or drive the rapid car
Or on wide-waving wings expanded bear
The Flying-chariot through the fields of air.[40]

By the turn of the century, however, the reaction begins. Part of this turn of events is to be attributed to the growing perplexities caused by didactic poetry, which as it got closer and closer to actual scientific description and explanation,

[38] He estimated that the evolutionary scale was in the magnitude of several hundred million years, not 40 million, as grandson Charles later believed.

[39] Thomas Watt (1736–1819), chemist and mechanical engineer, perfected the steam engine, crucial to the Industrial Revolution. Henry Cavendish (1731–1802), physicist and chemist, worked on gases and discovered hydrogen, prepared the path for A. -L. Lavoisier's "chemical revolution." Joseph Priestly (1733–1804), another polymath, discovered over ten gases, among which oxygen.

[40] Ibid.

required a stilted versification, a pedestrian rhyming no longer imbued with wonder and wit. Another cause may have been the sea change occurring at the social and political level, with events that led to the French Revolution and its extensive impact. Not that the Romantics were not as well versed in the scientific disciplines as their enlightened precursors. Erasmus Darwin's own *Zoonomia* confirms precise descriptions we find in William Wordsworth's lake poetry, although his poetics as embodied in the *Lyrical Ballads* is already shifting toward a more conversational register and timbre, and technical lexicon is generally shunned. From the *Songs of Experience*, through *The Book of Thel* and even *The Book of Urizen* Darwin's science is presumed background knowledge to William Blake's visionary work. However, Blake also understood the broader philosophical and ideological implications of rushing headlong into the new disciplines, the new quasi-religious role taken on by Reason, and he does not spare invectives against Jean-Jacques Rousseau, Voltaire, Newton and the entire Enlightenment project. As far as the human condition is concerned, mired in "the mind-forged manacles" of the slums of London in 1802, Blake boldly declares that despite Newton, the world is still … flat. Percy B. Shelley was a collector of mechanical paraphernalia and read voraciously in non-humanistic subjects, perhaps also to better describe his *Prometheus Unbound*, who is symbolically the father of science and technology. John Keats put in verse what became, unfortunately, a trope in critical and cultural history: the notion that poets either hate or do not understand science, and that moreover they feel that science is robbing them of their catalogs or encyclopedia of themes and symbols. In "Lamia" we read:

Do not all charms fly
At the mere touch of cold philosophy?
There was an awful rainbow once in heaven:
We know her woof, her texture; she is given
In the dull catalogue of common things.
Philosophy will clip an Angel's wings,
Conquer all mysteries by rule and line,
Empty the haunted air, and gnomed mine –
Unweave a rainbow.[41]

But no emblematic figure embodies the interpenetration and interdependence of science and the humanities than Johann Wolfgang von Goethe (1749–1832),

[41] John Keats, "Lamia," 229–37.

who in Johann Eckermann's *Conversations with Goethe* (1836) states that of his poetry he is not after all that proud but was proud of having made significant contributions to the theory of light and color. Not bad for arguably the greatest writer in the German tradition and who practically launched a series of cultural revolutions, in lyric poetry, in fiction (the *Werther, Wilhelm Meister*) and in theatre (*Faust*), and who influenced directly the younger heralds of a new way of doing philosophy (Schiller, Johann Gottlieb Fichte, Friedrich Wilhelm Schelling, Hegel). Goethe had difficulty with Bacon's inductive method and thought instead in terms of syntheses, and he critiqued Newton's excessive mathematization of the universe. As a scientist, methodic and empirical (he kept tables of weather variations in five different cities, to figure out how winds impact on weather), he also saw things with an aesthetic sensibility, in a holistic, integrative yet dynamic vision.[42] He was well acquainted with Erasmus Darwin's writings, and himself made inroads into the budding theory of evolution, especially through his observations of plants. Goethe's *Story of My Botanical Studies* came out in 1831, the same year that Charles Darwin sailed on the *Beagle*. To complete the picture about the interrelation between science and the humanities, and the interim sociopolitical terrain they share, we recall the decades following the Congress of Vienna. In Europe and the Americas, the various nationalisms were stirring other fires. Utopianism, socialism, and the knowledge of "fantastic" places—think of the birth and growth of geographical societies—were carving new furrows in the relationship between science and literature, logic and rhetoric, the technical and the poetical. In fact, the impact of science and technology and its full-tilt acceptance and eventual hegemony in the most diverse sectors of society and culture began to raise questions about how far this new learning might go. Mary Shelley's *Frankenstein, or the Modern Prometheus*, written in 1818, though it may be read in the context of the then new literary genre of the gothic, it is a clear allegory of a legitimate philosophical concern about humans deciding to take the ultimate creation in their hands: making a new living human being. Artificially.[43]

[42] On Goethe's vision of science, see W. Heisenberg, *Across the Frontiers*, (New York: Harper & Row, 1974), 122–41. Here we read: "Schiller … in 1794 … made it clear to the poet that his ground phenomenon was really not an appearance but an Idea. An Idea, it may be added, in Plato's sense" (136). Today we would refer to Goethe's idea with the word "structure."

[43] Through the century there is also a current of writers who "use" science to promote or predict future perfect societies, though by the beginning of the twentieth century, basically, after H. G. Wells, the projections of Prometheanism (in the arts as in politics) turn into nightmares, the absurd, institutionalized dystopia. A different manner of illustrating the foundationlessness of being.

Binding Knowledge

Let us look at the relationship between *technē* and *poiesis* from the point of view of the third term in the subtitle, the *logos*. How much poetry, or literature, is present in scientific writing? Or, better stated, are there aspects that we might unselfconsciously call "literary" in scientific writing? And, more specifically, what expressive instruments, what rhetoric, what metaphors, or symbols based on myths, does science employ to stake out its territory? And are there faculties that work for both the technical and the poetical?

First of all, the role of imagination and spontaneous creativity. The truly committed artist, as the truly engaged scientist, is one who, with an idea or vision in mind, heightens his or her sensibility or focus and is always "on," so to speak. Think for instance of photographers, who seem to look past you when you speak to them face to face because they are considering light, shade, color, framing, focus, and composition all at once even while they are talking to you about lunch; or writers (and linguists, or actors and so on) who appear transfixed when a particular conversation, even if banal or irrelevant to them, is going on as they focus on sounds, semantics, metaphors, images, rhythms, accents, and so on. A thinker listens to another thinker (even if reading in silence) and operates on at least a double register (often several): they follow the discourse on its own terms and at the same time seek for that concept or hypothesis that may make the connection in their own theory on a particular subject. Seeking a correspondence, or a similitude, an analogue to yet a third theory in the mind. This needs to be made available through language, in language, by language.

Both philosophers and scientists have long sought to explain the meaning of the human condition, its ontological anchor, and the possibility of the creation of knowledge on the basis of systems of thought that aimed to be in some guise or another transcendent, detached, universal, *super partes* so to speak. Think of some of the great names of our Western tradition, from Aristotle down to John Locke, Immanuel Kant, or Isaac Newton. However, with the proper critical approach their thought, and their texts, can be rhetorically disassembled to show the sutures and the seams, the aporias or the "take it on good faith" spots of their systems. The putative father of modern rationalism, René Descartes, found the punctum of his theory of knowledge in an unquestioned yet questioning I, the ego who cogitates, laying a metaphysical foundation for a dualistic, algebraic model, composed of *res cogitans* and *res extensa*. His writings are replete with rhetorical devices even as he had no patience with literature and the classics. Yet, much like Dante in the *Vita Nova* envisions the dire possibility of offending Beatrice in a dream and thereafter comes up with the strategy of the "donna dello schermo," the foil of "the other woman," Descartes recounts three dreams in which all of his work in optics and geometry of the late 1620s comes to a head in what in 1637 will emerge as the *Discours de la méthode*, originally just an "Introduction" to his scientific research, yet destined to become one of the most influential small treatises in Euro-American culture. He claims that knowledge begins with a *tabula rasa*, which is an interesting fiction to hear from someone who by age thirty-five had read and assimilated practically all of the pertinent works in philosophy and relata produced since the dawn of civilization (at that time it was still possible). From an expository angle, it was an application of Cusanus' ruse in the *Docta ignorantia*. It was analogous to the comportment we see with Pablo Picasso, who discovered primitivism and the elementary (unlearned) gesture of the spontaneous brush stroke after he had gone through the academy and studied and imitated and often bettered, in a few years, all the major painters up to his time. It was the simplicity of Petrarch's sonnets in the *Canzoniere*, on which the poet worked assiduously for forty years during and while he studied everyone he could lay his hands on, from antiquity through the texts he himself discovered and the various genres he tried while committing his reputation to his Latin epics.

Leonardo da Vinci in his notebooks once wrote that the man of genius, even whilst he is walking about tending to quotidian affairs and seemingly unconcerned with a particular problem, is always thinking about *that* problem until he resolves it. We also know that Newton was neurotic, he didn't sleep for days at times, but that heightened awareness where everything one does is constantly scanned and scoured to find the key or image or formula seems to be common to both scientists and poets. Maybe the (apocryphal) anecdote of the apple that fell to his feet and triggered the equations that led to the law of universal gravitation is not insignificant. Marie Curie discovered the radiation emitted by radium quite by accident, when she noticed that a silver plate bore particular traces that could not but be the result of something as yet unseen but inferentially possible. Tinkering in his laboratory, Thomas Edison discovered that a signal in one room makes a noise in another room, and there you have the basic elements for the telephone. Two more examples in detail. In the late

1940s Hans Krebs (1900–1982) was working on glycolysis in the mitochondria of a leaf cell. He was trying to figure out how a glucose molecule breaks down without terminating a process that would have required an endless supply of pyruvate. He had to figure out the circularity of a process of the breaking down and recomposition of a particular four-carbon molecule. Known also as the citric acid cycle, the solution occurred to Dr. Krebs while he was shaving (we don't know whether he cut himself that morning). In 1895 a medical student named Vincenzo Tiberio, in Arzano, near Naples, found that in his pensione there were many people with intestinal problems. He noticed that when they cleaned the common fresh water well in the courtyard, the ailing increased, but when the rim of the well had a substantial amount of mold, the problem decreased. He did some experiments and isolated a bacillus, which he tested on rabbits. He figured out it was actually a fungus, later called penicillium. He published his results five years later. A French student picked up on it, but his work was also ignored by the scientific community. Then, in 1928, Alexander Fleming, on return from a weekend absence from his lab, noticed he had left one of his petri dishes uncovered, and one of the cultures exuded a substance that he found had antibiotic properties. For his discovery he received the Nobel Prize in Medicine in 1935. It is a curious coincidence and a fact that in the Middle Ages people already knew how to use blue mold of bread to treat suppurating wounds.

Science is called such when what it claims to have brought forth from nothing something that cannot be falsified. In other words, the result must be duplicated by other scientists, otherwise it is not called valid knowledge. This implies a concept of equivalence and correspondence on the basis of: (1) equal or standardized methods, and (2) employing the same language, or formulas (which is still a specific semiotic code whose messages are valid only if sender and receiver agree *a priori* that salt is salt or, better, that Na + Cl equals NaCl). The language of science is *univocal*: words are terms, one meaning to each lexeme. On the other hand, the language of conversation is typically *ambiguous* or imprecise, as so many other factors enter the communication field and can steer meaning in a number of different directions. The language of literature, instead, is *polysemous*, something known to ancient theorists such as Quintilian and Philo, and key notion in Dante, Milton, Blake and the epic tradition. Modern linguists and grammarians have rationalized the very workings of polysemy, how words can bear several meanings depending on different sentence structures and rhetorical exchanges.[44] This is an aspect of the constant technologization of the humanities, of the creative arts, explaining processes relying on calculus, statistics, taxonomies, models. But here, we speak of polysemy in a more general sense. Literature, discourse itself, is ab initio, from the very inception, multi-meaning-producing, the moment it is "actuated," set in being, where the exchange involves persuasion, awareness of the other. So, polysemy is here taken as enabling the reader to follow a variety of paths, enter into mythologies, reconstruct situations, plan the world. These worlds must be allegories of the mind, bearing conceptual schemas, but also require engagement.

Perhaps *that* is the deep main difference between the scientist and the poet. Or is it? Scientist or poet, it seems the quest is to find and present or explain the inexpressible or the mysterious, the origin of knowledge itself, or of a particular knowledge intrinsically. Whether we wish to explain who or what is behind thunder and earthquakes or why mold will cure my infection, the quest entails going from the unknown to what we can wrap our minds around, something tangible, something we can picture, something we can and must name. Going against the leading trends of his day, Giambattista Vico found in metaphor and allegory the origins of knowledge *tout court*, which in earlier epochs was influenced or marked by the sublime, divination, or magic. Behind modern chemistry there are thousands of years of alchemy. But in Modernity—roughly the last four hundred years of our recorded history—we have grown accustomed to *discovering the unknown starting from the known*: number and measurement are the key ingredients in this process. Sequences, deductions, continuity, solidity, representation were devised and given ironclad inevitability. 2 is to 4 as 4 is to x x: therefore, x must equal 8. The power of analogy, of algebra, is stunning. Metaphor, wrote Aristotle, the magus of Western logic, is an inappropriate analogy. Well, of course. Analogy allows us to go from the known to the unknown, but metaphor does the reverse. Imagination seems to be subdued. It is consigned to that sector

[44] See the work of Alan Cruse, *Meaning in Language: An Introduction to Semantics and Pragmatics* (Oxford: Oxford University Press, 2011). I was made aware of this tripartite distinction reading Galvano della Volpe, *Critica del gusto* (1960; English translation: *Critique of Taste* [London: NLB, 1978]). This allowed me to overcome the dread of having to say literature is ambiguous and science is not, a very simplistic and reductive grasp of the matter. Stating that some literary text is ambiguous does not tell me anything, and it may actually be an excuse for not saying what the sense of a given work is, not fashioning a plausible interpretation. See my position on the cooperation of the critic, and the necessary risk of having to take a stand in establishing meanings and values in any work, in my *Prefaces to the Diaphora*, 44, 170–3, 218.

of society that, since the seventeenth century, has been losing ground in terms of its acceptability as the purveyors of real, true knowledge. The creative explosion of the baroque and mannerism did not help. Having tackled the all-powerful systems of theology as the place to go to know anything (a struggle of many centuries), science now slowly edged out literature as the de facto queens of the faculties; the ruler over methods and finalities of what is known; and the where, when, and how to expand more into the unknown. Science becomes progressive, it lurches forward. The idea of progress makes *sense*. But a parallel development in the culture required precisely that pruning of the language toward that univocity we just saw, toward specialized metalanguages, so that the scientist is obliged to keep his lexicon and sentence structure to mimic the laws of logic, correspondence, and consequentiality, so sparse and so hyper-precise, that one wonders how the creative sparks just mentioned above can survive the strictures of their professional rhetoric.

Oh yes, did I say rhetoric in conjunction with science?

Well, scientific discourse is no less rhetorical, in its broadest sense, than that of the literati. I already alluded to how Plato and Descartes were uniquely literary (but don't tell that to a philosopher or a scientist). First of all, the claim that their language is methodical whereas that of the writers is rhetorical is a misleading statement, since *method and rhetoric are the recto and verso of each other*, and there is no such thing as discourse that does not intend to persuade: *es gibt keine unrhetorische sprache,* thundered that enfant terrible who wanted to do philosophy with a hammer: *there is no unrhetorical speech*. For methods too aim at persuading on the ground that they rest on an assumption (a theory, an axiom) and guide a series of steps (method) toward a projected (hypothetical) result, to prove a claim. Enough people within a legitimate social body or organism accept the result, and it is considered official, trustworthy, abiding knowledge, first for a small cadre of the elect, then progressively in larger and larger circles until even the unlettered are persuaded and become believers in the *Novum Organum*, as Bacon called it. Yes, knowledge is a social construct (we can talk about this after the lecture). This process is not unlike what takes place with political discourse in the assembly, where the speaker anchors his argument on a general claim—say: poverty is a problem, justice is good, the homeland must be secured, and so on—and then goes through a series of examples (which are the corrispective of the logical steps in a mathematical proof) builds up by an interplay of deduction and inference a conclusion that is to be accepted by the audience. Enough people accept the claim of the speaker, say: terrorism is something evil, and that becomes common knowledge in the given community. We do not wish to consider that this process obtains whether on one occasion the terrorist is a freedom fighter and on another, or from the point of view of people on the other side of the fence, they are the evil enemy. Alas, even universalism is constantly flirting with relativism.[45]

Ancient rhetoric had structured public speech this way: *Exordium*, *narratio*, *partitio*, *probatio*, *repetitio*, and *a peroratio*. The classical scientific method is structured in parallel fashion, as follows: come up with a hypothesis, survey the problem, breakdown the specific pertinent cases, produce demonstrations or proofs toward validating the hypothesis, repeat the original claim to show that the adduced experiments or proofs are coherent and verifiable, and make the conclusion of the hypothesis a law or new thesis.

But there is another side to this, one engulfed in the politics and power of discourse. Despite the long-held claim that scientific discourse is objective and aims at some sort of universal knowledge above and beyond subjective claims, science is not *wertfrei*, or value free. Because stating the hypothesis is already a metaphysical or political decision: to decide to investigate new sources of energy is not done simply to accumulate the stores of universal knowledge, but it is done in view of a possible development or application in a specific area of society with the aim of generating a new machine, or equipment, please a population or bring us relief… happiness we used to call it. This machine or equipment enters into the broader network of production, manufacturing, reproduction, commerce, and so on. Too often, as Heidegger had suggested, we believe *that* is the only way to go: more production, more reproduction, more contrived invention of products whose basic destiny is actually *not* that of adding to universal knowledge for all of mankind in some sort of utopian fantasy but to put something new on the market. Modernity is rooted in the modus, the self-regenerating now, which we saw is constantly appropriating not just the past but the future as well.

This state of affairs leads to another issue that I cannot fully develop here but is important enough to mention given its deep philosophical ramifications: is science really giving us *new* knowledge about the world? Well, it depends on the statute ascribed to knowledge, whether with a capital or lowercase "K." For centuries we convinced ourselves that knowledge is cumulative: well, that idea too has had a historically short life span. Consider the history of science

[45] The preceding and the following paragraphs condense, perhaps in too skeletal a way, the main tenets of my more technical work, *The Elusive Hermes*.

itself: how many doctoral students in physics and chemistry would today study the physics and chemistry of the eighteenth or nineteenth century (outside of the lone historian of science)? When I was in college, we learned there were only 103 elements (14 or 15 of which did not exist in nature or the universe, but had been created … artificially!). Now I check and we are up to 114 elements (113 is actually missing, but it must be there, someone will discover it, otherwise the chart is incoherent). Would you trust a pilot whose flight school manual was written in 1935? The laws of fluid mechanics that keep a plane afloat may have remained the same, but there are available new sources of information and organization of materials, and the equipment is surely incomparable. But even the laws of mechanics change if you go above thirty kilometers up in the sky or practice medicine as in the years before antibiotics or anaesthesia or X-rays. In fact, one peculiar aspect of science and technology appears to be that it is always on the verge of something new, which tends to overwrite what was known yesterday. To be a scientist means to live on the threshold of invention at all times, at the boundary of what language allows us to say, at a critical point: this IS new knowledge; I hold that this is not so much different from a poet's predicament, whose best work is always the next book, the one he has not written yet.

Ever since Vico, we have known how our very characterization of the universe depends on metaphors, which are essentially anthropomorphic. From the neck of the bottle to the legs of the table, it appears that the very descriptions of matter and energy, to be understood, to allow us to make sense of the world (that is, the world of human beings) one way or the other refer back to our humble domain in everyday life; at best we extrapolate imaginatively. Books have been written on the unavoidable use of metaphor and imagery in science. So much is this a reality that scientists refuse to consider, that the moment we entered the realm of the very very big—the size of the universe—or the very very small—subatomic particles—scientists had to either stay within the precincts of higher level calculus and algebra, topology, and other ultimately poetical domains such as Riemann space, Hilbert space, non-Euclidean geometry, Circadian clocks (self-regenerating mechanisms), Chaotic logic (for example, the definition of a holon: one part within a larger whole that is itself also a whole containing smaller parts!). Or else bow down and accept to reflect upon what to poets is their everyday armamentarium. Humanists can be as creative as scientists, but typically—history *docet*—can explain things better! Let me give you an example.

Most people, even in academia, have an idea of science that is perilously dated. From the sixteenth to the beginning of the twentieth century, we explained science using images from antiquity, all based on harmony, symmetry, balance, a deeply ingrained idea of perfection that each successive discovery or invention was supposed to confirm (we saw that earlier with the panegyrics of Newton coming from religious and didactic poetry).[46] When I was studying physics and engineering in college I learned that internal combustion engines were perfectly, "naturally" balanced if they had 2, 4, 6, 8, 12, or 16 pistons. Note the arithmetic progression. The three-cylinder two-stroke Kawasaki and Saab engines required so many crankshaft counterweights to make them engineering aberrations. Now we have five-cylinder engines in several standard cars and even a V-10! Things just had to work according to an ideal of symmetry. Equilibrium was thought to be a state where forces canceled each other out: not true at all, as you can tell if you can balance yourself on a sphere in the gym (ask your muscles if the forces cancel out, so they can relax). With the arrival of Albert Einstein's theory of relativity, Erwin Schrödinger's wave equation, Werner Heisenberg's uncertainty principle, and Niels Bohr's statistical quantum theory, the classical universe was burst asunder.[47] Forever. Newton's universe seems to work only in the kitchen and for an acquired common sense. But what we call reality has shown itself to be as complex as *Finnegans' Wake*. Representation was challenged, and thinkers in the sciences faced not only a mathematical task but also a rhetorical problem as well. In a 1925 paper titled "Materialism, Past and Present," Bertrand Russell wrote:

> Matter, for common sense, is something which persists in time and moves in space. But for modern relativity-physics this view is no longer tenable. A piece of matter has become, not a persistent thing with varying states, but a system of interrelated events. The old solidity is gone, and with it the characteristics that,

46 I am of course generalizing out of necessity. The transformations in worldviews impacted the structure and content of public discourse, whose legitimation became a battleground, triggering new "discursive formations," Michel Foucault called them (in *The Order of Things*), but that are still particular rhetorical arrangements, designations, and taxonomies to control the runaway polysemy (which could be "dangerous") and the hidden allegories (which must fall within a pre-established mapping of cultural values and memes.).

47 For a clear explanation, both theoretical and historical, of the revolutionary contributions by these giants of modern science, see Robert Crease, *The Great Equations: Breakthroughs in Science from Pythagoras to Heisenberg* (New York: Norton, 2008), esp. chs. 9 and 10, and the Interlude on "the double consciousness of scientists," 230–4. On the relationship art-physics, or beauty and mathematics, see Werner Heisenberg, *Across the Frontiers*, cit., "The Tendency to Abstraction in Modern Art and Science," 142–53, and "The Meaning of Beauty in the Exact Sciences," 166–83. But see also Karl Popper, *The Logic of Scientific Discovery* (New York: Harper Torchbooks, 1959), esp. ch. 9, 215–50.

> to the materialist, made matter seem more real than fleeting thoughts. Nothing is permanent, nothing endures; the prejudice that the real is permanent must be abandoned.[48]

The fact that there is a reality out there that I can observe (according to the vaunted principle of objectivity from earlier science) no longer holds. Niels Bohr writes in 1927:

> Our usual description of physical phenomena is based entirely on the idea that the phenomena concerned may be observed without disturbing them appreciably ... Now, the quantum postulate implies that any observation of atomic phenomena will involve an interaction with the agency of observation not to be neglected. Accordingly, an independent reality in the ordinary physical sense can neither be ascribed to the phenomena nor to the agencies of observation ... This situation has far-reaching consequences.[49]

If the observer cannot be detached from the object of his observation, we are cast into an interrelational universe where the presence of the self, or its instruments, impact to the degree that an ever new phenomenon is actually presented to the observer each and every time he engages the object. In phenomenology Maurice Merleau-Ponty established that perception itself is never neutral, that merely looking at the world outside of our bodies is already an interpretation of the world.[50]

You might recall that at this time there were two competing theories on the composition of light: the wave theory and the corpuscular or quantum theory. Light behaved in ways that proved each of them right. How could that be, asked our theological and Platonizing minds: only one of them can be right, right? Wrong. The philosophical/mathematical mytheme of some necessary transcendent unity to the universe was proven to be wanting, insufficient. Bohr had to come up with *the principle of complementarity* to make this apparent paradox intelligible. For if matter is discontinuous, energy is invisible, and the removal of the observer is no longer possible, how do you represent this unstable, unpredictable, unimaginable domain? How is the logic given voice? But a poet has in part already spelled it out. In "The Second Coming" William B. Yeats writes:

48 Bertrand Russell, *Basic Writings* (New York: Routledge, 2009), 241.

49 Niels Bohr, *Philosophical Writings of Niels Bohr*, volume 1 (Cambridge: Ox Bow, 1987), 53.

50 Cf. Maurice Merleau-Ponty, *Phenomenology of Perception*, translated by Colin Smith (London: Routledge Classics, [1945] 2003).

Turning and turning in the widening gyre
The falcon cannot hear the falconer;
Things fall apart; the center cannot hold.[51]

And in another poem, he qualified this image, this situation, as "the artifice of eternity."

There is a beautiful discussion of this conundrum in Daniel Tiffany's *Toy Medium*[52] where we learn that a certain direction of research was imposed on quantum physics by the problem of how to represent it, and in a sense, therefore, communicate and teach phenomena that go beyond our age-old mental habits:

> The poetic function most compatible with quantum representation is thus not abstraction or extreme formalism, but a symbolic mode in which literal images of ordinary experience betray, but do not represent, an invisible world of impossible bodies and events.[53]

The issue here is that, as physicists, we can investigate only what, in a sense, we can possibly imagine. Sort of visualize, project, "see." The word-image harks back to *eidos*, idea. Further, if we still have problems imagining four- or multi-dimensional space, then there is no alternative but to resort to allegory, *allo-agourai*, which is not a speaking of others as a set of other known entities, one thing standing for another (which is basic semiotics: *aliquid stat pro aliqui*, the definition of the sign: one thing stands for another, which once again, is analogy, algebra of the missing fourth term); but, rather, allegory ought to be thought of as *other-speaking*, an attempt to bring the unknown into the known by letting the unknown inscribe what was previously inconceivable, that is, without concept: "The unreal, material world is depicted in this case by what it is not, by the intuitive features of ordinary things. Hence the allegorical picture is best understood … as a map, referring by convention to the terms of the picture."[54] Old fashioned terms reemerge: phenomena, ether, forces of soul, phantoms … back to magic. If a poet can handle three years of college math, they may be a candidate to

[51] William B. Yeats, "The Second Coming," in *The Collected Poems of W. B. Yeats*. 1989.

[52] Daniel Tiffany, *Toy Medium: Materialism and the Modern Lyric* (Berkeley: University of California Press, 2000).

[53] Ibid., 273.

[54] Ibid.

enter into and perhaps depict for us what goes on in the infinitesimally small pluriverses of our mostly empty spaces.

But even this use of allegory does not satisfy me, for the censored observer cannot be kept out of the picture thus redefined. If science is still, nevertheless—above its intrinsic difficulties when confronted with a universe made up of strings or spaces folding upon themselves or holes where matter disappears entirely—a social project, then, the observer will still be there to impact and determine, to guess and to imagine, and in the last analysis, even mathematics and super-engineering feats must yield to the power of discourse. The limits of cognition are the limits of language, the limits of the imagination are the limits of language.

Autopoetics

I want to wrap this up with a fourth but much shorter frame. The notion of *autopoetics* was first launched by Humberto Maturana with reference to biological "self-making" of living creatures, and adopted by Niklas Luhmann when describing social processes.[55] Throughout the twentieth century we have learned that language is arbitrary with respect to what it represents: there is no absolute reason why when I say chair this particular object I am sitting on comes to mind; if enough of us agree (whether by chance or by design) to call it mercury, then soon we will all be sitting on mercuries. It is a convention: that is what arbitrariness means. I could say "sedia," but then only people from another country would understand me. Even onomatopoeias are culturally determined. Not all dogs bark "arf arf," some bark "bau bau." And yes, anthropologists seem to have confirmed Vico's intuition on the origin of human speech, starting from the hunt, the need to communicate to survive, as can be seen in higher mammals such as whales and elephants. But language is not only *that*, and therein lies the mystery. Language is also self-conscious and self-referential, and in fact according to Roman Jakobson this feature is really exploited in creative writing, in poetry in particular. Pulling attention away from *what is being said* toward *how it is being said*, poetry stands on the opposite side of referential discourse.

[55] See on this the work of Humberto Maturana, *Autopoiesis and Cognition: The Realization of the Living* (Boston: Reidel, 1980), and of Niklas Luhmann, *Organization and Decision*, translated by Dirk Baecker and Rhodes Barrett (Cambridge: Cambridge University Press, 2018).

The latter tends to efface itself, as in the popular expression "language is a tool" of the scientists (actually the majority of people) and grants us the possibility of realism (or the belief that this is how reality can be described). But in self-referentiality, we turn constantly back unto ourselves, as if to confirm the now famous and emblematic dictum: the medium is the message. In reality all five functions of language are operating or happening at the same time, though one typically prevaricates over the others. Self-referentiality can take place at various levels, from the phonemic to the morphological, from the stylistic to the semantic and symbolic levels. Structuralist and deconstructivist critics have shown us how this works. Language can be used to speak about language, as in analytical philosophy, thus becoming a metalanguage of itself. At the highest level of thematization, we have standardized batches of symbols, glossaries that spill into the common idiom. Some become tokens and shorthand techniques, notes Ira Livingston, such as plays within plays, or poetry itself being represented by harps, singing birds, or babbling brooks are well known. But this panoply of self-references can produce multiple and apparently contradictory effects.

First, self-referentiality calls into question the accepted, habitual, unconscious idea of realism and attracts attention to the fact that representation is its own universe, a necessary terrain to traverse, a basic element in the process. Yet,

> producing parallels, permutations and oppositions between the text (or language event) and the way it represents itself, the self-referential function often tries to level the difference between signifier and signified, to enhance "the ring of truth."[56]

Entering the symbolic economy of what lies outside the text, language may induce (rather than *re*present) notions of beauty, or peace, or the natural. In brief, by echoing the split between itself and the world outside of it, the system of self-reference, in the words of Niklas Luhmann, "copies the difference between system and environment into itself and uses it as a premise of its own operations."[57]

The question Livingston asks is what might have already occurred to you:

How could the system copy the difference between itself and its environment to use as a premise of its own operations if this difference is what brings it into

[56] See Ira Livingston, *Between Science and Literature: An Introduction to Autopoetics* (Carbondale: University of Illinois Press, 2005), 58–9.

[57] Ibid., 59.

being in the first place or, rather, what brings it being? Doesn't the system have to be operative to perform the act of copying supposed to premise its "operations?"[58]

The answer is surprising: *a self-referential system simply is and operates as a nest of paradoxes.* Kind of an epistemological quandary, as we saw with astrophysics and subatomic mechanics.

On the other hand, we have another distinct feature of language that I introduced above as the rhetorical, but some recent schools in philosophy and linguistics call the performative. "The sky is blue" is not a performative, "go and sit down" is. But if a speaker of another language asks me to define the sky, and I say it is the blue over our head, then that same utterance becomes a performative for that questioner, for I have conferred authority to the statement and it acted on the listener's stock of knowledge. Well, the sky's blue is also constructed, but within certain delimitations. *A performative statement cannot be analyzed in terms of its truth or falsity, only in terms of its effectiveness within a stated idiom and context.* J. L. Austin suggests that performatives be evaluated in terms of whether they lead to happiness (echoes of Aristotle?), and that can only happen within a given community, not in the abstract. The only way out of the apparent impasse between self-referentiality and performativity is by accepting that one subtends or encapsulates the other, whereby we as speaking humans—*homo sapiens loqui*—are both inside and outside the system at the same time.

The questions asked by physics and taken up most recently by molecular biology is that in living bodies it is not substance that is the central concern but patterns, fractals, *homeorrhesis* (Greek for flow). The waves move across the surface of the ocean, not the water. The eyes move over the letters on this page, not the letters, which remain where they are for another reading by the brain and vanish as they await the next batch of corpuscles, metaphorically speaking, to invest the retinas. But each sentence is grammatically structured and the thought it carries is no mere filler to plug into diagrams. Meanings are altered in the process and, in Heraclitean fashion, no two sentences are alike. Words and grammar are really what one thinks with, and often against what we are trying to think.

An autopoietic system is, like a wave or a whirlpool, a self-sustaining patterned movement, but it does more than merely show what is already present; it actually "*produces its own components*."[59] Unlike what happens with

[58] Ibid., 59.
[59] Ibid., 79.

structuralism, which tends to model systems as spatial organizations frozen at a single moment in time, autopoiesis understands them as patterns of ongoing events continually under construction. This is what happens in quantum mechanics, where the notion of a solid or stable object is meaningless and useless; in fact, a true solid anything ultimately does not exist. The electron comes into being the moment I observe it, but as I do it has already vanished and is being replaced by another and then another, constituting a continuum of waves and recurrences that enter into relation with an *x* number of recurring patterns of other waves. You might have heard of chaos theory in this context. Something similar occurs with language, which insists on the formulation of autopoiesis by foreclosing it:

> I write many sentences to explain the co-emergence of subject/verb/object, and because the way I explain (that is, with subject, verb, and object) keeps undermining my explanation, my job security as a language worker is guaranteed, like Sisyphus and Old Man River: we just keep on reinventing the wheel.[60]

The final word here is that the organization of our lives, our understanding of the world, our critical interpretive system are often no more and no less than variously complex systems, which have built into them the double feature of self-legitimation and pragmatic impact outside themselves. Similarly, Claude Lévi-Strauss spoke of *bricolage*, self-sustaining loops we "pathologize as vicious circles." Perhaps meaning ultimately derives from the straddling or exceeding of categories? Still, "in the grammar of relativity, autopoiesis and performativity theory, all nouns are participles. We are fractal creatures, crazed through and through with cleavages, we are not to be understood as nouns and structures,"[61] as delimiting, boundary and discipline-bound thinking entities, but rather as interactions, self-sustaining patterns in relentless metamorphoses, participles, and processes, autonomous creatures who can exist only because we are dependent on other creatures, and therefore not autonomous. In the end, when confronted with all the possible possibilities, there the questions come down to language and interpretation. Science, poetry, and the inevitable politics that intrudes in or exudes from their interaction are the three main vital springs of the human project.

[60] Ibid.
[61] Ibid.

Figure 8 "Communication, 2" by Angela Biancofiore.

7

Poetics of Translation as Migration

We are on a quest, and are not discouraged by our collective suspicion that the perception we look for in art is about as likely to turn up as is the Holy Grail. That is one of the reasnos we, I mean we humans, are not only the creators, translators and consumers of literature, but also its subjects.
Michael Cunningham, "Found in Translation"

The topic to discuss is the following: whether, what, and how much the translator and the migrant have in common. The generalities they share are several, and can be described in terms of spatial analogies:

1. Translating is a *trans-latio*, a setting-apart, a removing in a different place for a different community, a circling until a livable balance in the new social reality is achieved.
2. Migrating entails a moving-towards, a removing oneself to another spot, whether out of necessity or choice, which is a subsequent problem.[1]

Naturally, migrating means moving through space, but spaces are never devoid of meaning or specific symbolisms, in fact, cultural studies in the past twenty years prefers to speak of *places,* whereas the logicians may still prefer to speak of sets or domains, the cultural anthropologist of habitat, or the scientist of environment. This is conventional wisdom on the subject.

But right at this juncture, we have enough to prod the mind further: is a migrant a "translated man"? Or, even more intriguing, is a translator a migrant of sorts, and if so what kind of traveler? Someone who removes their psyche (intellect, ideas) through language into an alternative cultural/intellectual milieu, while not migrating physically, existentially? In other words, is the

[1] See the fuller articulation on the connection between history and human migration, and the description of twenty different kinds of travelers, in my "Migration, History, Existence," in Peter Carravetta, *After Identity*, 3–37. See also the more recent Thomas Nail, *The Figure of the Migrant* (Stanford: Stanford University Press, 2015), a major contribution to migration studies.

translator not, to some degree, a traveler who goes abroad, lives and masters a culture, and then wants to carry home a novelty (a particular book), and does so by writing it in the target language, the translator's original language. Is not the translator sort of "returning" home with a prize, a secret, from abroad? Just like a number of immigrants would, whether exiles, expatriates, or members of a diaspora.[2]

I propose that much can be gleaned by developing these analogies into a critical *figura*, let's call it provisionally *the erring condition*. Consider the case of writers who are from one country and relocate to another while continuing to write in the "native language":[3] the body is elsewhere but the language-world is "back there."[4] Now by juxtaposition consider that the migrant is the one who, in transposing their body, their person, from one specific cultural (linguistic, historic, geographical) place to another (a new society in a different location, typically a country) *is also leaving something behind, necessarily so* since they are outside of the original or earlier sociocultural space, however vaguely defined. Further, they are not yet entirely in the new world either (as we will see, the inevitable culture shock is a rite of passage, its completion varying tremendously on the basis of geography, class, age, and gender). Like the translator, the migrant is therefore functioning in an *interim*, a *non-space* or *non-time* in the common acceptations of these terms, between languages, between societies, or ever just dwelling with one foot inside and one outside these realms, living on the thresholds, as it were. No longer A, not yet B, what is the status of this dimension, of this condition? According to M. Cronin,

> A translated man … [moves] from a source language and culture to a target language and culture so that translation takes place both in the physical sense of

[2] Cf. Stephen Castles, Hein De Haas, and Mark J. Millers, eds., *The Age of Migration: International Population Movements in the Modern World*, 5th edition (New York: Guilford Press, 2014); and Robin Cohen, *Global Diasporas: An Introduction* (London: Routledge, 2008).

[3] This topic has been explored widely, and one can think of Franz Kafka or García Márquez, for example. There are deep psychological and political implications at stake. On this, see Deleuze and Guattari, *Kafka*, 16–27. Relying on previous researches, the two thinkers use a tetralinguistic model anchored on (1) a vernacular or maternal language; (2) a vehicular or public (business, governmental) language, which signal deterritorialization; (3) a referential level of senses and culture, signaling reterritorialization; and (4) a mythic dimension, caught up in the spiritual and the religious (23) (and which comes close to what I have been calling allegorical). But from the point of view of the author, he/she is a "stranger" in his/her own language at this point (26). The condition I am sketching is rather that of the expatriates or exiles, though in certain cases it applies to any immigrant.

[4] The case of writers who are bi- or trilingual raises a different set of problems, whose influence in this context we shall keep in the back of our minds.

movement or displacement and in the symbolic sense of the shift from one way of speaking, writing about and interpreting the world to another.[5]

But beneath the easily conjectured dichotomies or logical dyads (world A vs world B; Origin vs Destination, etc.) that both translation and migration foreground, on the assumption they can be resolved into some higher unity, there emerges the tension of the life-world that's in-between, caught in a Nietzschean *Zwischen*, that speaks directly to what it means existing in the "transposing, a transporting, from one world to another," and to the condition of dwelling in an unstable intermundium literally along the way (and often for a long time).

In studying migrations, I came to parallel conclusions. For instance, the processes of second-language acquisition,[6] which all migrants experience, metaphorically applies to the translator as she begins the work of actually translating a book: she is acquiring, assimilating, making choices, and setting into motion an entire semiotic realm, an exemplar from a national tradition, itself inevitably made up of specific subcodes, regional variants, and idiolects and so on. But this sets in motion another set of responses, which are typically studied in sociology or ethnopsychology. For instance, the phases that a translator must go through before they can deliver an author in another culture, parallel the stages of culture shock, in which deep transformation occurs in the actor, the subject, in stages of varying duration and magnitude. These interconnected phases of experience have been mapped, they provide us with a (often statistically) determined set of symptoms or markers and suggest possible intellective and emotional developments. These stages include *contact*, *refusal*, *alienation*, *negotiation*, *absorption*, *participation*, *assimilation*, *independence*, or *autonomy* of judgment.[7] Eventually, the "new" individual can go from one world into the other and back without any significant problem. We have the transnational, translinguistic self. Johann Wolfgang von Goethe's cosmopolitan citizen, perhaps.

Let us look closer at how each of these stages may apply to the translation of given works. As a matter of actual practice, a translator will deal, at different

[5] Michael Cronin, *Translation and Identity* (New York: Routledge, 2006), 45.

[6] For some of the general constraints and solutions, see Ellen Bialystok and Kenji Hakuta, eds., *In Other Words: The Science and Psychology of Second-Language Acquisition* (New York: Basic Books, 1994).

[7] See "The Transitional Experience View of Culture Shock," in *Journal of Humanist Psychology* (1975), a chart that is reproduced and interpreted in my *After Identity*, 20–6, 36.

times, with dynamics of first impact upon reading the original (say, reading it in high school, then college again); they may then have heavy doubts about whether to undertake the project, and consider survival strategies to avoid or circumvent the challenge. But then slowly begins a process of negotiation with their personal *and* cultural unconscious, that perhaps the original text *can* indeed be brought over into the home/target language/culture. The translator now reads and rereads in isolation or in context. Eventually, the translator achieves a status of autonomy or independence, being able to decide which road to take, that is, which word or construct to use, which reader they have in mind. Then takes to the journey. Long hours. Long days. In a hermeneutic communion with the text to be translated.

There will be, as I know from the history of *Divine Comedy*'s translations into English, differences in the finished renditions, but this is directly related to each individual translator's world (their experience, reputation, community, skill), but the thought and visions of Dante Alighieri come through *nearly* unscathed. Consider the first three lines of the *Divine Comedy* by different translators:

> In the middle of the journey of our life, I came to
> myself in a dark wood, for the straight way was lost.
>
> (R. M. Durling)

> Midway along the journey of our life
> I woke to find myself in a dark wood,
> For I had wandered off from the straight path.
>
> (M. Musa)

> When I had journeyed half of our life's way,
> I found myself within a shadowed forest,
> for I had lost the path that does not stray.
>
> (A. Mandelbaum)

We get the picture. *Even* in translation, we are immediately catapulted into a grand story, an epic journey, an exploration into the soul.[8] Which one is … better? If you are a poet in the English language, Mandelbaum takes the laurel, Musa does try to make it poetical and measures his iambs and trochees, and Durling is matter of fact, and definitely "trustworthy" (and great to teach Dante, especially for his extensive commentary). But we *do* get the sense of what Dante's poem is trying to convey. Yet I want to avoid the question, more like an ancient

[8] One can hear echoes of this in John Bunyan's *The Pilgrim's Progress*, "As I walk'd through the wilderness of this world, I lighted on a certain place where was a Den, and I laid me down in that place to sleep; and as I slept, I dreamed a Dream."

querelle, surrounding the old conceit of *traduttore/traditore*, or worse yet, about translations being "beautiful unfaithful" (!) these prejudgmental conceits are not relevant to the present inquiry.[9] A loss in any transaction occurs as if by a law of thermodynamics. Metaphorically as well. The question is deciding how much of what *does* get through is, first of all, acceptable, and in second place how "beautiful" it emerges in new clothing, reason for which it usually takes a great poet in the target language to translate a great poet from a different tradition. But is this "beauty" an entirely objective parameter? Not likely. For, in fact, the idea of a perfect copy in a different language makes no sense. Translation is, to a degree, an imitation, but in an alternate linguistic/cultural reality. But it is also a rebirth.

Are there differences between the translator and the migrant? Of course. Unless we equate words with life, translating and migrating are two different orders of existence. Further, to flesh out the *erring condition* figura, although the migrant may, in many instances, return to the home soil, the purpose of a translation is typically one way.[10]

But we are not focusing on what they do not have in common. We want rather to explore how they are alike to the degree, figurative or metaphoric, that they share certain patterns and dynamics.

Now to avoid falling into an involuntary dichotomy myself, I have to stretch my critical field to comprise at least a third focal point, something that would allow me to keep both in view, triangulating, so to speak. That is, the concept of interpretation.

That a translation is *also*, inevitably, intrinsically, an interpretation is well known. Less known or studied, by comparison, is that a migrant's perception/interpretation of the world is challenged to the point that they will be compelled to keep on actively sorting out the changing environment around and in a way redesign as best as possible the (new) world. Thus, *the lived experience and concurrent critical self-reflection/readjustments about codes and habits that both translator and migrant gain along the way are fundamental to their interpretation of the world/culture in which they live, as "home."* Whoever meets an immigrant (exile, expat, refugee), will quickly learn that they have immediately available

9 Nevertheless, one can by analogy think of how an emigrant, once they leave their native soil (town, family), may often feel they have "betrayed" either the family or the motherland. Migration literature, especially in fiction, attests to this.

10 I am aware that often a translation into a different language may trigger, somewhere down the line, an interest in the original on its own home turf: cf. Baudelaire's Poe, Michelet's Vico.

another socioculturally specific set of values or frames for comparison, whether at the level of language, mores, behavior, what is lawful, and so on. What this person may have to say about the world of the resident host may not always be appreciated, but it must be dealt with, if we are going to explore and understand this in-between world, this extended threshold existence. For one thing, is there a time frame for how long an immigrant, as a translator, has to live through the journey, stay in the host country, and then return? A year? Twenty years? These are not immaterial questions. They also bring into the mix the question of temporality.

In a similar but clearly less dramatic way, a translation interprets a work by the sheer act of introducing (or reintroducing if times and communities have substantially changed) a novel way of looking at the world: one can think of Mao Zedong's planned translations of the famed Red Book propounding certain social and political beliefs in distant social contexts, such as Latin America or Africa, where this ideology appeared to be strange, unrealizable, riddled with inconsistencies, and so on. A translation appears into a given culture like a foreigner: how are we going to deal with this new perspective, this other worldview? What if anything will change in the host country as a result of the introduction of this stranger? This foreign text?

A general theory of translation that would set a standard for principles and rules that would apply to all languages or countries appears to be impossible. That is one important observation made by George Steiner in his fundamental book, *After Babel*,[11] which in turn spurs one to wonder, if this is so, what are the philosophical consequences? What happens to universals? And language universals in particular? But we are running ahead of ourselves. Steiner gives ample evidence that our very civilization could not exist were it not for the possibility and existence of translations, with their intriguing history, their multifaceted motivations, and the impact they had in a culture's sense of self. Translations are not solely contingencies in a culture, often they are necessary to its very definition. *Translations have existed and will continue to proliferate at the interstice between free choice, destination, and chance (or contingency).* These decisions and these external facts have determined, from a realm of other possible outcomes, a specific social history, the introduction of a specific concept, an

[11] Cf. George Steiner, *After Babel: Aspects of Language and Translation* (Oxford: Oxford University Press, [1975] 1998).

ideology, a political agenda. These latter are in turn those *particulares* of history that act as switchboards to redirect traffic of ideas and values. These *particulares* represent the lives of people, social beings, who constitute and set in motion cultural forces that become, albeit in an ever fluid way, the receptive community for the arrival of a foreigner (the original text, the immigrant).

A general theory of translation cannot be given outside of the broadest generalities: *translation seems forever linked, in a co-foundational, and co-enabling, mode, to the instance and place of its entering the scene of history, the proscenium of a specific society's immanent present tense.* In this Steiner was bold: he dared to pose the question: translation is a philosophical problem, but philosophy has not addressed the problem of translation.[12] Translations are the backbone of the *Überlieferung*, of *Tradition* as transmission.[13]

But my greater point is the following: much like Steiner, I discovered, and accepted as constituent of any practice of interpretation, the instability of the referent, the shifty identity of the canon, the unstable configuration of a given transcendent Truth, typically equipped with yardsticks for comparisons and resolution.[14] In a critical stance and idiom quite unlike what we might find in a French thinker from those days like Michel Foucault or from the Anglophone Heideggerians, Steiner places language and the creation of meaning in the dialectic between *contingency* and *necessity*, and accepts that as an inescapable condition: *for it is in the "trans" that the translation, the migrating occurs and where categories (world views, belief systems) are challenged and seen in their groundlessness, in their own spatio-temporal contingency, in their flow.* Owing to this precondition, a general theory, a universal theory, as stated, cannot be given: this fact, this phenomenon, this activity, is simply too deeply implicated in the very construction of meaning in language that always entails some co-participation, a rhetorical exchange across codes, a wading into emptiness, doubt, yet ever in a somewhere. It is the opposite of suspended animation: the translator/migrant lives in animated suspension, and that is always subject to the vagaries of contingency.

[12] Other than in terms of continually discussing the use and abuse (or misuse according to stern-faced philologists of Ancient Greek and Old German or French) of prefixes and prepositions and adverbs, and notoriously etymologies, in Martin Heidegger and Jacques Derrida, even Giorgio Agamben, without ever questioning whether they had it right to begin with.

[13] See on this Georg-Hans Gadamer, *Truth and Method* (New York: Seabury Press, 1980); republished by Bloomsbury Academic in 2013.

[14] For detailed discussion on origins and developments of the idea of canons, see Chapter 8, "The Canon(s) of World Literature."

This introduces us to a new problem, for the situation is further complicated by the philosophical question of: (1) whether the word expresses the thought about a thing, or (2) whether the word stood for the thing in such a way that the mind could make use of it to decode or grasp the order of reality. In other words, we come upon the noted, and still problematic, Sapir–Whorf hypothesis.

The origin of this theory goes back to Edward Sapir and his studies on Native American languages. In his landmark *Language*,[15] Sapir writes: "Walking is an organic, an instinctive, function (not, of course, itself an instinct); speech is a non-instinctive, acquired, 'cultural' function."[16] Further down, we read: "Language is a purely human and non-instinctive method of communicating ideas, emotions and desires by means of voluntarily produced symbols."[17] So far, the big news is that language and reality are two separate orders of existence, that language predates us and is a conventional, albeit complex, system of communication.[18] But what about ideas, thoughts? How does language impact on the creation of ideas, of specific concepts? Can we think without language? For Sapir, we can think only as far as we have the language to do it. This means also tying what the mind can express to the knowledge and possibilities of a *specific* language. The resultant theory is unsettling: we are prisoners of our own language:

> The birth of a new concept is invariably foreshadowed by a more or less strained or extended use of old linguistic material: the concept does not attain to individual and independent life until it has found a distinctive linguistic embodiment. … Language, as a structure, is on its inner face the mold of thought.[19]

We are thus introduced to the notion of *linguistic relativity*: such is the language, such are the (possible) thoughts. The story is long and complicated and goes back to Wilhelm von Humboldt (1767–1835), and the first rumblings *against* the search for and belief in a universal language for all mankind.[20] The latter camp is championed by the Cartesians, the likes of Bertrand Russell, Rudiger Frege, and Noam Chomsky. Add to the mix behaviorism and we have Edward Wilson, B. F. Skinner, and now Steven Pinker. Sapir on the other hand enters

[15] Edward Sapir, *Language: An Introduction to the Study of Speech* (New York: Harcourt, [1921] 1949).

[16] Ibid., 4.

[17] Ibid., 8.

[18] It may not be sheer coincidence that during the same years, Ferdinand de Saussure's *Cours de linguistique générale* was published (1916). Clearly the thrust to rethink what language is and where its boundaries are was coming from a variety of philological (or linguistic), scientific, and philosophical quarters.

[19] Sapir, *Language*, 17, 22.

[20] See on this Umberto Eco, *The Search for the Perfect Language* (London: Blackwell, 1995).

the field in the footsteps of anthropologist Franz Boas, is inspired by Einstein's theory of relativity,[21] according to which all measurement and proportion is ever dependent on the point of observation.[22] For the linguist, the starting point is the utterance, speech *in a given language*. His disciple Benjamin Lee Whorf (1897–1941) in the 1930s developed the theory further, raising it to thought-provoking heights. In his studies on the Hopi language, he claimed, there is no word, grammatical form, or expression that refers "directly to what we call time."[23] But that theory has been contested heavily. Guy Deutscher gives a translation of a passage from Hopi that demonstrates that, in fact, the Hopi did have a way to express time, as in our sense of today, tomorrow, years ago.[24] Thus, the suggestive premise that "the limits of my language are the limits of my world"[25] did not stand up to further empirical arguments to the contrary.

A position that counters Whorf was being advanced in those years by Lev Vygotsky (1896–1934): "Progress in thought and progress in speech are not parallel. Their two growth curves cross and recross."[26] Yet we are presented here again with a dilemma:

> From the point of view of psychology, the meaning of every word is a generalization or a concept. And since generalizations and concepts are undeniably acts of thought, we may regard meaning as a phenomenon of thinking. It does not follow, however, that meaning formally belongs in two

[21] See Albert Einstein, *Relativity: The Special and General Theory* (New York: Crown, [1916] 1961). A book written for those not conversant with higher mathematics, but yet presumes "a standard of education corresponding to that of a university matriculation examination."

[22] On the complex development of measurement, a veritable historical drama involving scientists and artists and everyone in-between, see Robert Crease, *World in the Balance The Historic Quest for an Absolute System of Measurement* (New York: Norton, 2011). That the observer cannot be theorized out of any involvement in the process itself of making a determination, outside of physics, see Maturana, *Autopoiesis*, and Humberto Maturana with Berhard Porksen, *From Being to Doing: The Origins of the Biology of Cognition* (Heidelberg: Carl Auer Verlag, 2005/2011), ch. 1: "Without the observer, there is nothing" and, further down, "how can we claim to know of the existence of that absolute [the reference was to Immanuel Kant] reality and at the same time assert its unknowability? This is just an absurd kind of conceptual acrobatics because any talk about that supposedly independent reality is inevitably dependent on the persons talking … It is the observer whose operations I want to understand by operating as an observer; it is language I want to explain by living in language … there is no way of approaching what we want to explain from outside of ourselves."

[23] As cited in Guy Deutscher, *Through the Language Glass* (New York: Holt, 2010), 143. Deutscher offers a lively history of the main issues in linguistics and how the Sapir–Whorf hypothesis, despite an early acceptance, was discussed and critiqued from the 1970s on. Though most of the work focuses on how language theory changed as it tried to deal with how to express colors, from Goethe to Ludwig Wittgenstein, he does attempt to save some aspects of linguistic relativity.

[24] Ibid., 143.

[25] Ibid., 147.

[26] Cf. Lev Vygotsky, *Thought and Language*, translated by A. Kozulin (London: MIT Press, 1986), 68.

> different spheres of psychic life. Word meaning is a phenomenon of thought only insofar as speech is connected with thought and illuminated by it. It is a phenomenon of verbal thought, or meaningful speech – a union of word and thought.[27]

This may be a middle-of-the-road approach, but it tends toward a "rational" explanation of a paradox: language is simply a means to convey thought, but yet it appears as though thoughts exist independently of language. Well, how is that possible? The result is to have to accept the underlying dualism of Western metaphysics once again:

> Language has two lives. In its public role, it is a system of conventions agreed upon by a speech community for the purpose of effective communication. But language also has another, private existence, as a system of knowledge that each speaker has internalized in his or her own mind.[28]

A much better explanation can be furnished if we think of W. V. Quine's *ontological relativity*,[29] and his contribution to this debacle, significantly handled by making recourse to translation:

> Empirical meaning is what remains when, given discourse together with all its stimulatory condition, we peel away the verbiage. It is what the sentences of one language and their firm translations in a completely alien language have in common. So, if we would isolate empirical meaning, a likely position to project ourselves into is that of the linguist who is out to penetrate and translate a hitherto unknown language.[30]

The conclusion to this line of thought is that concepts *can* be communicated or decoded by an outside culture even if the languages are incomprehensible to each other. This is the ideal case. The ground for this is that we have enough nonlinguistic cues and signs and stimuli to "figure out" what the utter foreigner is saying. So we might say that communication of concepts *can* occur even if language A and language B are profoundly alien to each other (don't have similar syntax, or vocabulary, or language-family derivations) *because* of that lowest common denominator, the concept (or idea, or symbol, as the case may be).

[27] Ibid., 212.

[28] Deutscher, *Through the Language Glass*, 233.

[29] See W. V. Quine, *Ontological Relativity and Other Essays* (New York: Columbia University Press, 1969).

[30] W. V. Quine, "Meaning and Translation," in Lawrence Venuti (ed.), *The Translation Studies Reader* (London: Routledge, 2000), 94.

What Quine suggests is that *we are not prisoners of our language,* and that we may still communicate and establish bonds with speakers from a totally different world than ours. So, there will be profound differences between cultures and that "loss" when translating from one language to another (not to speak of "misunderstanding" and "distortion"), but a meaning can and does get across.[31]

Steiner doesn't really contest the Sapir–Whorf hypothesis, just as he doesn't contest outright the neurological study of translation or the statistical approach: they all enlighten us on some aspect, on a peculiar intersection of forces, but they all collectively seem to suggest that there are no definite patterns, there is no law or general rule about the process unless linked to the language/culture in question. The relationship between mind and reality goes through language and, as such, through an actually existing language with its traditions and evolution of its grammars and lexicon.

The other aspect of Steiner's provocative inquiry surfaces when he asks whether, from a rationalistic/philosophical point of view—that is, according to the existing philosophical currents up to the 1970s (not the ones that he, and now I, invoke)—the cognitive processes involved in translating a book from one language into another do not differ substantially from what is involved when we look at the world and decide that a given sign is saying something about that particular object or event. The word/thing connection proved particularly difficult to disentangle. Historically, we have had thinkers, writers, and translators who believed that language (or each person's speech) is fundamentally nomadic, and always an idiolect, thus irreducible, and therefore untranslatable. But to believe that there are some specific texts that are definitively untranslatable is to be myopic: all texts are translatable to some degree, and it is a question of when the receiving society has changed to a point where it can accept the arrival of the foreign text. In other words, effecting a translation, like undertaking to emigrate,

[31] The discussion here could, of course, veer toward a postcolonial critique, since the above explanations and examples are largely theoretical. Let us recall real-life scenarios where the total incomprehension of another's language, and with that its unintelligible mythologies and customs, is cause for disaster and tragedy. For an exemplary demonstration of how that boundary determined the outcome of early modern explorations, see Tzvetan Todorov, *The Conquest of America*, translated by Richard Howard (New York: Harper & Row, 1984), a brilliant application of a structuralist/semiotic approach to grasp a concrete historical event. For the more diachronic aspect of how the language of the invader slowly coopted the host countries, see the several studies by Walter Mignolo, in particular, *The Darker Side of the Renaissance: Literacy, Territoriality, and Colonization* (Ann Arbor: University of Michigan Press, 2003); and his theory of "Border Thinking," as developed in *Local Histories/Global Designs*. On the relationship between border and boundary, see Edward Casey, *The World On Edge* (Bloomington: Indiana University Press, 2017), ch. 1: "Borders are clearly demarcated edges that serve to distinguish one place (region, state, territory) from another … Boundaries, in contrast, resist linearization; they are inherently indeterminate, porous, and often change configuration" (8).

requires a lot of thinking as to when, with whom, and where exactly you want to land. Thus, another critical focus must be accounted for. When the social dynamics of *reception* change,[32] when there may be a documentable "demand" for the importation into the local language of a classic, or even of a previously black-listed or morally reprehensible, book then it does get translated. On the other hand, no one can deny that even the unrepeatable, or unduplicable, words that come to life in a real, person-to-person dialogue, move over time, and as such cannot be redone, relived: it is the Heraclitean principle Steiner adopts as fundamental to an understanding of translation as at once an existential process, a cultural fact, and a profound philosophical issue.

Thus, we find that translations, a bit like migrations, make us aware that interpretation is rooted in the specific contingency of its occurrence. Without resorting to the metalanguage of the theorists of the postmodern or referring to them, Steiner deconstructs the metaphysical assumption of both Western monotheism and Platonism. We are entreated to reckon with the foundationlessness, *die ungrundliche*, of the experience of translation as an inroad into understanding the boundaries of language. The theory of the black box on translation is another chimera the MIT positivists are exploring, with predictable results: (1) we don't know enough, and (2) statistically cause and effect still work! What mad pursuit to locate the neuron with the infobit or imprint of the French word "bois" so that now we can study how and when we can put next to it the Italian "bosco," or the English "wood." The idea of translation machines has long been a utopic dream. Language is not just made up of univocal terms, the semantic envelope varies with the particular grammar and syntax that organize meaning and by what communities speak it and for how long. Stories about some hilarious renditions by Google translator abound and do give credence to the belief in the impossibility of a formal, predictable, dependable method or mechanism of translation.

However, these very same researches in translation studies and practices may be important to glean what were the concerns of the host country or society in terms of values and what were their beliefs when it came to their conception of language. A way to a post-metaphysical understanding of our societies and their differences may come precisely by understanding that translations and

[32] Steiner would not use this metalanguage, which echoes terms developed within analogous systems by Umberto Eco, Wolfgang Iser, and Stanley Fish.

migrations are *ab origine*, from their emerging into any one social reality, marked ontologically for instability, constant change, flows often enough not controlled or not even wanted. To state what so many have already ascertained: translation is metamorphosis and must live in a state of constant risk, indeed it must risk in order to live.

Let us turn for a moment to an overly glorified theory of translation: Walter Benjamin's idea that amidst so many languages and communities the task of translating is to seek some *Ursprache*. He writes: "All higher language is a translation of lower ones, until in ultimate clarity the word of God unfolds, which is the unity of this movement made up of language."[33] There are so many other passages in the essay "The Task of the Translator" that are confusing, contradictory, and ultimately mystifying. But that goes with a mind bent on finding the unitary trans- or supra-temporal presence of a deity behind all phenomena, an imaginary axiom of sorts. But when any single language proved unable to name or express this elusive spirit, which is like a destiny for all humanity, he sought it in the nonverbal space between languages. Benjamin was looking for the ultimate language in what we may metaphorically assume is that paradise of communication that existed before the tower of Babel came crumbling down.[34] Steiner, much more realistic and philosophical at the same time, begins with the rubble left by the fallen tower of The Language. With this premise, he stays close to the empiria, the experience, the appearance and givenness of each bungling, each mis/communication, but still effective transaction, the transit itself. To say that whether in the original or the translation of Dante's *Divine Comedy* there is still a search for grace is to place understanding at the level of metaphysical, transhistorical idealizations: we saw above that philosophy in the twentieth century has managed to secure an independence of the mind, and the concepts it produces, from language. Though, alas, it cannot do without its *dicibilité*, its being capable of being cast into language. Still, what must be brought across the boundary are the *arché* of the good, of justice, of beauty, and other mythemes such as heroism, love, violence, freedom, and so on. These exist as part of a long-hewn tradition in the West, the universal vs particular dichotomy, each bearing in its bosom its opposite or denial. These too are believed to be … universal.

[33] Walter Benjamin, *Illuminations* (New York: Harper, 1996), 74.

[34] Cf. Gen. 11.

But that is erroneous. Studies in anthropology will bear that out. Rather, I suggest we look at these grounding notions:

1. metaphysical ideas are as *regulatory* as they may be universal, and *change through time*, meaning from society to society;
2. these same "immutables" exist *relative to one another*, that is, there exist different conceptions of what is universal from culture to culture, from individual to individual (unless imposed by force) and each impacts the ultimate sense of the other;
3. it is the debris, the detritus left behind that speaks to the unrepeatability of any single event, but this is also where we find a point of entry into the chain(s) of signification.

As Francis Bacon taught, we begin with the datum, collect materials, and eventually make inferences toward some general principle. Among these imperfect yet still manageable concepts we saw above: that translating requires matching to some degree two words from two entirely different language-worlds; but that we ought never aspire to, because it is impossible, a general theory, a metaphysical theory, or worse a theological doctrine, which explains all such processes and can be counted on to guide future translations.

The crux of the problem can be brought back to the inflated meaning we tend to attribute to a putative original text, thence to an original language. There may be several reasons for the emergence of this mytheme. Historians of literature and philosophy for the past two centuries have identified two very strong, deeply entrenched traditions, with their own sets of satellite notions and practices, and these are the religious (biblical) and the secular (national literatures), masterfully explicated by Erich Auerbach in his opus *Mimesis* (1946). This also tells us that there are unseen but impactful relations between the two. Auerbach identified them as interlocking canonical forms of discourse through over two millennia, and the development into modernity is that the secular is winning a greater following. Benjamin on the other hand continued to seek and identify this higher (biblical) language, which turns out to be a speechless language. In brief, whereas in secular interpretation we have, over the course of centuries, developed techniques and expanded the range of considerations (textology, transcriptions, circulation, interested or sponsoring individuals/groups), including more and more the actual material lives of the actors and sociality surrounding the appearance of the original text as a way to build a set of points and hypothesize the author's intentions.[35] In biblical exegesis, however, there remains one incontrovertible punctum: the author is God; whatever we do with the translation, it must be true … to God's intended meaning! In other words, we can argue about Dante's or Miguel de Cervantes' possible intentions when they sketch a character with such and such features—they are, after all, allegories of humans, and as the linguists told us, above, a number of valid conceptual assumptions can be made about possible meaning across the language boundary. But God?

Just think of the arrogance of theology and with it of the droves of experts who are believers and so essay to actually give us, translate, the word of the deity, a deity who by definition and consensus is above anything we can ever imagine, whose will remains a mystery (and must be a mystery), whose logic is, well, ethereal, unfathomable. Yet that message imported into the community must be True, must be all pervasive, must speak to *all of humanity* … only to have to fall back upon the material conditions of a specific exegete's rendition of this allegedly sacred text. Looking at the development of Bible studies,[36] we soon learn that the sacred texts are studied now *not* for what God might have said or meant (well, not as much as in past centuries), but *for* what a community at a given time and place thought that God said. In other words, aesthetic reception applies to sacred as well as to secular texts. It opens the field to researches of the neohistoricist current, as conducted by Stephen Greenblatt,[37] or of the ethnographic "thick description" of Clifford Geertz and his followers. And in an even broader sense this is also what historical hermeneutics has taught us,[38] that is, the meaning of a text is also intrinsically bound to the history of its interpretations and canonization of these.[39]

[35] The notion that the interpreter could and should recreate the author's "intended meaning" in any passage of their work goes back to Romantic hermeneutics, to Friedrich Schleiermacher, developed by the great historians and literary critics of the nineteenth century, and was influential until the New Criticism, which helped to put an end to it, separating the text from its author. It was reframed as an "intentional fallacy," by W. K. Winsatt and Monroe Beardsley: what an author might have though in composing a work is no longer the business of criticism.

[36] For general background see Lee Martin McDonald, *The Biblical Canon: Its Origin, Transmission, and Authority* (Peabody, MA: Hendrickson Publishers, 2007); and Duncan S. Ferguson, *Biblical Hermeneutics: An Introduction* (Atlanta, GA: John Knox, 1986).

[37] See Greenblatt, *The Swerve.*

[38] Cf. Gadamer, *Truth and Method.*

[39] See Chapter 8, below.

Soon we discover that a translation can indeed turn into a full-fledged hermeneutic exercise. I am thinking of Giovanni Pico della Mirandola's *Heptaplus*, which tackles the sevenfold meaning of the first word in Genesis. It is a tour de force: a single word, *Bereshit*, "In the Beginning," in order to be properly understood, required over twenty individual glosses and then connections with and expansions of these to traditions and to the semantics of other texts, so that in the end, coming from a believer who risked being accused of heresy for putting on the same level the Christian Bible and religious thought from Iran, Turkey, Lebanon, and others ancient peoples, the proper rendition was truly an-*other* text, an original in its own right, but one which the Papacy did not appreciate: "The father, in the Son and through the Son, the beginning and end or rest, created the head, the fire, and the foundation of the great man with a good pact."[40]

One may say that Pico went into hermeneutical overdrive, that is a separate issue. What matters is the hermeneutic implication that change, often radical change, in going from one language to another, is inevitable and, in fact, this can be something that gives the traveler/translator some freedom of movement and of choice, in brief, they can be creative, add a new layer to the palimpsest. Moreover, we also became aware that keeping to the sociohistorical reality of material, personal dynamics, even in post-metaphysical days, we can study and analyze the meaning of the text as it arrives at its *destination*, worry less about the *origin*. Here the translator, like the migrant, brings into the interrelated codes and subcodes of a society a different perspective, one which by sheer reflection might allow us to see our own worlds in a different light. It's the most we can expect. But it is a crucial reflection.

Translation, like migration, is the very act or process of living in the no man's land of the in-between, perhaps the only place where the translator/migrant is truly immersed in the creative mind of the original in a friendly embrace, in an attempt to dance with the author so he/she can tell his/her friends outside the ballroom how fantastic the author is. The longer the dance, the embrace, the better. But the translator is not out to be, or become, the author. Perhaps the translator has more in common with the actor: you willingly want to be, need to

[40] Cf. Giovanni Pico della Mirandola, *On the Dignity of Man, On Being and the One, Heptaplus*, cit., 172. Clearly there is behind Pico a long tradition of allegorical exegesis, just think of Philo's "De Opificio Mundi" or "Legum Allegoria," in *Philo*, volume 1, translated by F. H. Colson and G. H. Whitaker (Cambridge, MA: Harvard University Press, 1929).

be, pretend to be, someone else. The translator becomes profoundly aware of this status as an individual wandering through forests of signs, symbols, ideas, facts, and so on. Like the migrant we saw above, they can carry only so much across, and only so much will be understood, but at this juncture the focus slowly shifts to what's at hand, the game of life/logos, and this in turn quickly devolves into where it all will land. The translator is not supposed to explain, but a translation carries with it a great deal of explanation. Translations do tend to *inflate* the text because they have to (re)create a context that is either forever gone or irremediably far away. Nevertheless, despite these *diaphorai*, these *differentiae*, communication is somehow assured. Simply put, there would be no history, no memory of culture without translations. There would be no clans or towns or cultures or civilizations without immigrants.[41]

Finally, George Steiner reminds us that translation can take different forms, from plain imitation in a different language to outright recreation with little or no resemblance to the mythic original. Here we are back to the street, to actual blood, sweat, and tears reality, because translations have to be printed, sold, distributed, accepted as valid, recommended or imposed on students, communities, used to nudge a colleague up the professoriate ladder, or to destroy a reputation, worse yet, in some cases a translated text starts a revolution.

One concluding point Steiner made that, once again, neither hermeneuticians nor literary critics and professional translators have explored to its fullest implications, is the question of *asymmetry*. Thinking/comparing different *languages* we quickly learn they *are asymmetrical with respect to reality and with respect to one another.* There are no mirror images of anything with anything, there are no two entities exactly alike, there are only productions over time that at best we can gather under a temporary category, a functional aegis. Since things are in continuous change, and translation itself is ontologically mired in metamorphosis, asymmetry as a fundamental principle of reality should not surprise us. This very notion would be a great starting point to think of translation as a practice and discipline that continues to make us understand not only our cognitive processes but also the relativity of values in our social world and the need to keep on crossing boundaries.

41 Within the semantics of this term I include, as categorical subsets, the several distinctions between exiles, expatriates, nomads, fugitives, refugees, and so on. See my "Migration, History, Existence," in *After Identity*, 3–37.

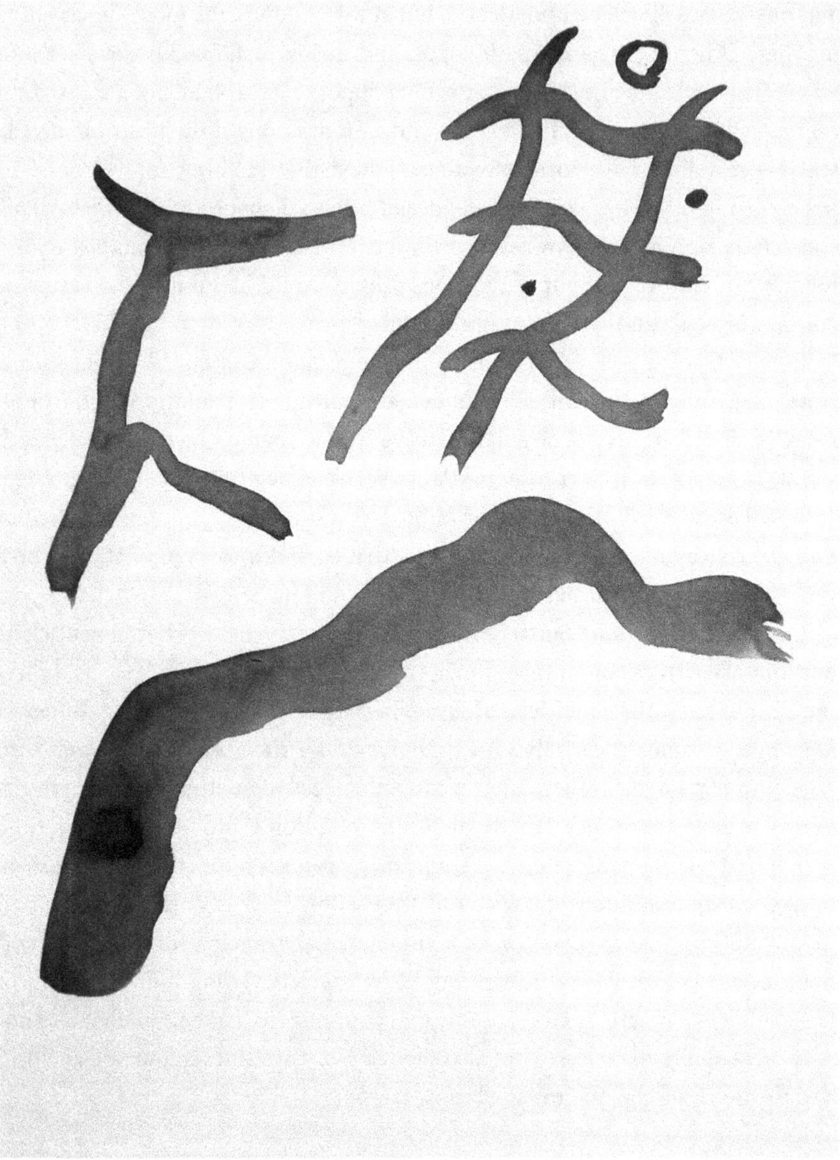

Figure 9 “Communication, 3” by Angela Biancofiore.

8

The Canon(s) of World Literature

Premises to a Postcolonial, Transnational Poetics

Failing to fetch me at first keep encouraged
Missing me one place search another,
I stop somewhere waiting for you.
Walt Whitman, "Song of Myself"

Although the actual roots of the word "canon" are obscure, scholars believe it is a Sumerian concept with parallels in Babylonian/Assyrian *kannu* and Semitic *kaneh*, indicating "a measuring rod."[1] In the ancient Greek, *kanōn* means "a standard or norm by which all things are judged or evaluated, whether the perfect form to follow in architecture or sculpture or the infallible criterion (*kritērion*) by which things are to be measured."[2] I single out this definition because it alerts us to the concomitant idea of *criterion*, present already in Epicurus (341–270 BCE), who wrote *Of the Standard, a Work Entitled Canons* (*Peri Kritēriou ē Kanōn*), and implicitly reminds us that with the establishment of the standard goes the necessity to exercise critique. This key term in Greek (*krinein*) is usually rendered as "to judge," which entails the identification of the proofs in jurisprudence before judgment is passed, in a sense determining what the standard is, what is right and what is wrong. It also extends to medicine, as in the determination of the symptoms of a disease. In the same semantic field we find the Latin word *cernere*, which in agriculture means the activity of separating the wheat from the chaff,[3] and from which we derive the English verb "to discern." The polyvalent notion of determining what is right, or just, or

1 Ezek. 40:5.
2 McDonald, *The Biblical Canon*, 38–9.
3 Jean Starobinski, *L'Oeil vivant II. La relation critique* (Paris: Gallimard, 1970), 114.

proper, subsequently took shape as an icon, a rule, a practice or even a myth, against which to determine what is worthy of conservation and circulation for the collective memory and, conversely, what was deemed acceptable to be excluded, left by the wayside, or ignored at a particular juncture in the life of a given culture.

There have always been fierce battles between competing canons since antiquity, as the case of the Bible makes patent.[4] It is no different today, where different splinter groups, recently emerged, vie for inclusion into what constitutes a common Hebrew canon.[5] It took centuries for the texts of Western monotheism to coalesce into a stable text, the *Septuagint*, a canon that is now closed, with its writings assumed to have come from, or to have been revealed by, God. They are not subject to change or criticism, only to interpretation of possible latent meanings according to the *regula fidei*, or canon of faith, similar to what we call "in the spirit of the letter," a critical attitude that has been extended to such disparate texts as Dante Alighieri's *Divine Comedy* and the Constitution of the United States of America. Thus the sacred text, of any culture, tends to become authoritative, or a *norma normata*, having achieved a fixed shape, and is ideally unchangeable. What bears on our discussion is the function these "eternal" texts exercise on succeeding generations, as they inscribe a process and its protocols, or a *norma normans*,[6] whereby all extracanonical texts about the primary text constitute the tradition that becomes authoritative for the community. Referred to as hermeneutics, this process of interpretation has long been associated with paradigmatic authorities that range from Philo (25 BCE–50 CE) to Friedrich Schleiermacher (1768–1834). The interpretive tradition exemplified by these prototypical figures of interpretation has developed techniques of reading that have by and large condensed around the figure of allegory, or the search for hidden meanings.

Applied to secular texts, this process makes the *norma normans* the real issue, for the "normatizing" and therefore perennially homogenizing—and/or "nationalizing"—process is now compounded by the presence of the author as a fallible human being subject to the vagaries of time and place. Still, we must

[4] See Lee Martin McDonald, *The Biblical Canon: Its Origin, Transmission, and Authority* (Peabody, MA: Hendrickson Publishers, 2007); Bernard M. Levinson, "'You Must Not Add Anything to What I Command You': Paradoxes of Canon and Authorship in Ancient Israel," *Numen*, 50 (2003): 1–53.

[5] See Lital Levy, "Reorienting Hebrew Literary History: The View from the East," *Prooftexts*, 29 (2009): 127–72.

[6] McDonald, *The Biblical Canon*, 56.

recognize that a canon becomes central to establishing the identity of a people and, more to the point, the specific values—be they aesthetic, ethic, political—that the given community refers to in determining whether a particular text functions constructively, albeit subtly coercively, within or outside the community. The history of nationalisms and nation-building bears this out spectacularly, as the processes of codification of specific texts that occurred in the nineteenth century as European and South American countries became formally independent nation-states are typically reproduced, *mutatis mutandis*, in post-Second World War Africa. A canon, then, clearly exercises both a *legitimizing* and a *censorship* function, even while it constantly generates one or several splintered anti- or extracanonical "minor" or "marginal" textualities.

Italian literary history can furnish us with an exemplary case in point in this context. Under the influence of philosopher Benedetto Croce, the canon of Italian literature was required to meet the standards of his particular brand of idealism and historicism. Despite some variations and elaborations, for over six decades the literary canon systematically kept texts that identified with movements of the avant-garde and social realism out of the schools. This situation lasted until in the second half of the twentieth century, when various Marxist, neo-Marxist, and structuralist approaches opened up a broader range of authors and perspectives.[7] Most recently, the Italian literary canon is facing the difficulty of dealing with textualities produced in Italian by authors who come from as far away as Senegal, Iraq, Argentina, and the Philippines. More than that, attempts are under way to minimize the attachment to (northern) Europe and explore the long-ignored impact of the Mediterranean world.[8]

The creation of a single canon of world literature, however circumscribed, cannot realistically be construed, although critics have at different times essayed to do precisely that, inevitably starting from within one national perspective. Insofar as literature is concretely made up of words that are always given in specific languages, one must immediately ask: in *which* language is the canon cast, from within *what* tradition, and in terms of *what kind* of relationship to the collective memory of a group, a people, or a nationality is it built upon? These questions elicit the further critical question: what is the proper, or at least suggested, itinerary through this canon? In different ways, and with a

[7] Peter Carravetta, "Italian Theory and Criticism; 20th Century," in *The Johns Hopkins Guide to Literary Theory & Criticism*, 2nd edition, 534–41 (Baltimore: Johns Hopkins University Press, 2005).

[8] See Armando Gnisci. *Per una storia diversa*. Rome: Meltemi, 2001.

transnational sensibility, both Jean Starobinski and Edward W. Said have drawn attention to this critical issue, namely, in the name of what values, aesthetic or otherwise, and in view of what social purposes, is a canon authorized, or become authoritative enough, to select and propose its "best" or "great" books such as to claim worldwide resonance or viability? A discussion on canons must from the very start set in motion a methodology that accounts for the social and ideological position of the critic, the specificity of the text, and the circumscribed environment in which they interact.

A salutary reminder for students and readers at large is that they are always reading and therefore interpreting a work from a very specific sociohistorical location in the world. Critics have long recognized that we interpret from the point of view of the present, *our* present, and it is only through a second process that one can claim to understand how, for instance, Montesquieu interpreted Persian culture *as if* the succeeding two centuries had not occurred. That task, which is carried out through exegesis, is still in the end brought to bear on our present, where one might conceivably ask: to what degree does the Enlightenment conception of Eastern cultures contribute to our present conceptions of the East? This line of reasoning has been amply explored in postcolonial studies and is responsible in part for relaunching the question of the validity of any one canon.

We thus introduce students and other readers to a set of interconnected problems that bear upon our inevitable involvement in the text we happen to be discussing: historical relativity, the multiplicity of interpretations, and the necessity to place the ideas, symbols, and suggestions that arise during the reading in the mental encyclopedia we happen to bring to class on any given occasion. Inevitably, then, we seek an understanding in view of *our* social reality, *our* world. A world, once again, which is not an ideal or universal bubble but, in the case of myself and my students, a twenty-first-century Anglophonic and urban society with a particular geohistory that cannot be confused with the collective memory of someone who lives in Iran or China. Even the very medium, the material support of the text, is often radically alien from what some readers might be accustomed to. One need only recall that for extended periods of time, from antiquity and often down to our own age, literature has been written in stone, on wax tablets, on papyrus, in a different alphabet, handed down orally, and most recently, may exist only in an electronic format.

Here, translation itself becomes a topic of analysis, spurring reflection on the role it has played over time in determining the modes of transmission and incorporation of literary works in the weave of canons from different countries, across continents and centuries. We must confront the fact that by and large the majority of students cannot realistically be expected to read canonical works, however defined, from other cultures in the original languages, and that their encounter with the literary text must therefore occur in a translation. The question of the relationship of the literary text to the literacy of the intended audience plays into social and pedagogical specificities and language registers of the society of provenance of the text as well as those of the target language.[9] One need only recall that classics such as Homer's *Odyssey*, Dante's *Divine Comedy*, and the Bible have become standard bearers of world literature in translation, in fact through numerous translations and reductions within the same national language. Thus, the question that canon formation compels one to ask is: why is a given, and to all effects "foreign," work translated, and how is it presented to a specific society, to us? Who translated it and when? How does it compare/contrast with works written by, say, a writer of one's own country and deemed important in the receiving culture at this juncture in time? And what supporting materials help explain the relevance of this particular canonical "import"?

These considerations lead us to confront, at both the theoretical and the pragmatic levels, the issue of the definition of literature itself. A proven approach is to draw up a list of features, or qualities, which a literary work is traditionally expected to embody. The discussion about whether literature represents in various guises universal or eternal values has a very long and tormented history. We have all been exposed to certain notions that have themselves become canonical at different periods in history. These include: literature is essentially an aesthetic construct, or it embodies the spirit of the people, or is concerned with humanity's tragic destiny, or represents the story of freedom, or what lasts in a transient world. Each of these ideas, however, implies a metaphysical assumption about reality itself, one which cannot be ignored. The emergence and great influence in Euro-American academic and literary groups of postcolonial studies, feminisms, ethnic studies and neohistoricism have had a salutary impact in cutting down to size the notion of a canon with a capital C, which pretended to speak for the whole of humanity, and has introduced texts previously ignored or literally expunged from reading and publishing lists.

An unintended consequence of this ideological swerve, however, is that there is now a generation, perhaps two, which has never read Percy B. Shelley or Victor

[9] John Guillory, "Canon," in Frank Lentricchia and Thomas McLaughlin (eds.), *Critical Terms for Literary Study* (Chicago: University of Chicago Press, 1995), 238, 241.

Hugo or Thomas Mann. In the case of Hugo, for example, it is important to know that if we wish to understand the evolution of the French literary canon, he sits at the juncture between Romanticism and nationalism, and that Baudelaire's early career was marked by what Harold Bloom would call the "anxiety of influence" vis-à-vis the literary giant. One need only reread Hugo's *Contemplations* (1855) to assess the range and breadth of this monumental figure. This was a time when poets in countries such as Italy, France, England, and by extension in some of the newly independent countries such as Greece, Argentina, and Mexico, were considered *vates*, prophets and speakers of and for the people of that particular country. Their inclusion in a world literary canon would have to downplay their more "nationalistic" texts and emphasize their more "universal" themes. But as claims to universality have in recent history also been considered, if not ethnocentric, then certainly Eurocentric, some formerly canonical authors—such as Henry Wadsworth Longfellow, Alfred Lord Tennyson, Gabriele D'Annunzio, Theodore Dreiser, Émile Zola … and Hugo himself—have faded from our attention.

This situation may be seen as symptomatic of how a canon, and a universalist world canon in particular, changes over time and not only reflects internal, national traditions but also supports and exemplifies concerns that the previous generations did not and could not have. A case in point is the appropriation and institutionalization of the Classics from antiquity. There have been distinct periods in which a culture has turned back to ancient times in order to construe literary values for its present and future generations. In the fourteenth and fifteenth centuries, Italian humanism rediscovered, translated, and set as canonical standard texts from the Greek and Roman traditions. Literature here was conceived not only as a strictly literary and aesthetic model but also as an ethical and civic one as well. This process established the premises for what would become the "quarrel between ancients and moderns" in the following century, as European cultures dealt with the stimuli coming from interfaith clashes, growing process of secularization, the opening up and colonizing of the "New World," and the nascent scientific and technological revolutions that imposed a rethinking of what of the past to retain for the present cultural baggage of its denizens. There were of course occasional radical voices from the side of the neo-ancients that reached beyond the Graeco-Roman *oekumene*, such as Giovanni Pico della Mirandola, who would have wished to include in his syncretic canon texts from Persia, the Hittites, the Chaldeans, the Sumerians, the Alexandrians, and so on. During the Enlightenment, however, as the very discipline of philology was coming into its own, and impacted royal courts, academies, universities, and religious schools, a study of canon formation will reveal the systematic exclusion of non-European literatures (and with that the connected cultural worlds) but also the continuous interpenetration of science and the humanities.[10] Similarly, during the heyday of Romanticism, it was the medieval texts that were the rage and influenced to no small degree the values, the styles, and the ideologies of the early- to mid-nineteenth century. The rise of the novel during the Enlightenment period, moreover, displaced the epic to some extent, allowing for various levels of subjectivity to be explored in more detail and drawing attention to the contemporary as opposed to the perennial. The question is crucial when dealing with literatures from countries that did not have a parallel evolution in any of our highly codified genres, once again placing the onus on the critic who wishes to represent the prose production in various extra-European contexts.

During the epoch of nation-building, the Classics were reintroduced and interpreted in terms of what they said about nationalistic tenets, such as love of country, language, territory, allegiance to the people—*das Volk*, *el pueblo*, *la raza*, *il popolo*. Here again one might find such concerns in the literature produced in countries that achieved statehood only in the twentieth century. Much more all-encompassing were the grand projects ushered in by Columbia and Harvard universities in the 1920s and 1930s, as well as the ideologies behind them, though retrospectively one would be hard put to find sustained references to texts such as the *Ramayana*, *Sundiata*, *The Song of Igor's Campaign*, or the Norse eddas. Yet despite these constant revisions and often profound revolutions, clearly a world literature canon remained essentially a Eurocentric canon until well into the 1970s.

Given the present state of the world as marked by globalization, the internet, porous borders, and the waning distinction among disciplines, political ideologies, and indeed between fact and fiction, the national literature canon has been challenged. As a result, there is an emphasis on a transnational and transhistorical process of formation and reformulations in which subjectivities are transacted and languages, value systems, and specific codes remapped. A similar position has been advanced by Matthew Potolski, who argues that what needs to be introduced into any notion of a canon are "dispersed, cosmopolitan,

10 See Chapter 6, above.

and self-selected" communities no longer anchored in the dominant triad of race, geography, and language.[11] We might add, in view of the past three or four decades, that there is less support today for the multiculturalist claim that every culture or subgroup must necessarily be validated under the aegis of a vague egalitarian worldview, needing to be represented in the spectrum of, say, American or British literature as the mainstream norm or *metron* of validation. The reason is that this notion of challenging and redrawing the canon plays by the same rules, and in a sense obeys the same dialectic. Vindicating a rhetoric of "we were here too," this approach may have had its reason for being during the Cold War years, where much revisionism took center stage, but in the twenty-first century it seems to have lost its edge. Paul Lauter has convincingly argued that the multicultural paradigm is being replaced by "immigration shock," suggesting that it may be time to recalibrate the measuring rods implicit in canon formation.[12]

A canon of world literature must reflect on this critical paradigm shift. Perhaps the concerns of identity ought to shift not to difference but to multiplicity, to hybridity, and in more practical terms, given the role of translation as an encounter, to content, to processes of assimilation, and to variable modes of relation. A conceptual and ideological transformation of a world literature canon occurs when, besides the introduction of previously unknown or ignored texts, the texts of the established canon are reinterpreted in view of a different set of issues. A text such as William Shakespeare's *The Tempest* shows not only power relations between ruler and subjects but also the early manifestation of a colonial attitude toward non-European peoples. Studies in early modern European literatures have amply demonstrated the heterogeneous, multilayered presence of subjects who embody *avant la lettre* the condition of hybridity, dotted as they are with mestizos, mulattoes, creoles, and other multiracial, multiethnic characters. In this sense, a world literature canon has always existed, though it has not always been visible under the screening protocols of a national or even nationalistic literature.

A world literature canon could well begin with travel narratives and a focus on travel itself, on how notions of origins and authenticity have been no more than transactional categories that *homo viator* has used as symbolic currency.

[11] Matthew Potolski, "Decadence, Nationalism, and the Logic of Canon Formation," *Modern Languages Quarterly*, 67 (2) (June 2006): 213–44, 216.

[12] Paul Lauter, "Contexts for Canons," Pedagogy, 10 (1) (Winter 2010): 107–16, 108.

Travel—of ideas, texts, values, ultimately people—ought not be considered a mere genre among others but as an underlying modality of human existence itself. Only recently construed as a critical concept whose application extends beyond its use in economics and sociology, migration lends itself to the study of the transmission of texts and their metamorphoses through time and place, for "migration is the engine of history." Focusing on the different types of travelers who have crisscrossed the planet, one finds not only the more studied exiles, work migrants, refugees, and expatriates, with all the symbolisms they imply. One would also find explorers, missionaries, conquerors, escapees, spies, evacuees, soldiers, diplomats, reporters, Romas, vagabonds, traditional nomads, and so on. As literary characters, these travelers highlight a variety of interactions among languages and peoples, ethical values and worldviews. One has to go beyond the formula "migration literature," which would consign certain texts to a typology wherein we can read of a negotiation between two locales, or focus on the inner drama of a character who has been uprooted and now must find some substitute real or ideal land to recompose an identity of sorts. The suggestion being made here is that literature itself, and world literature in particular, is at bottom an experience of migration, that is to say, of transposition, a moving from place to place linguistically, existentially, socially. The traveler brings worlds together, or at least links them within a more fluid conception of the one planet we inhabit.

The notion that literature as migration is most apt at creating or recreating a world canon draws strength from the fact that during the past several decades avant-garde texts (typically aggressive, iconoclastic, disruptive) have been more widely accepted or "mainstreamed," fueling much of that amorphous notion of the postmodern that critics still grapple with. Equally, the notion of the literary itself has been expanded and made more malleable, receptive to forms that older canonical ideas would have excluded. In other words, besides poems, plays, and novels, today we include texts written in various vernaculars, transcribed oral literature, biographies and autobiographies, memoirs, historical documents, hypertexts, and a variety of travelogues. *The idea is to make the inevitably censoring function of canon formation not a tool for literary ideologies of inclusion and exclusion, but rather a compass for selected itineraries ever open to engage the texts that literally and metaphorically speak a different language, manifest forms utterly new to us, and compel a humbling self-critique.* Depending on where one is located on the globe, a good collection of travel literature can set the premises for itineraries at various levels, allowing for landings that can permit the retrieval of texts from lesser-known cultures, and emphasize the transmission of ideas and values that literature always bears along. A focus on traveling texts can allow for the relaunching of a classic as well as for the introduction of a masterwork into a different culture where it might plant new roots or graft itself on previously unquestioned or ossified productions. Owen Lattimore's old anthology *Silk, Spices and Empire* (1968), for example, contains excerpts not only from Ptolemy and Pliny but also and most importantly from writers from "the other side," as it were, who were cultural mediators in their countries, such as Chang Ch'in, Ch'ang Ch'un and Ibn Battuta.[13] Grounded on need, desire, and the lure of the different and the distant, this literature makes the entire world—or at least that huge section of it which extends some 6,500 kilometers across what today would be several countries—the locus of its existence and exchange, offering a window into radical cultural diversity, intertwined ideologies, and transient commonalities.

With this new orientation, which implicitly includes translation and the crossing of a variety of social borders and epistemological frontiers, we may then seek to locate the existence of world canons lodged already within national literatures. Here, one could profitably take inspiration from the study of premodern societies through that masterwork that is Ernst Robert Curtius's *European Literature and the Latin Middle Ages* (1948), where notions of topics, rhetoric, metaphorics, philosophy, and symbolism become the key elements to map out and analyze the endless interpenetrations of societal values above and beyond (and before) national literatures and ethnicities. An important factor here is to think of literature as a rhetorical construct that speaks *about*, and relates *to*, nonliterary concerns. As such literature both represent and creates worlds, suggesting alternative modes of understanding. To stay with the present, Roland Pérez, for example, has persuasively argued that Latino/a literary theory has, over the course of several decades, "invented new modes of imagining the American experience," reminding us "of the limits and possibilities of American democracy."[14] A similar position has been argued for African American literature already since the 1970s, where the contribution of religious, political, and musical values to the American canon extends its roots across the Atlantic, and not just

[13] Owen Lattimore, *Silk, Spices and Empire: Asia Seen through the Eyes of Its Discoverers* (New York: Delacorte Press, 1968).

[14] Rolando Pérez, "The Bilingualism of Latino/a Literatures," in Ilan Stavans (ed.), *The Oxford Handbook of Latino Studies*, 282–305 (New York: Oxford University Press, 2020), 299.

to Africa. In this sense, a world canon links attitudes and perspectives that are no longer very distant in time and space or, and most importantly, that "foreign."

The notion of "traveling theory"[15] is already available to strengthen this view. In fact, all national literatures ought to be rethought this way. To give but one example, the critic who wishes to include writers such as Adonis, Elias Khoury, Naguib Mahfouz, and others whose original language is Arabic would in part have to contextualize the fact that before they became accessible in English these writers struggled within their national or pan-national canons to revitalize their vernacular and were caught in the throes of parallel, but not identical, processes of canon formation and reformulation. Arabic literature has long been canonized under the aesthetic value of *adab*, a term that includes *belles-lettres*, but for centuries it has also meant educational literature, propriety, *Bildung*, even "*humanitas*." Clearly here the aesthetic and the ethic were interwoven, and literature was presumed to touch upon the "spiritual." But under successive stages of globalization, writers have been exposed to multiple non-Arabic forms of thinking and writing, and the national canons have had to make adjustments. One need only think of the huge influence of Persian and later Turkish literature. Once again, translation surges to the forefront as a key element in the establishment of any canon, whether national or world. The latest stage of Arabic literature, writes Nadia Al-Bagdadi, is characterized by "dispersion" and issues of intertextuality, migration, and reconceptualization of any value expressed in the writing itself demand new critical approaches, a different hermeneutics of culture.[16]

A world canon can therefore be reconstructed in any given semester by a critic/educator who rests for a while in the oasis of the classroom, sets up a flexible methodology, and directs their students toward endless heterologies and possibilities of understanding, none of which is or can ever be the last word.

[15] Edward W. Said, *The World, The Text, The Critic* (Cambridge, MA: Harvard University Press, 1983).

[16] Nadia Al-Bagdadi, "Registers of Arabic Literary History," *New Literary History*, 39 (2008): 437–61, 451.

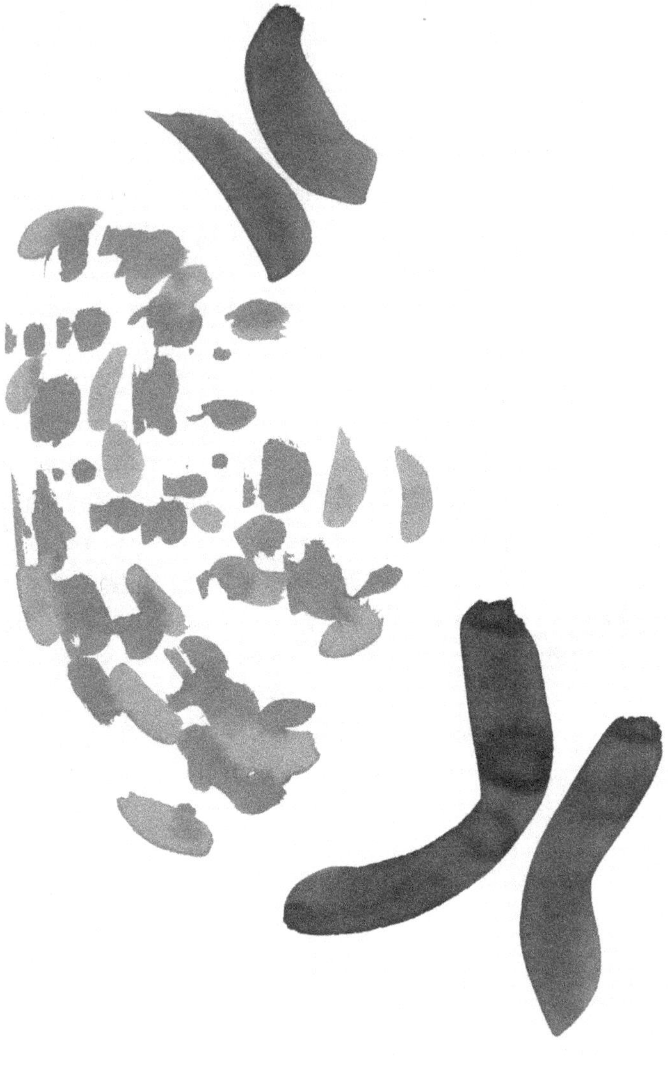

Figure 10 "Communication, 4" by Angela Biancofiore.

Bibliography

Abrams, Richard M., ed. *The Issues of the Populist and Progressive Eras, 1892–1912.* Columbia: University of South Carolina Press, 1969.

Abu-Lughod, Janet. *Before European Hegemony: The World System AD 1250–1350.* New York: Oxford University Press, 1991.

Ahmed, Ali Jimale, ed. *The Invention of Somalia.* Lawrenceville, NJ: The Red Sea Press, 1995.

Al-Bagdadi, Nadia. "Registers of Arabic Literary History." *New Literary History* 39 (2008): 437–61.

Alcalay, Ammiel, ed. *Keys to the Garden.* San Francisco: City Lights, 1996.

Alcalay, Ammiel. *Poetry, Politics and Translation: American Isolation & The Middle East.* Newfield, NY: Palm Press, 2003.

Alderman, Harold. *Nietzsche's Gift.* Athens: Ohio University Press, 1977.

Alexander, Meena. *Poetics of Dislocation.* Ann Arbor: University of Michigan Press, 2012.

Alexei, Sherman. *The Lone Ranger and Tonto Fistfight in Heaven.* New York: Open Road Media, 2013.

Anceschi, Luciano. *Autonomia ed eteronomia dell'arte.* 1936. Milan: Garzanti, 1976.

Andersen, Earl R., and Gianfranco Zanetti. "Comparative Semantic Approaches to the Idea of a Literary Canon." *Journal of Aesthetics and Art Criticism* 58, no. 4 (2000): 341–60.

Anderson, Benedict. *Imagined Communities: Reflections on the Origin and Spread of Nationalism.* London: Verso, 1983.

Anderson, Quentin. *The Imperial Self.* New York: Vintage, 1971.

Anzaldúa, Gloria. "La Conciencia de la Mestiza." In *In Other Words: Literature by Latinas of the United States*, edited by Roberta Fernández, 266–82. Houston: Arte Publico, 1994.

Appadurai, Arjun. "Disjunction and Difference in the Global Cultural Economy." *Theory, Culture & Society* 7, no. 2 (Spring 1990): 295–310.

Apter, Emily. *Against World Literature: On the Politics of Untranslatability.* London: Verso, 2013.

Aristotle. *The Complete Works of Aristotle.* 2 vols. Edited by Jonathan Barnes. Princeton, NJ: Princeton University Press, 1984.

Artioli, U., and F. Bartoli, eds. *Il viandante e la sua orma.* Bologna: Cappelli, 1981.

Baca, Jimmy S. *Working in the Dark: Reflections of a Poet of the Barrio.* Santa Fe, NM: Red Crane Books, 1992.

Bacon, Francis. *Francis Bacon: A Selection of His Works*. Edited by Sidney Warhaft. New York: Odyssey Press, 1965.

Balibar, Etienne. "Paradoxes of Universality." In *The Anatomy of Racism*, edited by David Goldberg, 283–94. Minneapolis: University of Minnesota Press, 1990.

Barolini, Helen, ed. *The Dream Book: An Anthology of Writings by Italian American Women*. New York: Schocken Books, 1985.

Baudrillard, Jean. *The Illusion of the End*. Translated by Chris Turner. Stanford, CA: Stanford University Press, 1992.

Beach, Christopher, ed. *Artifice and Indeterminacy: An Anthology of New Poetics*. Tuscaloosa: University of Alabama Press, 1998.

Benjamin, Walter. *Illuminations*. New York: Harper, 1996.

Benso, Silvia, and Brian Schroeder, eds. *Contemporary Italian Philosophy*. Albany: State University of New York Press, 2007.

Benveniste, Émile. *Problems in General Linguistics*. Translated by Mary E. Meek. Coral Gables: University of Miami Press, 1971.

Benveniste, Émile. *Le Vocabulaire des institutions indo-européennes*. 2 vols. Paris: Minuit, 1969.

Bernstein, Charles, ed. *The Politics of Poetic Form*. 1993. New York: Roof, 2008.

Bhabha, Homi K. *The Location of Culture*. New York: Routledge, 1994.

Bhabha, Homi K., ed. *Nation and Narration*. London: Verso, 1990.

Bialystok, Ellen, and Hakuta, Kenji, eds. *In Other Words: The Science and Psychology of Second-language Acquisition*. New York: Basic Books, 1994.

Blake, William. *The Poetry and Prose of William Blake*. Edited by David V. Erdman. Garden City, NY: Doubleday, 1970.

Boas, Franz. *Race, Language and Culture*. New York: The Free Press, 1940.

Bohr, Niels. *Philosophical Writings of Niels Bohr*. Vol. 1, *Atomic Theory and the Description of Nature*. Cambridge: Ox Bow, 1987.

Braudel, Fernand. *On History*. Translated by Sarah Matthews. Chicago: University of Chicago Press, 1980.

Brenner, Michael, Peter Marsh, and Marylin Brenner, eds. *The Social Contexts of Method*. New York: St. Martin's Press, 1978.

Brown, Kurt, ed. *The Measured Word: On Poetry and Science*. Athens: University of Georgia Press, 2001.

Brown, Lee M. ed. *African Philosophy. New and Traditional Perspectives*. Oxford: Oxford University Press, 2013.

Bruns, Gerald L. "The Invention of Poetry in Early German Romanticism." *Wordsworth Circle* 47 (2–3) (Spring/Summer 2016): 110–14. Available online: https://www.questia.com/library/journal/1G1-460573840/the-invention-of-poetry-in-early-german-romanticism (accessed October 7, 2020).

Calderón, Héctor, and José D. Saldìvar, eds. *Criticism in the Borderlands: Studies in Chicano Literature, Culture, and Ideology*. Durham, NC: Duke University Press, 1991.

Camus, Albert. *The Essential Writings*. Ed. by Robert E. Meagher. New York: Harper, 19 1979.

Carravetta, Peter. "Gertrude Stein." In *Magill's Critical Survey of Poetry*, edited by Walter Beacham, 8:2731–41. Los Angeles: Salem Press, 1982.

Carravetta, Peter. "Poetica e scrittura: Praeludium a Gertrude Stein." In *Arte e conoscenza*, edited by E. Bonessio Di Terzet, 37–85. Genoa: Università di Genova, 1985.

Carravetta, Peter. "Luciano Anceschi." In *Critical Survey of Literary Theory*, Frank N. Magill, 1: 29–35. Pasadena, CA: Salem Press, 1988.

Carravetta, Peter. *Prefaces to the Diaphora: Rhetorics, Allegory, and the Interpretation of Postmodernity*. W. Lafayette, IN: Purdue University Press, 1991.

Carravetta, Peter. "The Other Columbiad." *Differentia* 6–7 (Spring/Autumn 1994): 311–20.

Carravetta, Peter. "Vital Crossings and Histories: Recent Tendencies in American Poetry." *Poetry NZ* 18 (1999): 76–82.

Carravetta, Peter. "Italian Theory and Criticism; 20th Century." In *The Johns Hopkins Guide to Literary Theory & Criticism*, 2nd edn., 534–41. Baltimore, MD: Johns Hopkins University Press, 2005.

Carravetta, Peter. *Del postmoderno: Critica e cultura in America all'alba del duemila*. Milan: Bompiani, 2009.

Carravetta, Peter. *The Elusive Hermes: Method, Discourse, Interpreting*. Aurora, CO: Davies Publishing, 2012.

Carravetta, Peter. "No Longer a Paradox: The Sophists as Philosophers of Language and Existence." In *Paradoxes*, edited by Stefano Arduini, 61–80. Rome: Edizioni di Storia e Letteratura, 2012.

Carravetta, Peter. "An Introduction to Italian Poetry in the United States." In *Poetry of the Italian Diaspora*, edited by Luigi Bonaffini and Joseph Perricone, 1061–71. With introductions to twenty italophone poets in the United States. New York: Fordham University Press, 2014.

Carravetta, Peter. *La funzione Proteo: Ragioni della poesia e poetiche della fine*. Rome: Aracne, 2014.

Carravetta, Peter. "After Thought: From Method to Discourse (Rhetoric)." *RSAJ: Rivista di Studi Americani* 26 (2015): 121–40.

Carravetta, Peter. *After Identity: Migration, Critique, Italian American Culture*. New York: Bordighera, 2017.

Carruth, Hayden, ed. *The Voice That Is Great within Us*. New York: Bantam, 1971.

Carter, Paul. *Meeting Place: The human encounter and the challenge of coesistence*. Minneapolis: University of Minnesota Press, 2013.

Casey, Edward. *Imagining: A Phenomenological Study*. Bloomington: Indiana University Press, 1976.

Casey, Edward. *The World on Edge*. Bloomington: Indiana University Press, 2017.

Castles, Stephen, Hein De Haas, and Mark J. Miller, eds. *The Age of Migration: International Population Movements in the Modern World.* 5th edn. New York: Guilford Press, 2014.

Caws, Mary Ann. *Manifesto: A Century of "isms."* Lincoln: University of Nebraska Press, 2001.

Chow, Rey. *Writing Diaspora.* Bloomington: Indiana University Press, 1993.

Cicero. 28 vols. Vol. 2, *De Inventione; De optimo genere oratorum; Topica.* Translated by H. M. Hubbell. Cambridge: Harvard University Press, 1949.

Charters, Ann, ed. *The Portable Beat Reader.* New York: Penguin, 1992.

Clifford, James. *The Predicament of Culture.* Cambridge, MA: Harvard University Press, 1988.

Cohen, Robin. *Global Diasporas: An Introduction.* London: Routledge, 2008.

Coleridge, Samuel T. *Biographia Literaria.* Edited by James Engell and W. Jackson Bate. Princeton, NJ: Princeton University Press, 1983.

Coleridge, Samuel T. *Coleridge's Poetry and Prose.* Edited by Nicholas Halmi, Paul Magnuson, and Raimonda Modiano. New York: Norton, 2003.

Contini, Gianfranco. *Altri esercizi.* Turin: Einaudi, 1973.

Crease, Robert. *The Great Equations: Breakthroughs in Science from Pythagoras to Heisenberg.* New York: Norton, 2008.

Crease, Robert. *World in the Balance: The Historic Quest for an Absolute System of Measurement.* New York: Norton, 2011.

Cronin, Michael. *Translation and Identity.* New York: Routledge, 2006.

Cruse, Alan. *Meaning in Language: An Introduction to Semantics and Pragmatics.* Oxford: Oxford University Press, 2011.

Cruz, Victor H. *Beneath the Spanish.* Minneapolis, MN: Coffee House Press, 2017.

Cruz, Victor H. *In the Shadow of Al-Andaluz.* Minneapolis, MN: Coffee House Press, 2011.

Cruz, Victor H. *Maraca: New and Selected Poems, 1966–2000.* Minneapolis, MN: Coffee House, 2001.

Curtius, Ernst R. *European Literature and the Latin Middle Ages.* 1948. Princeton, NJ: Princeton University Press, 1973.

Dante. *Literature in the Vernacular.* Translated by Sally Purcell. Manchester: Carcanet New Press, 1981.

Dante. *The Portable Dante.* Edited and translated by Mark Musa. New York: Penguin, 2013.

Danto, Arthur. *The Transfiguration of the Commonplace.* Cambridge, MA: Harvard University Press, 1980.

Dash, Michael. *The Other America: Caribbean Literature in a New World Context.* Charlottesville: University of Virginia Press, 1998.

da Vinci, Leonardo. *Leonardo on Painting.* Edited by Martin Kemp. New Haven, CT: Yale University Press, 2001.

De Campos, Haroldo. "Poesía y Modernidad: De la muerta del arte a la constelación: el poema posutópico." *Vuelta* (Mexico), February 1985, 23–30.

De Laurentiis, Allegra, and Jeff Edwards, eds. *The Bloomsbury Companion to Hegel*. London: Bloomsbury, 2015.

Deleuze, Gilles, and Felix Guattari. *Kafka: Toward a Minor Literature*. Translated by Dana Polan. Minneapolis: University of Minnesota Press, 1984.

Deleuze, Gilles, and Felix Guattari. *A Thousand Plateaus: Capitalism and Schizophrenia*. Translated by Brian Massumi. Minneapolis: University of Minnesota Press, 2003.

Della Volpe, Galvano. *Critique of Taste*. Translated by Michael Caesar. London: NLB, 1978. Originally published as *Critica del gusto* (Milan: Feltrinelli, 1960).

De Man, Paul. *Allegories of Reading*. New Haven, CT: Yale University Press, 1979.

Derrida, Jacques. *Marges de la Philosophie*. Paris: Minuit, 1972.

Derrida, Jacques. *Of Grammatology*. Translated by Gayatri Spivak. Baltimore, MD: Johns Hopkins University Press, 1974.

Derrida, Jacques. *Speech and Phenomena*. Translated by David Allison. Evanston, IL: Northwestern University Press, 1973.

Descartes, René. *Discourse on Method and Meditations*. Translated by Laurence Lafleur. New York: Bobbs-Merrill, 1960.

Detienne, Marcel. *The Creation of Mythology*. Translated by Margaret Cook. Chicago: University of Chicago Press, 1986.

Deutscher, Guy. *Through the Language Glass*. New York: Holt, 2010.

Dolnick, Edward. *The Clockwork Universe: Isaac Newton, the Royal Society, and the Birth of the Modern World*. New York: Harper, 2011.

Eco, Umberto. *The Search for a Perfect Language*. London: Blackwell, 1995.

Eco, Umberto. *A Theory of Semiotics*. Bloomington: Indiana University Press, 1975.

Einstein, Albert. *The Special Theory of Relativity*. 1916. New York: Crown, 1961.

Eliade, Mircea. *Myth and Reality*. Translated by Willard R. Trask. New York: Harper & Row, 1963.

Emerson, Ralph W. *Selections from Ralph Waldo Emerson*. Edited by S. E. Whicher. Boston: Houghton Mifflin, 1960.

Enzensberger, Hans M. *Civil Wars: From L.A. to Bosnia*. New York: New Press Reader, 1994.

Esdale, Logan, and Deborah M. Mix, eds. *Approaches to Teaching the Works of Gertrude Stein*. New York: Modern Language Association, 2018.

Ferguson, Duncan S. *Biblical Hermeneutics: An Introduction*. Atlanta, GA: John Knox, 1986.

Fernández, Roberta, ed. "Preface." In *In Other Words: Literature by Latinas of the United States*. Houston: Arte Publico Press, 1994.

Ferrini, Vincent. *Before Gloucester*. New York: Lost and Found [Center for the Humanities, CUNY/Graduate Center], 2013.

Février, James. *Histoire de l'écriture*. Paris: Payot, 1995.

Feyerabend, Paul. *Against Method*. London: Verso, 2010.
Foreman, Richard. *The Manifestoes and Essays*. New York: Theatre Communications Group, 2013.
Foucault, Michel. *The Archaeology of Language and Discourse on Language*. 1969. Translated by A. M. Sheridan Smith. New York: Harper & Row, 1976.
Foucault, Michel. *The Order of Things*. New York: Penguin, 1974.
Fraser, Julius T. *The Genesis and Evolution of Time: A Critique of Interpretation in Physics*. Amherst: University of Massachusetts Press, 1982.
Friedrich, Hugo. *The Structure of Modern Poetry*. Translated by Joachim Neugroschel. Evanston, IL: Northwestern University Press, 1974.
Gadamer, Hans-Georg. *The Relevance of the Beautiful and Other Essays*. Edited by Robert Bernasconi. Cambridge: Cambridge University Press, 1986.
Gadamer, Hans-Georg. *Truth and Method*. New York: The Seabury Press, 1975. London: Bloomsbury Academic, 2013.
Gargani, Aldo. *La frase infinita*. Milan: Feltrinelli, 1976.
Garraty, John A., ed. *Labor and Capital in the Gilded Age*. Boston: Little, Brown and Company, 1968.
Gaster, Theodor H. "Myth and Story." In *Sacred Narrative: Readings in the Theory of Myth*, edited by Alan Dundes, 110–36. Berkeley: University of California Press, 1984.
Gates, Henry Louis, Jr. *Loose Canons*. Oxford: Oxford University Press, 1992.
Gates, Henry Louis, Jr., ed. *Black Literature and Literary Theory*. New York: Methuen, 1984.
Geertz, Clifford. *The Interpretation of Cultures*. New York: Basic Books, 1973.
Geertz, Clifford. *Local Knowledge: Further Essays in Interpretive Anthropology*. New York: Basic Books, 1983.
Genette, Gerald. *L'Oeuvre de l'Art: Immanence et transcendance*. Paris: Minuit, 1993.
Gilson, Simon. "Medieval Science in Dante's *Commedia*: Past Approaches and Future Directions." *Reading Medieval Studies* 27 (2001): 39–77. Available online: http://centaur.reading.ac.uk/84398/1/RMS-2001-02_S._Gilson%2C_Medieval_Science_in_Dante%27s_Commedia.pdf (accessed October 8, 2020).
Gioia, Dana. *Can Poetry Matter? Essays on Poetry and American Culture*. St. Paul, MN: Greywolf Press, 2002.
Gioia, Dana. *The Gods of Winter*. St. Paul, MN: Greywolf Press, 1991.
Giroux, Henri. *Border Crossings: Cultural Workers and the Politics of Education*. London: Routledge, 2007.
Glissant, Édouard. *Poetics of Relation*. Translated by Betsy Wing. Ann Arbor: University of Michigan Press, 1997.
Gnisci, Armando. *Per una storia diversa*. Rome: Meltemi, 2001.
Gnisci, Armando. *We, The Europeans. Italian Essays on Postcolonialism*. Transl. by M.F. Rusnak. Aurora CO: Davies Group Publishers, 2014.

Goldberg, David, ed. *The Anatomy of Racism*. Minneapolis: University of Minnesota Press, 1990.

Gómez-Moriana, Antonio. "Narration and Argumentation in the Chronicles of the New World." In *1492/1992: Re/Discovering Colonial Writing*, edited by René Jara and Nicholas Spadaccini, 97–120. Minneapolis: University of Minnesota Press, 1993.

Gonzalez, Ray, ed. *Currents from the Dancing River. Contemporary Latino Fiction, Nonfiction, and Poetry*. New York: Harcourt Brace, 1995.

Gramsci, Antonio. *Cultural Writings*. Cambridge, MA: Harvard University Press, 1975.

Grassi, Ernesto. *Heidegger and the Question of renaissance Humanism*. Binghamton, NY: Center for Medieval and Renaissance Studies, 1983.

Grassi, Ernesto. *Rhetoric as Philosophy*. Carbondale: Southern Illinois University Press, 2001.

Greenblatt, Stephen. *The Swerve: How the World Became Modern*. New York: Norton, 2011.

Grosholz, Emily. "Poetry and Science in America." In *The Measured Word: On Poetry and Science*, edited by Kurth Brown, 69–89. Athens: University of Georgia Press, 2001.

Grušovnik, Tomaž, Eduardo Mendieta, and Lenart Škof, eds. *Borders and Debordering: Topologies, Praxes, Hospitableness*. New York: Lexington Books, 2018.

Gugelberger, Georg M. "Decolonizing the Canon: Considerations of Third World Literature." *New Literary History* 22 (1991): 505–24.

Guillory, John. "Canon." In *Critical Terms for Literary Study*, edited by Frank Lentricchia and Thomas McLaughlin, 231–59. Chicago: University of Chicago Press, 1995.

Gungwu, Wang, ed. *Global History and Migrations*. Boulder, CO: Westview Press, 1997.

Handlin, Oscar. *Race and Nationality in American Life*. Garden City, NY: Doubleday, 1957.

Harjo, Joy. *An American Sunrise*. New York: Norton, 219.

Harjo, Joy. *She Had Some Horses*. New York: Thunder's Mouth Press, 1983.

Hawthorne Deming, Alison. "Science and Poetry: A View from the Divide." In *The Measured Word*, edited by Kurt Brown, 181–97. Athens: University Press of Georgia, 2001.

Heidegger, Martin. *What Is Called Thinking?*. Translated by J. Glenn Gray. New York, Harper & Row, 1968.

Heidegger, Martin. *Being and Time*. Translated by John Maquarrie and Edward Robinson. New York: Harper & Row, 1969.

Heidegger, Martin. *On the Way to Language*. Translated by P. D. Hertz. New York: Harper & Row, 1971.

Heidegger, Martin. *Time and Being*. Translated by Joan Stambaugh. New York: Harper & Row, 1972.

Heidegger, Martin. "What Are Poets For." In *Poetry, Language, Thought*, translated by Alfred Hofstadter, 89–142. New York: Harper & Row, 1975.

Heidegger, Martin. *The Question Concerning Technology and Other Essays*. Translated by William Lovitt. New York: Harper & Row, 1977.

Heidegger, Martin. "What Is Metaphysics?." In *Basic Writings*, edited by David F. Krell, 91–112. New York: Harper & Row, 1977.

Heidegger, Martin. *Elucidations of Hölderlin's Poetry*. Translated by Keith Hoeller. New York: Prometheus Books, 2000.

Heisenberg, Werner. *Across the Frontiers*. Translated by Peter Heath. New York: Harper & Row, 1974.

Higgins, Kathleen. *Nietzsche's Zarathustra*. New York: Lexington Books, 2010.

Hirschberg, Stuart, ed. *One World, Many Cultures*. New York: Macmillan, 1992.

Hodge, John L. "Equality: Beyond Dualism and Oppression." In *The Anatomy of Racism*, edited by David Goldberg, 89–107. Minneapolis: University of Minnesota Press, 1990.

Holden, Jonathan. *Style and Authenticity in Postmodern Poetry*. Columbia: University of Missouri Press, 1986.

Hölderlin, Friedrich. *Selected Poems and Fragments*. Translated by Michael Hamburger. New York: Penguin, 1998.

Hoover, Paul, ed. *Postmodern American Poetry*. New York: Norton, 1994.

Husserl, Edmund. *Ideas, I*. 1913. Translated by F. Kersten. London: Kluwer Academic Publishers, 1998.

Jakobson, Roman. *On Language*. Cambridge, MA: Harvard University Press, 1990.

Jara, René, and Nicholas Spadaccini, eds. *1492/1992: Re/Discovering Colonial Writing*. Minneapolis: University of Minnesota Press, 1993.

Jarrell, Randall. *Poetry and the Age*. 1953. Gainesville: University of Florida Press, 2001.

Jatosti, Maria, ed. *Poesia dell'esilio*. Rome: Alem, 1998.

Johnson, Walter R. *The Idea of the Lyric: Lyric Modes in Ancient and Modern Poetry*. Berkeley: University of California Press, 1982.

Jones, Richard F. *Ancients and Moderns*. New York: Dover, 1982.

Jones, W. Powell. The *Rhetoric of Science: A Study of Scientific Ideas and Imagery in Eighteen-Century English Poetry*. London: Routledge & Kegan Paul, 1966.

Joris, Pierre. *A Nomadic Poetics: Essays*. Middletown, CT: Wesleyan University Press, 2003.

Jost, Walter, and Michael J. Hyde, eds. *Rhetoric and Hermeneutics in Our Time: A Reader*. New Haven, CT: Yale University Press, 1997.

Jung, Carl G. *Seminar on Nietzsche's "Zarathustra."* 1934–9. Edited by James L. Jarrett. Princeton, NJ: Princeton University Press, 1998.

Kadir, Djelal. *Memos from the Besieged City. Lifelines for Cultural Sustainability*. Stanford: Stanford University Press, 2011.

Kaplan, Robert B. *The Anatomy of Rhetoric*. Philadelphia: Center for Curriculum Development, 1972.

Kaufmann, Walter, ed. *Existentialism from Dostoievsky to Sartre*. New York: Penguin: 1975.

Keats, John. Selections in *The Norton Anthology of English Literature*. Major Authors edn., edited by M. H. Abrams et al., 1669–751. New York: Norton, 1968.

Kenner, Hugh. "'Writing is an Abnormal Act' in Today's Electronic World." *U.S. News and World Report*, February 14, 1983.

Kenny, Maurice. *Tekonwatonti/Molly Brant: Poems of War*. Freedonia, NY: White Pine Press, 1992.

Kersten, Fred. *Phenomenological Method: Theory and Practice*. Dordrecht: Kluver, 1989.

Khlebnikov, Velimir. *The King of Time*. Translated by Paul Schmidt. Cambridge, MA: Harvard University Press, 1985.

King, Desmond. *Making Americans: Immigration, Race, and the Origins of the Diverse Democracy*. Cambridge, MA: Harvard University Press, 2000.

Kohl, Herbert, ed. *The Poetics of Multiculturalism: Victor Hernández Cruz*. Farmington Hill, MI: Gale, 2018.

Kostelanetz, Richard. *Autobiographies*. 1975. Santa Barbara, CA: Mudborn Press, 1980.

Kostelanetz, Richard, ed. *Essaying Essays: Alternative Forms of Exposition*. New York: Out of London Press, 1975.

Lagos, Ramiro, ed. *Poetas sin fronteras*. Madrid: Editorial Verbum, 2000.

Lampert, Laurence. *Nietzsche's Teaching: An Interpretation of "Thus Spoke Zarathustra."* New Haven, CT: Yale University Press, 1986.

Lattimore, Owen. *Silk, Spices, and Empire: Asia Seen through the Eyes of Its Discoverers*. New York: Delacorte Press, 1968.

Lauter, Paul. "Contexts for Canons." *Pedagogy* 10, no. 1 (Winter 2010): 107–16.

Leopardi, Giacomo. *Tutte le opere*. 2 vols. Firenze: Sansoni, 1965.

Leopardi, Giacomo. *Zibaldone*. Edited by Michael Caesar and Franco D'Intimo. Rev. edn. New York: Farrar, Straus and Giroux, 2015.

Levinson, Bernard M. "'You Must Not Add Anything to What I Command You': *Paradoxes of Canon and Authorship in Ancient Israel." Numen* 50 (2003): 1–53.

Levy, Lital. "Reorienting Hebrew Literary History: The View from the East." *Prooftexts* 29 (2009): 127–72.

Livingston, Ira. *Between Science and Literature: An Introduction to Autopoetics*. Carbondale: University of Illinois Press, 2005.

Löwith, Karl. *From Hegel to Nietzsche: The Revolution in Nineteenth-Century Thought*. New York: Columbia University Press, 1991.

Lucretius. *The Nature of Things*. Translated by Alicia Stallings. New York: Penguin, 2007.

Ludlow, Peter, ed. *Readings in the Philosophy of Language*. Cambridge (MA): MIT Press, 1997.

Luhmann, Niklas. *Organization and Decision*. Translated by Dirk Baecker and Rhodes Barrett. Cambridge: Cambridge University Press, 2018.

Lyotard, François. *The différend: Phrases in Dispute*. Translated by Georges Van Den Abbeele. Minneapolis: University of Minnesota Press, 1988. Originally published as *Le Différend*. Paris: Minuit, 1983.

Lyotard, Jean-François. *The Postmodern Condition: A Report on Knowledge*. Translated by Geoffrey Bennington and Brian Massumi. Minneapolis: University of Minnesota Press, 1984.

Magnus, Bernd, and Kathleen Higgins, eds. *The Cambridge Companion to Nietzsche*. Cambridge: Cambridge University Press, 1996.

Margolis, Joseph, ed. *Philosophy Looks at the Arts*. Philadelphia: Temple University Press, 1987.

Marinetti, Filippo T. *Critical Writings*. Translated by Doug Thompson. New York: Farrar, Strauss and Giroux, 2006.

Marinetti, Filippo T. *Marinetti e il futurismo*. Edited by Luciano De Maria. Milan: Mondadori, 1973.

Marx, Karl. "The German Ideology." In *The Marx-Engels Reader*, edited by R. C. Tucker, 146–200. New York: Norton, 1978.

Maturana, Humberto. *Autopoiesis and Cognition: The Realization of the Living*. Boston, MA: Reidel, 1980.

Maturana, Humberto, with Berhard Porksen, eds. *From Being to Doing: The Origins of the Biology of Cognition*. 2005. Heidelberg: Carl Auer Verlag, 2011.

Mazziotti Gillan, Maria. *Where I Come From*. Toronto: Guernica, 1995.

Mazziotti Gillan, Maria, and Jennifer Gillan, eds. *Unsettling America: An Anthology of Contemporary Multicultural Poetry*. New York: Penguin, 1994.

McCormick, John. *Catastrophe and Imagination*. New Brunswick, NJ: Transaction Publishers, 1998.

McCormick, Peter J. *Modernity, Aesthetics, and the Bounds of Art*. Ithaca, NY: Cornell University Press, 1990.

McDonald, Lee Martin. *The Biblical Canon: Its Origin, Transmission, and Authority*. Peabody, MA: Hendrickson Publishers, 2007.

McElderry, Bruce R., Jr., ed. *The Realistic Movement in American Writing*. New York: The Odyssey Press, 1965.

McNeill, William H. *Polyethnicity and National Unity in World History*. Toronto: University of Toronto Press, 1985.

Merleau-Ponty, Maurice. *Phenomenology of Perception*. 1945. Translated by Colin Smith. London: Routledge Classics, 2003.

Miller, James E., Jr. *Walt Whitman*. Boston: Twayne Publishers, 1990.

Mignolo, Walter D. *The Darker Side of the Renaissance: Literacy, Territoriality, and Colonization*. Ann Arbor: University of Michigan Press, 2003.

Mignolo, Walter D. "Literacy and Colonization: The New World Experience." In *1492/1992: Re/Discovering Colonial Writing*, edited by René Jara and Nicholas Spadaccini, 51–96. Minneapolis: University of Minnesota Press, 1993.

Mignolo, Walter D. *Local Histories/Global Designs*. Princeton, NJ: Princeton University Press, 2012.

Moore, MariJo, ed. *Genocide of the Mind*. New Native American Writing. New York: Nation Books, 2003.

Morrison, Madison. *Engendering*. Norman, OK: Poetry Around, 1990.

Morrison, Madison. *Engendering*. Bilingual edn. Taipei: Cosmos Culture, 2002.

Morrison, Madison. *Magic*. Memphis, TN: The Working Week Press, 2000.

Morrison, Madison. *MM's Revolution: A Menippean Satire*. With a Chinese translation. East & West, 1998.

Morrison, Madison. *Particular and Universal: Essays in Asian, European and American Literature*. New Delhi: Crane Publishing, 1999.

Morrison, Madison. *Realization*. Verona: Anterem Edizioni, 1996.

Morrison, Madison. *SOLUNA Collected Earlier Poems*. New Delhi: Sterling Publishers, 1989.

Morrison, Madison, and Dan Boord. *Revolution*. Taipei: Bookman Books, 1985.

Mukherjee, Bharati. "Immigrant Writing: Give Us Your Maximalists!." *The New York Times*, "Book Review," March 1991.

Nail, Thomas. *The Figure of the Migrant*. Stanford, CA: Stanford University Press, 2015.

Ngugi, Wa Thiong'o. *Decolonizing the Mind: The Politics of Language in African Literature*. Portsmouth, NH: Heinemann, 1985.

Nietzsche, Friedrich. *Così parlò Zarathustra*. Translated into Italian by Sossio Giametta. Commentary by Giangiorgio Pasqualotto, 365–546. Milan: Einaudi, 1985.

Nietzsche, Friedrich. *The Portable Nietzsche*. 1954. Edited by Walter Kaufmann. New York: Viking, 1982.

Nietzsche, Friedrich. *Sämtliche Werke: Kritische Studienausgabe in 15 Bänden*. Edited by Giorgio Colli and Martino Montinari. Berlin: de Gruyter, 1977.

Norman, Charles, ed. *Poets on Poetry*. New York: Free Press, 1962.

O'Hara, Frank. *The Collected Poems of Frank O'Hara*. Edited by Donald Allen. Berkeley: University of California Press, 1995.

Opperman, Serpil and Serenella Iovino, eds. *Environmental Humanities: Voices from the Anthropocene*. New York; Rowman & Littlefield, 2017.

Owens, Craig. "The Allegorical Impulse: Toward a Theory of Postmodernism." *Oktober* 12 (Spring 1980): 67–86.

Padgett, Ron, and David Shapiro, eds. *An Anthology of New York Poets*. New York: Vintage, 1970.

Pakenham, Thomas. *The Scramble for Africa 1876–1912*. New York: Random House, 1991.

Palmer, Richard E. *Hermeneutics: Interpretation Theory in Schleiermacher, Dilthey, Heidegger and Gadamer*. Evanston, IL: Northwestern University Press, 1969.

Park, Robert. *Race and Culture*. Glencoe, IL: Free Press, 1950.

Pascoli, Giovanni. *Poesie*. Milan: Mondadori, 1958.

Pastor, Beatriz. "Silence and Writing: The History of the Conquest." In *1492/1992: Re/Discovering Colonial Writing*, edited by René Jara and Nicholas Spadaccini, 121–63. Minneapolis: University of Minnesota Press, 1993.

Paz, Octavio. *The Labyrinth of Solitude*. New York: Grove Press, 1985.

Pera, Marcello. *The Discourse of Science*. Translated by Clarissa Botsford. Chicago: University of Chicago Press, 1994.

Perelman, Chaïm. *The New Rhetoric: A Treatise on Argumentation*. South Bend, IN: University of Notre Dame Press, 1973.

Pérez, Rolando. "The Bilingualism of Latino/a Literatures." In *The Oxford Handbook of Latino Studies*, edited by Ilan Stavans, 282–305. New York: Oxford University Press, 2020.

Pérez Firmat, Gustavo. *Life On the Hyphen: The Cuban-American Way*. Austin: University of Texas Press, 2012.

Pessoa, Fernando. *Selected Poems*. Translated by Richard Zenith. New York: Grove Press, 1998.

Pfaff, William. *The Wrath of Nations: Civilization and the Furies of Nationalism*. New York: Simon & Schuster, 1993.

Phelps, Ron. "MM: The Sentence of Madison Morrison." MM's Web, n.d. Available online: http://www.madisonmorrison.com/sentenceofthegods/the-sentence-of-madison-morrison.html (accessed October 8, 2020).

Philo. "De Opificio Mundi," and "Legum Allegoria." In *Philo*. Vol. 1 of 12. Loeb Classical Library. Translated by F. H. Colson and G. H. Whitaker. Cambridge, MA: Harvard University Press, 1949.

Pico della Mirandola. *On the Dignity of Man, On Being and the One, Heptaplus*. Indianapolis, IN: Bobbs-Merrill, 1965.

Peirce, Charles S. *The Essential Peirce: Selected Philosophical Writings*. 2 vols. Edited by Nathan Houser and Christian Kloesel. Bloomington: Indiana University Press, 1992.

Pimenta, Alberto. *O silêncio dos poetas* [The Silence of the Poets]. Lisbon: A Regra do Jogo, 1978.

Plato. *The Collected Dialogues*. Edited by Edith Hamilton and Huntington Cairns. Princeton, NJ: Princeton University Press, 1975.

Popper, Karl L. *The Logic of Scientific Discovery*. New York: Harper Torchbooks, 1959.

Potolski, Matthew. "Decadence, Nationalism, and the Logic of Canon Formation." *Modern Languages Quarterly* 67, no. 2 (June 2006): 213 –44.

Pound, Ezra. *The ABC of Reading*. New York: New Directions, 2010.

Pratt, Mary Louise. "Arts of the Contact Zone." In *Profession 91*, 4:33–40. New York: MLA, 1991.

Quine, W. V. "Meaning and Translation." In *The Translation Studies Reader*, edited by Lawrence Venuti. London: Routledge, 2000.

Quine, W. V. *Ontological Relativity and Other Essays*. New York: Columbia University Press, 1969.

Radhakrishnan, R. "Ethnic Identity and Post-Structuralist Difference." In *The Nature and Context of Minority Discourse*, edited by Abdul R. JanMohamed and David Lloyd, 50–101. New York: Oxford University Press, 1990.

Ramazani, Jahan. "A Transnational Poetics." *American Literary History* 18, no. 2 (Summer 2006): 332–59.

Reed, Ishmael. "America: The Multicultural Society." *VIA: Voices in Italian Americana* 5, no. 1 (1994): 3–6.

Reed, Ishmael. *New and Collected Poems 1964–2007*. New York: Thunder's Mouth Press, 2007.

Renan, Ernest. "What is a Nation?" In *Bhabha* (1990): 8–22.

Ricoeur, Paul. *The Rule of Metaphor: The Creation of Meaning in Language*. 1975. London: Routledge, 2004.

Ricoeur, Paul. *Time and Narrative*. Vol. 1 of 3. Translated by Kathleen McLaughlin and David Pellauer. Chicago: University of Chicago Press, 1990.

Ritsos, Yannis. *Chronicle of Exile*. Translated by Maria Savvas. San Francisco: Wire Press, 1977.

Rodriguez, Richard. *Hunger of Memory*. New York: Bantam, 1982.

Rodriguez, Richard. "Mixed Blood: Columbus' Legacy: A World Made *Mestizo*." *Harper's Magazine*, November 1991, 47–56.

Rosaldo, Renato. *Culture and Truth*. Boston: Beacon Press, 1989.

Rosen, Stanley. *The Quarrel between Philosophy and Poetry*. New York: Routledge, 1988.

Rosenau, Pauline M. *Post-Modernism and the Social Sciences*. Princeton, NJ: Princeton University Press, 1992.

Rossi, Pietro. "Occidente e società extra-europee in K. Marx and M. Weber." *Rivista di Filosofia* 9, no. 1 (April 1988): 59–95.

Rothenberg, Jerome, and Pierre Joris, eds. *Poems for the Millennium*. Berkeley: University of California Press, 1995.

Rudrum, David, and Nicholas Stavris, eds. *Supplanting the Postmodern*. New York: Bloomsbury, 2015.

Russell, Bertrand. *Basic Writings*. New York: Routledge, 2009.

Russo, Jean Paul. *The Future without a Past: The Humanities in a Technological Society*. Columbia: University of Missouri Press, 2005.

Said, Edward W. *Orientalism*. New York: Columbia University Press, 1980.

Said, Edward W. "Reflections on Exile." In *One World, Many Cultures*, edited by Stuart Hirschberg, 422–7. New York: Macmillan, 1992.

Said, Edward W. *The World, The Text, The Critic*. Cambridge, MA: Harvard University Press, 1983.

Sánchez, Marta Ester. "Setting the Context: Gender, Ethnicity, and Silence in Contemporary Chicana Poetry." In *Contemporary Chicana Poetry: A Critical Approach to an Emerging Literature*, 1–23. Los Angeles: University of California Press, 1985.

Sapir, Edward. *Language: An Introduction to the Study of Speech*. 1921. New York: Harcourt, 1949.
Sartre, Jean-Paul. *Being and Nothingness*. Translated by Hazel Barnes. New York: Philosophical Library, 1956.
Sartre, Jean-Paul. *What is Literature*? Transl. by Bernard Frechtman. New York: Harper, 1965.
Saussure, Ferdinand de. *Course in General Linguistics*. 1916. LaSalle, IL: Open Court, 1983.
Searle, John. R. *Mind, Language, and Society*. New York: Basic Books, 1998.
Serres, Michel. *Hermes: Literature, Science, Philosophy*. Baltimore, MD: Johns Hopkins University Press, 1982.
Severino, Emanuele. *The Essence of Nihilism*. London: Verso Books, 2016.
Shelley, Percy B. *Shelley's Poetry and Prose*. Edited by Donald H. Reiman and Sharon B. Powers. New York: Norton, 1977.
Smith, Anthony D. *Theories of Nationalism*. New York: Holmes & Meier, 1983.
Smith, Susan H., and Melanie Dawson, eds. *The American 1890s: A Cultural Reader*. Durham, NC: Duke University Press, 2000.
Sollors, Werner. *Beyond Ethnicity*. New York: Oxford University Press, 1986.
Spalek, John M., and Robert Bell, eds. *Exile: The Writer's Experience*. Chapel Hill: University of North Carolina Press, 1982.
Spitzer, Leo. *Critica stilistica e semantica storica*. Bari: Laterza, 1966.
Sprague, Rosamond K., ed. *The Older Sophists*. Indianapolis, IN: Hackett Publishing, 1972.
Spurr, David. *The Rhetoric of Empire: Colonial Discourse in Journalism, Travel Writing, and Imperial Administration*. Durham, NC: Duke University Press, 1993.
Stalmaszczyk, Piotr, ed. *From Philosophy of Fiction to Cognitive Poetics*. New York: Peter Lang, 2016.
Starobinski, Jean. "The Meaning of Literary History." *New Literary History* 7, no. 1 (Autumn 1975): 83–8.
Starobinski, Jean. *L'Oeil vivant II: La relation critique*. Paris: Gallimard, 1970.
Stavans, Ilan, gen. ed. *The Norton Anthology of Latino Literature*. New York: Norton, 2011.
Stein, Gertrude. *Writings and Lectures 1909–1945*. Edited by Patricia Meyerowitz. Baltimore, MA: Penguin Books, 1974.
Steinberg, Stephen. *The Ethnic Myth: Race, Ethnicity, and Class in America*. Boston, MA: Beacon Press, 1981.
Steiner, George. *After Babel: Aspects of Language and Translation*. 1975. Oxford: Oxford University Press, 1998.
Steiner, Rudolf. *Zarathustra, Ermete, Buddha*. Translated by Lina Schwartz. 1911–34. Rome: Basaia, 1987 [in Italian].

Stepan, Nancy L. “Race and Gender: The Role of Analogy in Science.” In *The Anatomy of Racism*, edited by David Goldberg, 38–58. Minneapolis: University of Minnesota Press, 1990.

Stevens, Wallace. “Two or Three Ideas.” 1951. In *Poets on Poetry*, edited by Charles Norman, 363–75.

Stevens, Wallace. *The Collected Poems*. New York: Vintage, 1982.

Stevenson, Frank W. *Chaos and Cosmos in Morrison's “Sentence of the Gods.”* Bangalore: St. Joseph's Press, 2005.

Tabori, Paul. *The Anatomy of Exile: A Semantic and Historical Study*. London: Harrap, 1972.

Tate, Allen. “Tension in Poetry.” 1938. In *Poets on Poetry*, edited by Charles Norman, 349–62. New York: Free Press, 1962.

Thompson, Roger. *Emerson and the History of Rhetoric*. Carbondale, Southern Illinois University Press, 2017.

Tiffany, Daniel. *Toy Medium: Materialism and the Modern Lyric*. Berkeley: University of California Press, 2000.

Todorov, Tzvetan. *The Conquest of America*. Translated by Richard Howard. New York: Harper & Row, 1984.

Todorov, Tzvetan. *Introduction to Poetics*. Translated by Richard Howard. Minneapolis: University of Minnesota Press, 1981.

Turner, Frederick W., ed. *The Portable North American Indian Reader*. New York: Random House, 1986.

Vahinger, Hans. *The Philosophy of 'As If': A System of the Theoretical, Practical and Religious Fictions of Mankind*. Translated by C. K. Ogden. London, 1924; reprint London: Routledge & K. Paul, 1965. Originally published as *Die Philosophie des Als Ob* (Berlin, 1911).

Valesio, Paolo. *Novantiqua: Rhetorics as a Contemporary Theory*. Bloomington: Indiana University Press, 1980.

Valesio, Paolo. “The Writer between Two Worlds.” *Differentia* 3/4 (Spring/Autumn 1989): 259–76.

Vangelisti, Paul. *Embarrassment of Survival: Selected Poems 1970–2000*. New York: Marsilio, 2001.

Vattimo, Gianni. *The End of Modernity*. Baltimore, Johns Hopkins University Press, 1988.

Venuti, Laurence, ed. *The Translation Studies Reader*. London: Routledge, 2000.

Vico, Giambattista. *The New Science*. 1744. Translated by David Marsh. New York: Penguin, 1999.

Vico, Giambattista. *On Humanistic Education*. Translated by Giorgio A. Pinton and Arthur W. Shippee. Ithaca, NY: Cornell University Press, 1993.

Vico, Giambattista. *On the Most Ancient Wisdom of the Italians*. Translated by L. M. Palmer. Ithaca, NY: Cornell University Press, 1988.

Vico, Giambattista. *On the Study Methods of Our Time*. Translated by Elio Gianturco. Ithaca, NY: Cornell University Press, 1990.

Vygotsky, Lev. *Thought and Language*. Translated by A. Kozulin. London: MIT Press, 1986.
Walcott, Derek. "Origins." In *Collected Poems 1948–1984*, 11–16. New York: Farrar, Strauss and Giroux, 1986.
Waldenfels, Bernhard. *Topographie de l'étranger*. Translated by Francesco Gregorio, Frédéric Moinat, Arno Renken, and Michel Vanni. Paris: Van Dieren Editeur, 2009.
Waldman, Anne, and Lisa Birman, eds. *Civil Disobediences: Poetics and Politics in Action*. Minneapolis, MN: Coffee House Press, 2004.
Waldman, Anne, and Marilyn Webb, eds. *Talking Poetics from Naropa Institute*. 2 vols. Boulder, CO: Shambhala, 1978.
Wallerstein, Immanuel. *The Modern World-System*. 2 vols. New York: Academic Press, 1974–82.
Watten, Barrett. *The Constructivist Moment: From Material Text to Cultural Poetics*. Middletown, CT: Wesleyan University Press, 2003.
Webb, Barbara J. *Myth and History in Caribbean Fiction*. Amherst: University of Massachusetts Press, 1992.
Wecter, Dixon. *The Hero in America: A Chronicle of Hero-Worship*. Ann Arbor: University of Michigan Press, 1942.
Westerdale, Joel. *Nietzsche's Aphoristic Challenge*. Berlin: de Gruyter, 2013.
Williams, William C. *Imaginations*. New York: New Directions, 1970.
Wolf, Eric. *Europe and the People without History*. Berkeley: University of California Press, 1982.
Yeats, William B. *The Collected Poems of W. B. Yeats*. New York: Scribner, 1989.
Zangwill, Israel. *The Melting-Pot*. 1909. Charleston, SC: BiblioBazaar, 2008.
Zeidel, Robert. *Immigrants, Progressives, and Exclusion Politics: The Dillingham Commission, 1900–1927*. De Klab: Northern Illinois University Press, 2004.
Zinn, Howard. *A People's History of the United States*. New York: HarperCollins, 2003.
Žižek, Slavoj. *Living in the End of Times*. London: Verso, 2011.

Index of Names

Subject Index

www.ingramcontent.com/pod-product-compliance
Lightning Source LLC
Chambersburg PA
CBHW072236290426
44111CB00012B/2121
* 9 7 8 1 5 0 1 3 7 1 8 8 2 *